# The Informatics Guide to Healthcare

The latest American Association of Colleges of Nursing Essentials released in 2021 require nursing educators to incorporate the ten broad domains with included competencies and sub-competencies across four spheres of healthcare, the lifespan, and among diverse patient populations. Each of the ten domains includes Level 1 and Level 2 sub-competencies that differentiate between entry-level professional nursing education and advanced-level nursing education. As Heath Information Technology (HIT) professionals interact with each other, the need for interprofessional collaboration is essential. This book will bridge the gap between clinical and IT professionals in sharing their experiences through case studies with an emphasis on the practical application of sustainable templates that readers can customize and apply in their own healthcare or organizational settings. This book will integrate or put into practice competency-based learning through storytelling and narratives of subject matter experts in academia/education, leadership/practice, industry/entrepreneurial, and technology/computer programming arenas. The added values within this book are practical tools that exemplify use cases, best practices, and lessons learned.

# The Informatics Guide to Healthcare

## From Insight to Action

Edited by
Mary Joy Garcia-Dia, DNP, RN, FAAN, FHIMSS
Olga Kagan, PhD, RN, FAAAAI, FIEL, FHIMSS

Routledge
Taylor & Francis Group
A PRODUCTIVITY PRESS BOOK
HIMSS

Designed cover image: Shutterstock

First published 2026
by Routledge
605 Third Avenue, New York, NY 10158

and by Routledge
4 Park Square, Milton Park, Abingdon, Oxon, OX14 4RN

*Routledge is an imprint of the Taylor & Francis Group, an informa business*



For Product Safety Concerns and Information please contact our EU representative GPSR@taylorandfrancis.com. Taylor & Francis Verlag GmbH, Kaufingerstraße 24, 80331 München, Germany.



ISBN: 978-1-032-73489-7 (hbk)
ISBN: 978-1-032-73488-0 (pbk)
ISBN: 978-1-003-46445-7 (ebk)

DOI: 10.4324/9781003464457

Typeset in Garamond
by SPi Technologies India Pvt Ltd (Straive)

We dedicate this book with profound gratitude to our supportive families, our insightful contributing authors, and the dynamic healthcare informatics community. May it serve as an essential resource for aspiring professionals striving for excellence.

# Contents

# Preface

Welcome to *The Informatics Guide to Healthcare: From Insight to Action.* As co-editors, we are delighted to present a resource meticulously crafted for both aspiring and current professionals navigating the dynamic landscape of healthcare informatics. This book was born from a fundamental, recurring question we often encounter: "How does one become a successful informatics professional in healthcare?" We recognize that this field is uniquely diverse, welcoming individuals from a wide array of specialties, including nursing, medicine, pharmacy, and computer programming, among many others.

Within these pages, we have curated a rich collection of insights, frameworks, and narratives from leading subject matter experts. Our contributors, distinguished leaders across academia, clinical practice, industry, and technology, share invaluable examples and case studies that highlight essential leadership and informatics competencies. The practical tools, exemplary use cases, best practices, and hard-earned lessons shared throughout the book are designed to empower readers to hone their skills and confidently navigate their own informatics journey. Each chapter offers a unique perspective, providing comprehensive coverage from various experts in nursing and broader healthcare informatics.

Our exploration begins with a deep dive into Patient-Centered Care, tracing the evolution of patient-facing healthcare technologies (PFTs) and underscoring the informaticist's role in ensuring their ethical and secure implementation. Following this, we provide a comprehensive overview of Patient Portals, detailing their features, historical impact, and persistent challenges related to accessibility and security. The pervasive issue of Clinical Documentation Burden is then addressed, outlining its causes, historical context, and innovative technological and procedural interventions aimed at mitigation.

We then turn our attention to the critical intersection of Social Determinants of Health (SDOH) and Health Equity, emphasizing the informaticist's role in integrating SDOH data to address health disparities, followed by a dedicated discussion on Leveraging Technology and Data in Driving Health Literacy and Health Equity, showcasing how information communication technology (ICT) and data-driven strategies empower underserved populations. The Ethical Use of Emerging Technologies in Healthcare critically examines the moral considerations surrounding AI, robotics, and telehealth, grounded in established healthcare ethics principles. Subsequent chapters delve into Healthcare Interoperability, tracing its evolution and highlighting its crucial role in seamless data exchange, and a focused revisit of HIPAA, Privacy & Confidentiality, and Cybercrimes, detailing their critical importance in safeguarding patient information amid growing digital threats. We also address the pervasive Challenges with Integration, Access, Security & Electronic Medical Record (EMR), emphasizing the need for cohesive systems to ensure continuity of care.

The book continues with an Introduction to AI in Healthcare, defining its transformative applications and exploring the pivotal role of nurse informaticists in ethical AI adoption. We then explore Humanoid Technologies, discussing their rapid transformation of nursing practice and the theoretical frameworks influencing their design and acceptance. The Telehealth Evolution Toward Virtual Integrated Care chapter highlights telehealth's journey into comprehensive virtual care, presenting key modalities and practical applications. Our penultimate chapter, The Evolving Role of Nurses in Informatics and Healthcare, underscores nursing informatics' vital influence in leveraging technology to enhance care quality and decision-making. Finally, we conclude with Evangelizing a Culture of Innovation, focusing on cultivating a proactive approach to problem-solving within nursing informatics and healthcare.

It is our sincere hope that *The Informatics Guide to Healthcare: From Insight to Action* serves as an invaluable resource, guiding and inspiring you on your journey to becoming a successful and impactful informatics professional in healthcare.

# Acknowledgments

The creation of *The Informatics Guide to Healthcare: From Insight to Action* has been a journey enriched by the support and dedication of many, to whom we extend our sincerest gratitude.

First and foremost, we wish to thank our dedicated team at Routledge Productivity Press. Their collective expertise and unwavering support were instrumental in bringing this vision to fruition. A special acknowledgment goes to Kristine Rynne Mednansky, Senior Editor, Business & Management—Healthcare Management, for her guidance, patience, and commitment to this project from its inception.

To our esteemed contributing authors, we offer our deepest appreciation. Your invaluable expertise, dedication to sharing knowledge, and the rich diversity of perspectives you brought to each chapter have made this guide truly comprehensive and practical. This book would not have been possible without your diligent efforts and commitment to advancing healthcare information technology.

We are profoundly grateful to our families for their understanding, patience, and steadfast encouragement. The many weekends spent immersed in this project were made possible by their support, and for that, we are truly thankful.

Finally, we extend our thanks to the numerous professional organizations that champion professional development, foster innovation, and cultivate leadership within healthcare. The vibrant community they cultivate continually inspires us and provides the essential foundation for the advancements discussed within these pages.

It is our privilege to contribute this guide to the healthcare informatics community, and we are thankful for the collaborative spirit that made it a reality.

# About the Editors

**Mary Joy Garcia-Dia,** DNP, RN, FAAN, FHIMSS, is a nationally recognized author, nursing informatics specialist, and community advocate whose career spans over three decades at the intersection of healthcare innovation, digital transformation, and equity. As a thought leader, she has written extensively on topics including nursing leadership, informatics, resilience, and responsible technology adoption, contributing to foundational texts and peer-reviewed publications that shape the future of nursing practice. A fellow of the American Academy of Nursing, New York Academy of Medicine, and the Healthcare Information and Management Systems Society (HIMSS), Dr. Garcia-Dia holds leadership roles actively engaging in various committees (Information Technology Expert Panel, AI Taskforce, Nursing Education and Networking Taskforce, Nursing Informatics Committee workgroup on Social Determinants of Health (SDOH)). Her influence extends across professional nursing organizations such as American Nurses Association (ANA), Philippine Nurses Assocation of America (PNAA), National Coalition of Ethnic Minority Nurse Associations (NCEMNA), where she advances initiatives that promote ethical technology integration, inclusive leadership, and culturally responsive care. Dr. Garcia-Dia is widely recognized for her ability to bridge policy, education, and practice, and she actively mentors emerging nurse leaders. Her work exemplifies the power of informatics to drive meaningful change—empowering nurses, improving systems, and addressing disparities through data-driven, patient-centered innovation.

**Olga Kagan,** PhD, RN, FHIMSS, FAAAAI, FIEL, is a nurse educator, scientist, and entrepreneur, with expertise in nursing informatics. As a co-editor of *The Informatics Guide to Healthcare: From Insight to Action*, Dr. Kagan brings extensive experience in leveraging technology for improved healthcare outcomes and in driving innovation. She is the founder and president of the nonprofit Food Allergy Nursing Association (FANA) and President-Elect of Society of Scientists, Innovators, Entrepreneurs and Leaders (SONSIEL) where she co-founded the Collaborative Healthcare Innovation, Research & Problem Solving (CHIRPS) group. As a current chair of the New York Academy of Medicine (NYAM)'s Nursing Section, she works toward health equity and improving public health. As an associate professor, Dr. Kagan shares her expertise with students, contributes to textbooks, mentors nurses, and advises health-tech start-ups. A recognized thought leader, she has served on numerous committees and boards for organizations vital to healthcare technology and innovation, such as Health Information Management Systems Society (HIMSS), American Nurses Association (ANA), and American Academy of Allergy Asthma & Immunology (AAAAI). She has received multiple awards for her contributions to nursing leadership, mentorship, and research, and has been featured in media, TV, and online platforms. In 2025, she was a recipient of Nursing Informatics Leadership Changemaker, a Healthcare Information & Management Systems Society (HIMSS)-Alliance for Nursing Informatics (ANI) Partner Award.

# Contributors

**Kathleen Begonia, PhD, NI-BC, CCRN**
Clinical Associate Professor
Mount Sinai Phillips School of Nursing
New York, NY, United States

**Michael Joseph Dino, PhD, MAN, RN, LPT, FAAN, FFNMRCSI, ANEF**
Associate Professor
College of Nursing
University of Central Florida
Orlando, FL, United States
and
Director
Research Development and Innovation Center
Our Lady of Fatima University
Valenzuela City, Manila, Philippines
and
Vice President
Global Society for Philippine Nurse Researchers, Inc. Manila, Philippines
and
Past President Phi Gamma Chapter
Sigma Theta Tau International Honor Society of Nursing Indianapolis, IN, USA

**Mary Joy Garcia-Dia, DNP, RN, FAAN, FHIMSS**
Adjunct Associate Professor
Frances Payne Bolton School of Nursing
Case Western Reserve University
Cleveland, OH, United States
and
Associate Adjunct Professor
CUNY School of Professional Studies
New York, NY, United States
and
Past Board of Directors Member
HIMSS New York State Chapter
New York, USA

**Elaine Hui-Martinez, DNP, RN, NI-BC, CPHIMS**
Adjunct Associate Professor
Frances Payne Bolton School of Nursing, Case Western Reserve University
Cleveland, OH, United States

**Olga Kagan, PhD, RN, FHIMSS, FAAAAI, FIEL**
Faculty
The Barbara H. Hagan School of Nursing and Health Sciences
Molloy University
Rockville Centre, NY, United States
and
Associate Adjunct Professor
The City University of New York (CUNY) School of Professional Studies, New York, NY, United States
and
Founder & President
Food Allergy Nursing Association (FANA)
Great Neck, NY, United States
and
President-Elect
Society of Nurse Scientist, Innovators, Entrepreneurs & Leaders (SONSIEL)
Past Board of Directors Member, HIMSS New York State Chapter

**Virginia Lorenzi, MS**
Healthcare Informatics Specialist
New York, NY, United States

**Lilly Mathew PhD, RN, NI-BC, NPD-BC**
Associate Professor of Nursing Informatics
The City University of New York (CUNY) School of Professional Studies
New York, NY, United States
and
Nurse Scientist
Northwell Health – Glen Cove Hospital
Glen Cove, NY, United States

**Kathleen McGrow, DNP, MS, RN, PMP, FHIMSS, FAAN**
Chief Nursing Innovation Officer
Microsoft
Redmond, WA, United States
and
Adjunct Clinical Instructor
The University of Alabama at Birmingham School of Nursing
Birmingham, AL, United States

**Hiyam Nadel, MBA, RN, FIEL, CCG**
Director
Center for Innovations in Care Delivery
Massachusetts General Hospital
Boston, MA, United States
and
Inaugural Endowed Chair in Nurse Innovation
Founder & Immediate Past President
Society of Nurse Scientist, Innovators, Entrepreneurs & Leaders (SONSIEL)
Inaugural Johnson & Johnson Innovation Fellow

**Young-Shin Park DNP, RN, NI-BC, CNOR**
Information Technology Director
Mount Sinai Health System
New York, NY, United States
and
Associate Adjunct Professor The City University of New York (CUNY) School of Professional Studies
New York, NY, United States

**Anna Schoenbaum, DNP, MS, RN, NI-BC, FHIMSS, FAAN**
Vice President and Chief Digital Applications Officer
Penn Medicine (University of Pennsylvania Health System)
Philadelphia, PA, United States
and
Adjunct Faculty
University of Maryland School of Nursing
Baltimore, MD, United States

**Barbara Van de Castle, DNP, NI-BC, OCN-Emeritus**
Assistant Professor in Informatics
University of Maryland School of Nursing
Baltimore, MD, United States

# Foreword

We are living through one of the most profound transformations in the history of healthcare. Advances in digital health, artificial intelligence, and data science are reshaping how care is delivered, how clinicians work, and how patients engage with their own health. At the center of this transformation is a field that once worked quietly behind the scenes but is now taking its place on the front lines: healthcare informatics.

Informatics is no longer a niche discipline. It is now a critical enabler of safer, smarter, and more equitable healthcare. From unlocking the power of electronic health records to integrating social determinants of health into clinical workflows, informatics professionals are leading efforts to improve quality, reduce disparities, and drive innovation. Yet, for many, the field can feel both expansive and elusive. How do you enter the profession? What skills are essential? How do you lead effectively in such a rapidly evolving environment?

***The Informatics Guide to Healthcare: From Insight to Action*** offers timely answers to these questions.

In this book, Dr. Olga Kagan and Dr. Mary Joy Garcia-Dia have created a much-needed guide for both aspiring and experienced informatics professionals in healthcare. What makes this book stand out is its unique combination of practical guidance, real-world case studies, and multidisciplinary voices. It is not just a technical manual or a theoretical overview—it is a deeply practical resource grounded in the lived experiences of informatics leaders across the healthcare spectrum.

Each chapter addresses a pressing issue facing healthcare today: the evolution of patient-centered technologies, the growing challenge of documentation burden, the role of informatics in promoting health equity, the ethical use of emerging technologies like AI and robotics, and the transformation of telehealth into integrated virtual care. These are not abstract topics—they are the daily realities that define the future of modern healthcare systems.

What's especially valuable is how this book bridges disciplines. It recognizes that successful informatics work is not confined to one profession or background. It requires collaboration across nursing, medicine, IT, public health, education, and policy. Whether you're a nurse informaticist, a clinician curious about data, or a technologist building tools for the front lines, you will find insights here that inform your practice and sharpen your leadership.

Importantly, this book also highlights the human side of informatics. It reminds us that while we work with technology and data, our ultimate goal is better care for people. That means prioritizing equity, ensuring ethical implementation, and designing systems that reduce—not add to—clinician burden. It means seeing patients not as data points, but as partners in their own health journeys.

The authors have also made space for emerging issues that are reshaping the field, such as the rise of digital health literacy, the integration of AI into clinical workflows, and the need for robust cybersecurity in an era of increasing digital risk. They do so with clarity and purpose, offering not just information, but a path forward.

As someone who has spent a career at the intersection of healthcare, technology, and innovation, I see this book as more than a guide—it's a call to action. It invites all of us, regardless of role or title, to engage more fully in shaping the digital future of healthcare. It shows us what is possible when informatics is done well: systems that work, data that matters, and care that truly centers the person.

For anyone committed to improving healthcare through the thoughtful use of technology, *The Informatics Guide to Healthcare* is an essential resource. It's not just a book to read—it's one to keep close by as you chart your own informatics journey.

— **Tom Lawry**
Author, *Hacking Healthcare*
Managing Director, Second Century Tech

# Chapter 1

# Introduction

Olga Kagan and Mary Joy Garcia-Dia

We are delighted to present a practical guide for aspiring and current healthcare informatics professionals. This book was born from a recurring question: "How does one become a successful informatics professional in healthcare?" We recognize that there are numerous pathways into this dynamic field, welcoming professionals from diverse specialties such as nursing, medicine, pharmacy, and computer programming, among others.

Within these pages, we have curated a collection of stories, frameworks, and narratives from subject matter experts. These experts share invaluable examples and case studies, encompassing leadership and informatics competencies, designed to help readers hone their skills and navigate their own informatics journey successfully. Our contributors span various healthcare specialties and are leaders in their respective fields across academia, leadership, clinical practice, industry, and technology. The added value of this book lies in its practical tools, exemplifying use cases, best practices, and lessons learned. Each chapter offers unique perspectives from various experts in nursing and healthcare informatics.

Our journey through this book begins with a deep dive into **Patient-Centered Care**, where we explore the evolution of patient-facing healthcare technologies (PFTs) from early feedback devices to today's sophisticated smartphones and wearables. We emphasize critical considerations for PFT implementation, such as user engagement, robust data protection, and information accuracy, and introduce "Techquity" as a vital concept for equitable access. The discussion underscores the importance of user-centered design and addresses significant concerns regarding data security, privacy, and confidentiality, particularly with free applications. We also present methods for evaluating mHealth apps, such as the Mobile Application Rating Scale (MARS), and illustrate successes and challenges in PFT adoption through case studies. Ultimately, this chapter highlights the crucial role of informaticists in guiding technology choices, ensuring ethical considerations, and promoting secure, high-quality data use in the expanding mHealth market.

DOI: 10.4324/9781003464457-1

Following this, we provide a comprehensive overview of **Patient Portals**, defining them as online tools integrated with electronic health records (EHRs) that empower patients to access and manage their health information. We trace their history, noting the significant impact of the Health Information Technology for Economic and Clinical Health (HITECH) Act's Meaningful Use criteria and the 21st Century Cures Act. The chapter details the diverse features of modern portals, from administrative tools and secure messaging to medication management and telehealth scheduling. While emphasizing benefits like enhanced convenience and patient empowerment, we critically examine persistent challenges such as accessibility for vulnerable populations, varying eHealth literacy, and significant security concerns. The chapter concludes by stressing the importance of addressing these barriers for equitable and effective portal implementation.

Next, we address the pervasive issue of **Clinical Documentation Burden**, defining it as non-value-added work stemming primarily from extensive EHR management that contributes significantly to clinician stress and burnout. We outline the historical shift from paper to electronic documentation, driven by initiatives like the HITECH Act, and the subsequent efforts by the 21st Century Cures Act and Office of the National Coordinator (ONC) for Health Information Technology to mitigate this burden. The chapter details various interventions, including the Amer ican Medical Informatics Association (AMIA) 25x5 Documentation Burden Reduction Toolkit and the American Nursing Informatics Association's "Six Domains of Burden" framework, and explores innovative technologies like voice recognition and AI (Artificial Intelligence) scribes. Case studies illustrate successful strategies, emphasizing a multifaceted approach to alleviate burden and improve patient outcomes.

We then introduce **Leveraging Technology & Data in Driving Health Literacy and Health Equity**. This chapter examines how information communications and technology (ICT) improves health literacy and equity, especially for underserved populations who often rely on smartphones for health-related searches. It highlights disparities in broadband access and how digital health tools played a crucial role in health literacy efforts during the COVID-19 pandemic. Community-driven campaigns, such as the "Forging Partnerships" initiative, provided multilingual resources through social media and mobile apps, with groups like the Philippine Nurses Association of America sharing culturally tailored health content on platforms like YouTube and Facebook. The chapter also discusses how persuasive technology, including gamification and personalized digital health tools, enhances user engagement and fosters positive health behaviors. Data-driven strategies are presented as essential in identifying health disparities and informing targeted outreach, with examples of how disaggregated health data highlighted disproportionate impacts on specific communities, leading to focused interventions. Overall, this chapter demonstrates how ICT provides powerful solutions for overcoming barriers to healthcare access, emphasizing the integration of real-time data, community collaboration, and culturally relevant messaging to close information gaps and ensure equitable healthcare.

Our exploration then moves to the critical intersection of **Social Determinants of Health (SDOH) and Health Equity**, defining health equity as ensuring everyone has a fair opportunity for optimal health. We underscore that SDOH profoundly impact health outcomes, potentially accounting for up to 80% of health disparities, and highlight how historical discrimination contributes to unequal burdens of disease. The chapter outlines frameworks like the World Health Organization (WHO)'s SDOH model and emphasizes the vital role of nurse informaticists in integrating SDOH data into clinical workflows and IT systems, navigating regulatory mandates, and advocating for standardized data elements. Examples from various healthcare entities illustrate how nurse informaticists drive change through screening tools, predictive analytics, and community partnerships. The chapter concludes by emphasizing the continuous need for data-driven evaluation and adaptive strategies to address health disparities.

Following this, we delve into the **Ethical Use of Emerging Technologies in Healthcare**, critically examining the ethical considerations surrounding AI, robotics, telemedicine, and wearables. We organize these concerns into four key areas: Patient-Centered Concepts (informed consent, autonomy, and privacy), Data-Centered Concepts (responsible data access and security), Health Equity-Centered Concepts (bias and equitable availability), and Workforce-Centered Concepts (staff education and professional liability). Grounding these discussions in established healthcare ethics principles, five detailed case studies illustrate challenges in technology development, equity issues, informed consent, ethical leadership, and professional dilemmas. The chapter concludes with a call for proactive, interdisciplinary governance and continuous evaluation to ensure ethical implementation, patient safety, and health equity.

The discussion continues with **Healthcare Interoperability**, tracing its evolution in the United States and emphasizing its crucial role in improving care quality and efficiency. We define interoperability as the seamless, secure exchange of electronic health information "without special effort," as mandated by the 21st Century Cures Act. The historical journey highlights the foundational work of Health Insurance Portability and Accountability Act (HIPAA) of 1996) and the ONC, the patient advocacy movement for "free the data," and the impact of the HITECH Act. We detail how the 21st Century Cures Act directly addressed information blocking, promoted API (Application Programming Interface) access, and established Trusted Exchange Framework and Common Agreement (TEFCA). While progress has been made, challenges remain in achieving full data transparency, ensuring fine-grained privacy controls, and integrating patient-contributed data. Ultimately, ubiquitous interoperability promises to empower patients and providers, streamline operations, and enhance healthcare outcomes.

Next, we revisit **HIPAA, Privacy and Confidentiality, and Cybercrimes**, exploring HIPAA's crucial role in safeguarding patient privacy amid the exponential growth of digital technologies. The chapter highlights numerous instances of Protected Health Information (PHI) breaches and their severe consequences. We provide a detailed history of HIPAA modifications and discuss types of cybercrimes prevalent in healthcare, emphasizing the vulnerability posed by legacy systems and the alarming increase in PHI breaches. Case studies illustrate preventative and remediating strategies, stressing that continuous vigilance and proactive cybersecurity measures are essential to protect patient information.

The chapter on **Challenges with Integration, Access, Security, and Global EMR** highlights the critical need for integration among diverse healthcare information systems to ensure continuity of patient care. We address the "Best of Breed" strategy, which often leads to fragmented records and hinders a holistic view, emphasizing that disconnected systems negatively impact efficiency and safety. The text stresses that while interoperability enhances patient care and enables innovations, it also significantly increases cybersecurity risks. Case studies illustrate these complexities, from EHR data integration for infection prevention to medical device integration and the challenges of unifying patient records across merged systems. The conclusion reiterates that integration demands robust infrastructure, continuous adaptation, stringent data governance, and global policy alignment.

Our penultimate chapter, **Introduction to AI in Healthcare**, introduces Artificial Intelligence as an innovative force transforming healthcare, defining its application in enhancing diagnosis, treatment, and patient management. We highlight AI's relevance to nursing informatics (NI) through the Data, Information, Knowledge, Wisdom (DIKW) Framework and delve into key AI technologies: Machine Learning, Natural Language Processing, and Generative AI. Robotics and automation are also explored for their impact on clinical practice. Crucial ethical considerations like transparency, privacy, and the necessity of human–AI collaboration are emphasized, along with implementation challenges. The chapter concludes by highlighting the pivotal role of nurse informaticists in championing ethical AI adoption and optimizing clinical workflows.

Next, we explore **Emerging Technologies**, which are rapidly transforming nursing practice by offering innovative solutions to critical healthcare challenges such as staffing shortages, aging populations, and increasing care demands. This chapter introduces humanoid technologies (HTs) as anthropomorphic systems that simulate human appearance, behavior, or interaction patterns within healthcare. It traces the history of HTs from early mechanical representations to modern-day robots and digital avatars, highlighting Japan's pioneering role due to its aging population and technological advancements. The chapter delves into theoretical frameworks like Anthropomorphism, the Uncanny Valley, the Reality–Virtuality Continuum, and Human–Technology Interaction, explaining how these concepts influence the design and acceptance of HTs in nursing. It categorizes HTs into physical (e.g., humanoid service robots, human patient simulators) and digital (e.g., holograms, virtual agents) applications, providing examples and case studies of their use in education, patient care, and community health. Despite their promise, the chapter addresses significant barriers to widespread adoption, including safety, trust, ethical concerns, technical limitations, and economic factors. It concludes by outlining future directions, emphasizing advanced AI integration, collaborative care models, and the need for comprehensive regulatory frameworks to ensure HTs enhance human nurses and improve patient outcomes.

We then delve into **Telehealth Evolution towards Virtual Integrated Care**. This chapter highlights the transformative journey of telehealth into comprehensive virtual care, accelerated by the COVID-19 pandemic. It emphasizes the critical role of innovation in addressing persistent healthcare challenges like burnout, rising costs, and inefficiencies. The author effectively distinguishes between telehealth and the broader concept of virtual care, emphasizing the latter's integrated, patient-centered approach. Key virtual care modalities—virtual visits, chat-based interactions, remote patient monitoring (RPM), and technology-enabled tools—are presented, illustrating a "people, process, technology" framework for implementation. Case studies vividly demonstrate the practical applications and challenges of virtual nursing, RPM for chronic conditions, and telesitting. These examples highlight the importance of interprofessional collaboration, robust IT infrastructure, and careful patient selection for successful virtual care initiatives. The "Hospital-at-Home" model is also explored as a promising solution for delivering hospital-level care in a home setting. Overall, the chapter posits that telehealth and virtual care are not temporary fixes but essential, evolving components of modern healthcare, demanding thoughtful integration, continuous improvement, and a commitment to leveraging technology for enhanced access, outcomes, and efficiency.

In **The Evolving Role of Nurses in Informatics and Healthcare**, we explore the vital and expanding influence of NI in modern healthcare, highlighting how NI enhances efficiency, care quality, and decision-making by leveraging technology. We recognize inefficiencies in paper-based nursing documentation and the ongoing efforts to standardize nursing language, crucial for EHRs and AI training. The chapter stresses how data-driven initiatives advance patient care and the nursing profession, including potentially transforming reimbursement and addressing nursing shortages. It also discusses defining NI's value through outcome metrics and collaborative leadership. We address NI education and competencies, detailing the need for integrating AI and technology skills into nursing curricula, and differentiate between Informatics Nurses and Nurse Specialists. The chapter examines the impact of big data, emphasizing nurses' roles in ensuring data accuracy for training intelligent algorithms. It concludes by highlighting the rapid evolution of NI and the critical need for nurses to be involved in the entire lifecycle of digital tool development and deployment, advocating for NI education and roles.

Our final chapter, **Evangelizing a Culture of Innovation**, focuses on cultivating innovation in nursing informatics and healthcare, tracing its roots to pioneers like Florence Nightingale. Despite this history, significant barriers—organizational support, culture, training, staffing, funding, and regulatory hurdles—continue to impede progress. The chapter defines healthcare innovation, encompassing new solutions in policies, systems, technologies, and services, and specifically nursing innovation, which focuses on creative problem-solving. Key frameworks for fostering this culture, such as Design Thinking and Human-Centered Design, are introduced. The chapter emphasizes empowering leaders and nurses, creating safe environments for risk-taking, and leveraging external opportunities. It concludes that fostering an innovative culture is crucial for enhancing patient care and shaping the future of healthcare.

It is our sincere hope that this book serves as an invaluable resource, guiding and inspiring you on your journey to becoming a successful informatics professional in healthcare.

# Chapter 2

# Patient-Centered Care

Barbara Van de Castle

## Introduction

Patient-facing healthcare technologies (also known as patient technology or PT) are digital technologies that patients interact with to participate in their healthcare or clinical activities (Wells et al., 2014) in delivering patient-centered care. Terminologies associated with patient-facing technology (PFT) can include patient-facing mobile health technology such as mobile health applications (mHealth), smartphones, or online peer support community. Similarly, patient portals, personal health records, and the use of audiovisual tools for virtual visits are oftentimes associated with PFT. Telehealth, with its recent expansion of standards and increased adoption during and after the COVID pandemic, has been instrumental in moving patients toward technology-enabled advances and enabling patients to take control of their own healthcare. PFT provides a wide range of computer or internet-based services that support patient interactions and communication with their provider, clinical team, healthcare system, and the community (Leonardsen et al., 2020). This chapter will focus on system health technologies utilized or accessed in the communication and management of personal or population health.

## Evolution of Patient-facing Technology Applications

### *Early 1960–1990*

What was the first PFT? The weight scale can be considered one of the first pieces of equipment providing feedback to patients and providers alike. If someone did not want to know their weight, then they did not step on the scale. There was no need to accept an end user agreement just to learn their weight.

### *1990–2010*

The growing demand for more efficient communication between patients and their healthcare providers has increased the adoption of PFT and consumer e-health tools to promote patient


DOI: 10.4324/9781003464457-2

engagement and empowerment (Rozenblum & Bates, 2017). The convergence of the Internet of Things (IoT) with the Internet of Medical Things (IoMT), where medical devices such as smart scales, blood pressure machines, or continuous glucose monitoring devices are connected and monitored by healthcare professionals via the Internet, has encouraged and empowered patients to track their own data.

Current technology has stepped up by providing scales that connect with Bluetooth that will automatically upload (if the user had initially agreed to upload) their weight. Applications can also calculate the percentage of body fat and body mass index if the user agrees. The option to track these measures over time and to see them in graphical format is an excellent patient engagement tool. The healthcare data can be shared with providers or any group the patient wishes to have access to this information, such as focus groups, fitness apps, or social media.

Successful implementation and integration of PFT have increased access to timely, quality, specialty care, improved adherence to treatment, tracking and monitoring of disease progression, and improved patient outcomes (Wells et al., 2014).

## 2010–Present

Currently, there are many ways to access patient data generated from PFTs. Typical hardware equipment from desktop computers, laptops, tablets, smartphones with associated apps, and wearable devices are connected seamlessly, allowing data to be portable and available. Smartphones have become the most frequent connection for these technologies. These applications range from simple wellness tracking, such as physical activity (running, walking, biking, etc.) or a nutrition tracker (diet, calorie count, healthy menu). A person can count the number of steps or calories burned each day by wearing a smartwatch or fitness tracker. Other applications provide constant monitoring, troubleshooting, and real-time updates such as implanted insulin pumps, blood sugar levels, cardiac MEMS (a wireless monitoring system that utilizes a small, implantable device to measure pulmonary artery pressure in patients with heart failure). A smartphone application can track menses, food intake, or medication adherence. For these technologies to work well, the patient must be willing to participate in the process or encouraged by their healthcare provider to use technologies to help understand and track their own data. They need to experience the data entry process as well as see data that is automatically tracked. Tracking of one's own health data may be quite new to many people but healthcare providers who encouraged tracking tools will have to educate users on data privacy and confidentiality.

However, some patients see the importance of viewing some of their data over a web browser on a computer. For example, patient portals have become the foremost patient-facing technology due to the 21st Century Care Act[5], which mandated that healthcare organizations must provide patients with access to their health information in an electronic format. The processes that allow this communication are often linked to wearable devices and smartphone apps. Portal access allows patients to have direct communication with healthcare providers, verify and renew medications, and update their healthcare data. The category of mHealth includes all "mobile" types of portable devices such as smartphones, tablets, and wearable tech such as smartwatches. Mobile health applications are one of the biggest and fastest growing aspects of patient-facing technology today, reflected in the medical literature which already cites almost 6,000 articles exploring health care information systems and applications (Chan, 2021).

## Key Considerations with PFT Implementation

The incorporation of mobile health applications, patient portals and other emerging technologies can build a complete cycle of data and patient care when paired with patient-centered care and value-based care. Accessing these various options require key considerations such as user engagement; data use and the protection of that data (both input and output); and accuracy of the information provided through the technology. However, many PFTs may have poor design elements (Epizitone et al., 2022; Hyzy et al., 2024; Klug, 2023; Singh et al., 2016). There are valid concerns about privacy and security of data, particularly at the no-cost level. Ads can be distracting in a free application [Apps] and reduce user engagement, whereas the extra features in a paid version may enhance the experience as well as motivate a patient to get their money's worth. As the focus of healthcare moved away from a paternalistic to a patient-centered care model, techquity, user-centered design, security, privacy and confidentiality are key ingredients for the successful adoption of PFTs.

### *Techquity*

One vital aspect of PFTs is the concept of "Techquity," which as described by Rhee et al. (2021) is the "strategic development and deployment of technology in health care and health to achieve health equity." There are differences in access and the acceptance of technology throughout the globe (Goodman, 2020). How techquity is understood and maintained will be hard to accomplish but we cannot forget there can be gaps in the need to address it as research and products are created for improvement of healthcare outcomes (Johnson et al., 2023). Applying ethics to the entire use and design of PFTs should be a standard process for all health information technology.

### *User-Centered Design*

The plethora of apps provides many options; a study by Singh et al. (2016) found the top five categories of mHealth apps as defined by the highest needs and population were diabetes, hypertension, obesity, depression/bipolar disorder, smoking/alcohol, or drug abuse. Some apps have broad functionality, and others can be quite specific – but the apps are only going to be used if they can meet the patient's needs. Chronic diseases may be leading the PFT industry, but how we assess their use and impact is very important to get right.

Innovation has created numerous patient-facing applications, but not all of them provide quality end user designs. Healthcare applications comprise varying degrees of user-centric experience and design workflow. PFTs may have poor design elements (Epizitone et al., 2022; Hyzy et al., 2024; Klug, 2023; Singh et al., 2016). With so many different options of mHealth apps, it can be difficult to find a quality app that will keep the patient engaged with the activity the app is trying to promote.

### *Security, Privacy, and Confidentiality*

There are valid concerns about privacy and security of data, particularly at the no-cost level. Ads can be distracting in a free application [Apps] and reduce user engagement, whereas the extra features in a paid version may enhance the experience as well as motivate a patient to get their money's worth. Lack of quality information, healthcare data protection, and connections to healthcare experts all affect the usefulness of the data. Patients face a bewildering array of choices between paying for higher quality applications or using free applications that bombard them with ads and perhaps sell their information to various companies. A simple activity such as weight measurement may require consumers to accept an end user agreement just to learn and track their weight.

One site that monitors telehealth trends is the Medicare Telehealth Trends dashboard that provides filtering for different types of telehealth applications (Power BI Report, n.d.). This site only reflects the US Medicare and Medicaid visits; however, being able to drill down into this data shows the spike in telehealth visits at the beginning of the pandemic in 2020 (Power BI Report, n.d.). All these modalities are responses to the increasing demand from patients for engagement in their own healthcare. From tracking reproductive cycle, monitoring medication adherence, or calorie intake, users have chosen these mobile apps to manage their health. Perhaps they have been encouraged by their healthcare provider to use technologies to help understand and track their own data. However, awareness of the increase in available technologies, such as portals, desktop computers, smartphones, and watches, has been responsible for a surge in the research literature that relies on patient-reported outcomes (PRO), often termed electronic patient-reported outcomes (ePRO) (Raj et al., 2023). Finding the correct measurements for ePRO is important; the need to fit the correct measurement with the population it is studying is vital, as any error can cause data gaps and wrong outcomes. What we can learn from our work with applications and portals is well addressed in the 2017 article by Baldwin et al. (2017), indicating that the need to combine the ease of mHealth apps with the institutional data of a portal could be a better experience with the patient.

Applications are not heavily regulated, may provide incorrect information, and could be abandoned by the user in two weeks (Baldwin et al., 2017). The process involved is complex, aligning the correct Patient-Reported Outcome Measure (PROM) with the correct PFT, a process that Raj et al. (2023) describe in their effort to find the best match to improve patient engagement. PROMs need to efficiently capture and measure data in a way that keeps the patient engaged not only for research but also in a way that can improve patient outcomes over time. Consideration for respondent burden in PFTs must be chosen deliberately or patient engagement will not occur (Raj et al., 2023). Evaluating mHealth apps is not an easy task. The Mobile App Rating Scale (MARS) was created in 2015 by Stoyanov et al. (2015) because of a lack of valid and reliable tools to assess the quality of mHealth applications. The MARS consists of 23 items and four subscales, where the items are rated one to five (one is inadequate up to five being excellent). The subscales measure app engagement, functionality, aesthetics, and quality of information (Stoyanov et al., 2015).

As with all scales, there are benefits and challenges, so it is important to understand how to use MARS or other rating scales and be aware of shortcomings when using them as standards. Organization for the Review of Care and Health Applications (ORCHA) is a United Kingdom–based digital health company that assesses health applications used to evaluate 881 Android-based health apps (Hyzy et al., 2024). User ratings and number of downloads were assessed with objective quality measures, evaluating whether the higher rating and downloads could be equivalent to higher quality applications. Hyzy et al. (2024) findings suggested no meaningful link between user ratings and the number of downloads and with objective quality measures. Applications need to be selected based on high-quality actionable items – not the ratings and number of downloads. Understanding the barriers with the design of mHealth applications is essential in providing and improving the healthcare services these apps can provide (He et al., 2023).

Understanding the impact of these technologies and the influence they have on patients is important, yet it is not common practice for practitioners to recommend specific applications, due to the many variables that can occur for each patient, including concerns about privacy and their access and willingness to use the applications, all of which can be hard to assess for time-pressed staff (Singh et al., 2016).

## Case Studies

User engagement is the main ingredient for successful PFTs. With so many different options of mHealth apps, it can be difficult to find a quality app that will keep the patient engaged with the activity the app is trying to promote. There are good examples of PFTs losing patient engagement after a period. For example, weight loss is a common goal for PFTs, and studies have shown that patient engagement is high at the beginning of the user experience, correlating with more weight loss in the first three months of using the app. The authors found that early engagement occurs in many trials, but most drop off within three to six months (Lehmann et al., 2024). The findings show that patients trying out a new app that will track the calories consumed may have to add nutritional content manually because the app does not have an integrated barcode reader. In some cases, the weight-loss app integrates restaurant products with estimated calories, but may not include all food products, limiting the capability for the user to enter the calorie count. This lack of functionality can easily cause the user of the app to abandon it and not achieve the satisfaction of measuring caloric intake. Poor functionality and a lack of user design lead to incorrect feedback, contributing to loss of interest in an app.

On the other hand, the treatment of tuberculosis has used direct observation treatment for medication delivery for a long time, showing effectiveness in treating tuberculosis with direct observation (Tadesse et al., 2024). This treatment methodology requires a large amount of monitoring and support from various people. The ASCENT trial studied the use of a smart pill box and medication labels in a multicountry study for the treatment of tuberculosis. The authors found the use of a smart pill box was feasible; however, it had multiple challenges, such as power outages and poor networks. Limited infrastructure and downtime procedures need to be considered for PFT.

Using smartphones for the identification of ophthalmic needs in underserved areas has been highly successful. Retinal imaging can be accomplished with smartphone imaging, where fundus cameras are not readily available. In a study by Vishwanath et al. (2023), various conditions were identified with a smartphone using the camera in video mode with the flashlight on while the examiner held a +20 D lens on the other hand. These exams were accomplished at rural "eye camps," and over 100 patients (children and adults) were assessed and various conditions identified, such as glaucoma, retinal detachment, and toxoplasmosis. The growth in this area of ophthalmic care with smartphones has taken off and is growing each year. Jin et al. (2024) have a systematic review looking at the use of this technology and AI, assessing 52 articles from 2018 to 2023.

## Conclusion

For the working informaticist, it is important to understand the numerous responsibilities in making PFT choices. The application must engage the user both initially and over time as newer functionality and updates are developed. All the work with PFTs must take ethical considerations into their entire planning for the end user to trust and be engaged with their products. As the mHealth market continues to grow with AI and patient data, the need for secure data and its use must employ quality and standards that meet the values of transparency, veracity, and accountability (Goodman, 2020). Data protection is paramount, and the end user should understand how their data will be used. If you are evaluating these technologies, it is important to use the right standard measurements and scales for a quality assessment. We will continue to see a proliferation of healthcare apps connecting to our patients, and providers will turn to informaticists for guidance. Be prepared to provide that guidance by understanding the impact of this ever-growing technology.

## References

Baldwin, J. L., Singh, H., Sittig, D. F., & Giardina, T. D. (2017). Patient portals and health apps: Pitfalls, promises, and what one might learn from the other. *Healthcare (Amsterdam, Netherlands)*, *5*(3), 81–85. https://doi.org/10.1016/j.hjdsi.2016.08.004

Chan, J. (2021). Exploring digital health care: eHealth, mHealth, and librarian opportunities. *Journal of the Medical Library Association: JMLA*, *109*(3), 376–381. https://doi.org/10.5195/jmla.2021.1180

Epizitone, A., Moyane, S. P., & Agbehadji, I. E. (2022). Health information system and health care applications performance in the healthcare arena: A bibliometric analysis. *Healthcare*, *10*(11), 2273. https://doi.org/10.3390/healthcare10112273

Goodman, K. W. (2020). Ethics in health informatics. *Yearbook of Medical Informatics*, *29*(1), 26–31. https://doi.org/10.1055/s-0040-1701966

He, X., Zheng, X., & Ding, H. (2023). Existing barriers faced by and future design recommendations for direct-to-consumer health care artificial intelligence apps: Scoping review. *Journal of Medical Internet Research*, *25*, e50342. https://doi.org/10.2196/50342

Hyzy, M., Bond, R., Mulvenna, M., Bai, L., Frey, A. L., Carracedo, J. M., Daly, R., & Leigh, S. (2024). Don't judge a book or health app by its cover: User ratings and downloads are not linked to quality. *PLoS ONE*, *19*(3), e0298977. https://doi.org/10.1371/journal.pone.0298977

Jin, K., Li, Y., Wu, H., Tham, Y. C., Koh, V., Zhao, Y., Kawasaki, R., Grzybowski, A., & Ye, J. (2024). Integration of smartphone technology and artificial intelligence for advanced ophthalmic care: A systematic review. *Advances in Ophthalmology Practice and Research*, *4*(3), 120–127. https://doi.org/10.1016/j.aopr.2024.03.003

Johnson, K. B., Ibrahim, S. A., & Rosenbloom, S. T. (2023). Ensuring equitable access to patient portals: Closing the "techquity" gap. *JAMA Health Forum*, *4*(11), e233406. https://doi.org/10.1001/jamahealthforum.2023.3406

Klug, J. B. (2023). An overview of the Mobile App Rating Scale (MARS) in health care application assessment. *Journal of Hospital Librarianship*, *24*(1), 70–79. https://doi.org/10.1080/15323269.2023.2289804

Lehmann, M., Jones, L., & Schirmann, F. (2024). App engagement as a predictor of weight loss in blended-care interventions: Retrospective observational study using large-scale real-world data. *Journal of Medical Internet Research*, *26*, e45469. https://doi.org/10.2196/45469

Leonardsen, A. C., Hardeland, C., Helgesen, A. K., & Grøndahl, V. A. (2020). Patient experiences with technology-enabled care across healthcare settings: A systematic review. *BMC Health Services Research*, *20*, Article 779. https://bmchealthservres.biomedcentral.com/articles/10.1186/s12913-020-05633-4

Power BI Report. (n.d.). https://app.powerbigov.us/view?r=eyJrIjoiOGMzNGY1M2EtODkyMi00NzJiLTk5YzMtODMwODNiODc3NWIyIiwidCI6ImQ1OGFkZGVhLTUwNTMtNGE4MC04NDk5LWJhNGQ5NDQ5MTBkZiJ9

Raj, P., Cho, Y., Jiang, Y., & Gong, Y. (2023). Selecting patient-reported outcome measures for a patient-facing technology. *JAMIA Open*, *6*(4), ooad104. https://doi.org/10.1093/jamiaopen/ooad104

Rhee, K., Dankwa-Mullan, I., Brennan, V., & Clark, C. (2021). What is techquity? *Journal of Health Care for the Poor and Underserved*, *32*(2), xiii–xviii.

Rozenblum, R., & Bates, D. W. (2017). The role of patient-facing technologies to empower patients and improve safety. *PSNet Perspectives*. https://psnet.ahrq.gov/perspective/role-patient-facing-technologies-empower-patients-and-improve-safety

Singh, K., Drouin, K., Newmark, L. P., Lee, J., Faxvaag, A., Rozenblum, R., Pabo, E. A., Landman, A., Klinger, E., & Bates, D. W. (2016). Many mobile health apps target high-need, high-cost populations, but gaps remain. *Health Affairs (Project Hope)*, *35*(12), 2310–2318. https://doi.org/10.1377/hlthaff.2016.0578

Stoyanov, S. R., Hides, L., Kavanagh, D. J., Zelenko, O., Tjondronegoro, D., & Mani, M. (2015). Mobile app rating scale: A new tool for assessing the quality of health mobile apps. *JMIR mHealth and uHealth*, *3*(1), e27. https://doi.org/10.2196/mhealth.3422

Tadesse, A. W., Mganga, A., Dube, T. N., Alacapa, J., van Kalmthout, K., Letta, T., Mleoh, L., Garfin, A. M. C., Maraba, N., Charalambous, S., Foster, N., Jerene, D., & Fielding, K. L. (2024). Feasibility and acceptability of the smart pillbox and medication label with differentiated care to support person-centered tuberculosis care among ASCENT trial participants—A multicountry study. *Frontiers in Public Health, 12*, 1327971. https://doi.org/10.3389/fpubh.2024.1327971

Vishwanath, S., Swamy, D. T., & Gaddi, D. S. (2023). Smartphone for retinal imaging: Case series in resource-limited rural settings. *Indian Journal of Ophthalmology, 71*(5), 2008–2013. https://doi.org/10.4103/ijo.IJO_2077_22

Wells, S., Rozenblum, R., Park, A., Dunn, M., & Bates, D. W. (2014). Personal health records for patients with chronic disease: A major opportunity. *Applied Clinical Informatics, 5*(2), 416–429. https://doi.org/10.4338/ACI-2014-01-RA-0002

# Chapter 3

# Patient Portals

Kathleen Begonia

## Background and History of Patient Portals

Over the years, many people have turned to technology for better ways to securely organize and communicate their health information. Technology has proven its dominance in disrupting and creating change in society to improve the quality and safety of daily living. Many technological applications were created to improve user experience through knowledge empowerment. The field of healthcare is increasingly impacted by technological innovations, as seen by the implementation of patient portals.

The term 'patient portal' is defined consistently in healthcare literature as an online tool that integrates with the electronic health record (EHR) of a healthcare organization and is used by patients to view and track health information (Ammenwerth et al., 2011; Medline, 2018; Powell & Myers, 2018). Patient portals are bidirectional electronic pathways that allow patients to input data such as demographics and medication lists and provide patients with information about labs, diagnostic results, appointment scheduling, clinic visit summaries, patient education, and secure messaging with clinicians. They may be in the form of software applications or websites that integrate with the EHR to provide valuable information to patients.

Much of the information on the portal is standardized because of the Centers for Medicare and Medicaid's (CMS) Meaningful Use Stage 2 criteria, which allowed healthcare facilities to receive incentive payments for 5% of their patients actively using the portal (Office of the National Coordinator for Health Information Technology, 2017). When patients use their portals, they increase their knowledge about their health status and make lifestyle choices to improve health outcomes (Greene & Hibbard, 2011).

To promote the adoption and meaningful use of health information technology, the Health Information Technology for Economic and Clinical Health (HITECH) Act was enacted as part of the American Recovery and Reinvestment Act in 2009 (Department of Health and Human Services, 2017). Under the HITECH Act, Meaningful Use requirements, also known as the EHR Incentive Program, were created by the CMS to regulate and encourage the development of technology that supports quality care and patient engagement between 2011 and 2015. Due to federal

DOI: 10.4324/9781003464457-3

financial incentives offered to physician practices under Stage 2 of Meaningful Use, patient portals were widely implemented.

According to Meaningful Use Stage 2, 5% of patients must view, download, and transmit their health data and communicate with physicians via patient portals for providers to qualify for federal financial incentives (Anumula and Sanelli, 2012; Centers for Medicare and Medicaid Services, 2013). After Meaningful Use ended, CMS renamed the Meaningful Use EHR Incentive Programs to the Medicare and Medicaid Promoting Interoperability Programs in April 2018. Under the Promoting Interoperability measures, clinicians seeking incentive payment for services were required to 'Provide Patients Electronic Access to Their Health Information.' As of June 2024, the program is known as the **Medicare Promoting Interoperability Program** for eligible hospitals and clinics. For the most up-to-date information regarding the Medicaid Promoting Interoperability Program, please contact your state Medicaid agency or review the FY 2019 IPPS and LTCH final rule (83 FR 41676 through 41677) (CMS, 2013; U.S. Department of Health and Human Services, 2020).

The 21st Century Cures Act was introduced in 2021 with the goal of eliminating information blocking. This act allowed patients to see any of their health information, including progress notes and diagnostic test results, immediately and often without discussion with the patient's primary care provider. Prior to this act, many organizations suppressed or delayed the release of diagnostic test results, allowing time for providers to review results prior to patients; while such a delay potentially allows time for provider interpretation and communication, there is also a potential for 'information blocking' where patients do not have timely access to diagnostic results (Wood et al., 2023). The Cures Act has contributed to some of the challenges with patient portals.

## Features

Patient portal use and adoption have surged in the past five years, which makes them a crucial channel for timely healthcare access (Johnson et al. 2023). They facilitate a wide array of healthcare services, which include scheduling appointments, either in-person or virtual visits, secure messaging, preventive care alerts (i.e., flu shot reminder), pre-visit screening forms, and patient-reported outcome measures. For example, patients increasingly use portal-based secure messaging rather than calling the physician's office, they pay bills through a portal rather than mailing checks, and they schedule clinical visits and ancillary testing primarily using a portal (Table 3.1).

**Table 3.1 Features of Patient Portals**

| *Feature* | *Description* |
|---|---|
| Administrative tools | Patients can log in to make updates regarding contact information, patient preferences with care, advance directives, such as update DNR/DNI (Do not resuscitate/Do not intubate) status or designate a next of kin/emergency contact person, download and complete forms prior to going to the clinic (which saves time filling out forms at the office) |
| Appointment scheduling | Allows patients to make appointments or find a referral for another clinical appointment |

*(Continued)*

**Table 3.1 (*Continued*)**

| *Feature* | *Description* |
|---|---|
| Secure messaging | Allows patients to communicate with their care team, including nurses, physicians, and interdisciplinary clinicians, about various health conditions |
| Billing and payment | Clinicians are able to post patient bills on the patient portal, and patients can submit payments electronically |
| Insurance and benefits | Allows patients to update and view insurance coverage as it relates to the clinic or hospital they are associated with |
| Access to medical records | Allows patient ability to view health information such as lab results, allergies, or history of allergic reactions, immunizations, notes from hospital or clinic visits, and uploaded images from diagnostic tests or patient uploaded files (i.e., for skin appointments) |
| Patient education | Ability to find and view educational resources through a direct link provided by the medical organization |
| Medication list | Patients can view a list of their current and previous medications |
| Prescription refills | Patients can request a refill of their prescription if needed |
| Telehealth visits | Some clinics provide patients the option of scheduling a telehealth visit (i.e., dermatology visits, which allow a clinician to visualize a patient's skin easily) through the portal |
| Patient wearable data collection | Some portals allow a patient to link and upload their data from a wearable device (Apple watch, continuous glucose monitor, or even data from blood pressure, pulse oxygenation, or temperature monitor) |

# Benefits

## *Convenience*

Most portals provide patients with around-the-clock access to their medical records, which allows them to view and reflect on their health results and notes about their plan of care at any time. Patients enjoy the convenience, ease of use, and ability to engage in their health (El Yaman et al., 2023). With this convenient access, patients can follow up with other clinicians for a second opinion since they have a documented history of their health information. As long as the portal is available online and the patient has internet access, the patient has the ability to log on from anywhere in the world, while on vacation abroad, or overnight during the early morning hours.

Studies have shown that patients' ability to access their health information and test results at their convenience significantly facilitated future in-person patient–clinician communication (McAlearney et al., 2019). Patients can refer to specific diagnostic exam results or notes when discussing a plan of care during telehealth or in-person office visits; this contributes to their ability to make informed decisions about their health. Active portal users have demonstrated improvement in medication adherence, disease awareness and prevention, self-management of disease, and a decrease in office visits; they were increasingly satisfied with care and more likely to stay with their physician's practice (Kruse, Bolton, & Freriks, 2015).

### Empowerment

Patient empowerment describes a situation where the patients' role is changing from a patronized patient to an informed patient who is a responsible, autonomous, and competent partner in care (Ammenwerth et al., 2011). Empowerment gives people a sense of responsibility for their health. A concept analysis of the term 'empowerment' defines it as a process that helps people assert control over factors that affect their lives (Gibson, 1991). Studies show that portals contribute to a sense of independence and patient empowerment (Kelly et al., 2019; McAlearney et al., 2019). Qualitative research conducted on patient feelings about portal influence on empowerment resulted in two themes: (1) being heard and (2) moving forward (Risling et al., 2018).

Empowering a community with technology and technical skills can encourage people to realize their potential and increase individual productivity (Hägglund et al., 2022). When patients access their portals and engage in their health information, they may become empowered with knowledge and awareness of their health status. Patients can directly communicate with their care team by sending secure messages asking simple questions about their health and scheduling either telehealth visits or in-person appointments. Patients engaged with secure messaging feel heard by their care team and increase their health knowledge, which fosters a sense of self-efficacy while becoming competent in managing information. Evidence suggests that portals can improve self-efficacy by providing tools for enhanced self-management (Kelly et al., 2019; Risling et al., 2018). Increased engagement in health information has demonstrated improved health outcomes (Greene & Hibbard, 2011; Risling et al., 2017).

## Challenges

### Accessibility

Despite the rapid expansion of portals, there is minimal attention paid to the accessibility of portals for vulnerable patient populations, including individuals who may not easily use internet resources, such as people who are elderly, people with lower income, people of varied ethnic and racial backgrounds, and people with disabilities (Deshpande et al., 2023; Lyles, Fruchterman, Youdelman, & Schillinger, 2017; Nahm et al., 2020; Nishii et al., 2022). A majority of those who access portals are non-Hispanic white (Oest, Hightower, & Krasowski, 2018; Sorondo, Allen, Fathima, Bayleran, & Sabbagh, 2017). Vulnerable populations often need chronic medical care and face the most barriers to portal access due to factors such as health literacy and socioeconomic status (Lyles et al., 2017).

### eHealth Literacy

eHealth literacy, also known as digital literacy, is the ability of a patient to find, understand, and evaluate health information from the internet and electronic sources. Patients with low eHealth literacy skills are less likely to use the internet for health information, which makes them less inclined to use a portal (Deshpande et al., 2023). According to Nishii et al. (2022), adoption of portals is a challenge, and less than half of insured adult patients reported accessing an online portal in the prior 12 months; this was less common among patients who are male, are Hispanic, have less than a college degree, have Medicaid insurance, have no regular healthcare provider, or lack internet access. To log on to a portal, one must have a computer and secure internet service. To effectively navigate a portal, basic computer skills and portal training are needed. One of the reasons for not accessing a portal is discomfort with technology (Nishii et al., 2022). It would be helpful if portal training could be provided by physician practices offering portals since each portal is designed and maintained by the clinic's information technology team. Training ensures that patients and their caregivers know how to manage health information efficiently. Training should be provided yearly to ensure that the users remain competent in navigating their health information. The yearly competency training can also raise a flag to the clinic staff if a caretaker must be designated to manage health information.

As an unintended consequence, patient empowerment through portals may generate dependency on systems and the desire for instant electronic results (Calvillo et al., 2013). If results are not available due to a system downtime, patients may become anxious. Patients may feel powerless or unable to maintain health without technology. Additionally, the portal information may spark mixed emotions for patients; based on their clinical knowledge, they may feel relieved or overwhelmed. If patients with no medical background log on to their portal only to see concerning diagnostic results, they may feel overwhelmed with the medical terminology explaining the results. The 21st Century Cures Act allows notes and diagnostic results to be posted on the portal without any delay, which may mean that the patient can see the result, which may display in complex medical terminology, before their clinician has had the opportunity to review the result.

### *Security Concerns*

Maintaining the security of portals is one of the challenges as there are alarming amounts of cyberattacks that attack web servers, crack passwords, and harvest personal information of portal users (Hosseini et al., 2019). Patients may not be inclined to use a patient portal because of privacy and security concerns. Patients are concerned their health information may be at risk of a security breach due to ongoing cyberthreats. In addition, many caregivers access the patient portal on behalf of the patient; the reasons may be due to a disability, such as functional support needed when accessing the portal. In a study by Latulipe et al. (2020), almost half of the surveyed hospital staff encouraged password sharing, and few hospitals enabled patients to limit the types of information seen by those with proxy access. This concerning behavior may unintentionally contribute to the likelihood of a security breach of patient data.

## Case Studies

Three case studies are presented based on Walker and Avant's model to illustrate real-life example of eHealth literacy of a model case (Gunawan et al., 2023). A borderline, related, and contrary model will address factors such as access, language barriers, and vulnerable group (i.e., elderly population).

### *Model Case: Computer Literacy*

Dan is a 42-year-old man working as a high-school English teacher. In the evenings, he has been noticing consistent chest and back pain while using his laptop to grade his students' electronic assignments. At first, he thinks the pain is related to his posture while using his laptop; however, he starts to become fatigued and develops shortness of breath and intermittent episodes of coughing.

Remembering that he signed up for a patient portal, he signs on in-between grading assignments and sends his doctor's office a message about his symptoms. While checking his email the next morning, he sees a message from his doctor's office to schedule an appointment immediately. Dan logs on to his portal and schedules the next available appointment listed later that day. He goes to his doctor who examines and refers him to diagnostic imaging for body scans and chest X-rays. Dan waits for his results to post on the portal. As he consistently checks the portal, he realizes that there is patient education material available about lung diseases and what body scans can indicate. One evening at 8 pm, the results are posted and they are positive for a mass in the left lung's lower lobe. Shortly after the results post, he sees a message from his doctor notifying him that he will call the next morning at 9 am to discuss the results and next steps.

Despite seeing potentially life-changing diagnostic results on the portal before the doctor speaks with him, he feels empowered because he sees what the clinicians see at the same time they do. He also feels that the portal has provided him with the knowledge needed to participate in his care. This is a model case because it demonstrates the process of building the patient's confidence in navigating health information on a portal, active meaningful use, and feeling heard and acknowledged by the clinical team.

### *Related Case: Access*

John, 22 years old, lives with Down syndrome, a congenital heart defect, and a few other chronic conditions. To manage his lower leg weakness, dermatitis, hypothyroidism, and increasing anxiety, he requires numerous appointments scheduled with various physicians and therapists. To be able to accompany him to his appointments and help provide care, his parents work part-time and per diem. Many of John's healthcare costs are paid out of pocket, limiting finances for the internet and a computer.

John's parents were overwhelmed with tracking appointments, labs, and medications. They often had questions about his daily care, but had to wait months for available clinic appointments to ask these questions. In addition, John needs psychotherapy; however, he finds it difficult to go to yet another clinic office and would like to try one online. John and John's parents heard about patient portals at the doctor's office, but cost and guidance on the enrollment process were limiting factors.

Fortunately, John was financially and medically eligible for Medicaid. A Medicaid service coordinator reviewed his budget and was able to allocate a portion of funds toward internet costs and a personal computer. After signing up for the portal, John's parents were able to easily manage his care. John was able to see a psychotherapist virtually from the comfort of his home since he found a virtual therapist who accepted Medicaid. John's office visits decreased, and he maintained optimal health thanks to the help of his portal.

### *Contrary Case: Language Barrier*

A 55-year-old woman, Lina, who immigrated to the United States three years ago from Indonesia is encouraged by her daughter to go to the free mammography screenings offered by the local hospital. After the screening, Lina is mailed the diagnostic results, which show that she needs a biopsy to rule out breast cancer. The name of a clinic is provided and she schedules an appointment over the phone with her daughter's help since she speaks limited English. While she is at the clinic, they encourage her to sign up for the patient portal. Her daughter helps her sign up for the portal, but does not consistently help her use it to view results, patient education, or schedule follow-up appointments. Lina is confused about her diagnosis and wants to know the next steps, but feels limited by her inability to understand English or use computers. Lina waits for her daughter's availability to help navigate her care.

Lina is able to access a portal, but she cannot build the confidence to use it on her own to navigate her information. Lina can actively use the portal with her daughter's help, and she can acquire knowledge through the portal. However, due to the language barrier, she needs a language interpreter to translate the content to her, and the clinical team hears and acknowledges her daughter and not her directly. If the portal were available in various languages, reflective of cultural differences, and tailored to individualized experiences, many more people would be able to use it.

### *Borderline Case: Elderly Population*

A 65-year-old patient, Mr. Smith, has been diagnosed with diabetes and is encouraged by his healthcare provider to monitor his lab results, appointment schedules, and medication information through the hospital's patient portal. Mr. Smith is eager to take an active role in managing his health, so he attempts to access the patient portal from his home computer. Mr. Smith encounters multiple technical issues, such as forgotten login credentials and a lack of computer literacy, preventing him from successfully logging into the portal. Although the hospital offers technical support, Mr. Smith finds it difficult to navigate the process of contacting support due to long wait times and complex instructions. As a result, he is unable to resolve the issues on his own.

## Conclusion

Patient portals provide many features that patients use to help them become involved in their health. The benefits of self-scheduling, communication with the care team, and tracking healthcare notes can promote a sense of patient empowerment. Since patient portals have shown to improve self-efficacy and improve health outcomes, special attention should be focused on vulnerable populations in improving access to patient portals.

Despite government efforts to encourage widespread patient portal adoption and interoperability, significant access challenges persist, as highlighted in recent peer-reviewed literature. Cost remains a barrier, particularly for lower-income individuals (AnodynePay, 2024; McAlearney et al., 2024), while disparities in internet access continue to limit use (Fareed et al., 2021). Low digital literacy, especially among older adults, further impedes adoption (Gavin Publishers, 2023), and language barriers significantly affect engagement for non-English speakers (AHIMA Foundation, 2022). Moreover, ongoing cybersecurity concerns can deter patients from utilizing these platforms (Frontier Business, 2021; ReferralMD, 2024). Addressing these multifaceted challenges, including financial accessibility, infrastructure improvements, digital literacy support, multilingual options, and robust security measures, is crucial for achieving equitable and effective patient portal implementation.

## References

AHIMA Foundation. (2022). *Language access in health information: Key considerations.* https://ahima.oundation.ahima.org/understanding-the-issues/requesting-translation-of-patient-portals/

Ammenwerth, E., Schnell-Inderst, P., & Hoerbst, A. (2011). Patient empowerment by electronic health records: First results of a systematic review on the benefit of patient portals. *Studies in Health Technology and Informatics, 165* (63–67). Amsterdam: IOS Press. Retrieved from https://www.researchgate.net/profile/Elske_Ammenwerth/publication/51231049_Patient_empowerment_by_electronic_health_records_First_results_of_a_systematic_review_on_the_benefit_of_patient_portals/links/55b7c48108ae092e965743ff.pdf

AnodynePay. (2024). *Patient Portal Pros & Cons: SWOT & Cost Benefit Analysis.* https://www.anodynesimplepay.com/blogs/patient-portal-benefits

Anumula, N., & Sanelli, P. C. (2012). Meaningful use. *AJNR: American Journal of Neuroradiology, 33*(8), 1455–1457. https://doi.org/10.3174/ajnr.A3247

Calvillo, J., Román, I., & Roa, L. M. (2013). How technology is empowering patients? A literature review. *Health Expectations: An International Journal of Public Participation in Health Care and Health Policy, 18*(5), 643–652. https://doi.org/10.1111/hex.12089

Centers for Medicare and Medicaid Services. (2013). EHR incentive programs. Retrieved from http://www.cms.gov/Regulations-and-Guidance/Legislation/EHRIncentivePrograms/

Department of Health and Human Services. (2017). HITECH act enforcement interim final rule. Retrieved from http://www.hhs.gov/hipaa/for-professionals/special-topics/hitech-act-enforcement-interim-final-rule/index.html

Deshpande, N., Arora, V., Vollbrecht, H., Meltzer, D., & Press, V. (2023). EHealth literacy and patient portal use and attitudes: Cross-sectional observational study. *JMIR Human Factors.* https://humanfactors.jmir.org/2023/1/e40105

El Yaman, N., Zeitoun, J., Diab, R., Mdaihly, M., Diab, R., Kobeissi, L., Abou Ljoud, S., Antoun, J., & Bardus, M. (2023). Utilization of patient portals: a cross-sectional study investigating associations with mobile app quality.*BMC medical informatics and decision making, 23*(1), 177. https://doi.org/10.1186/s12911-023-02252-x

Fareed, N., et al. (2021). Disparities in patient portal use: A systematic review and meta-analysis. *Journal of Medical Internet Research, 23*(3), e21708.

Frontier Business. (2021). *The importance of cybersecurity in healthcare.* https://enterprise.frontier.com/dcaas-staticassets/enterprise/blogs/pdf/MNS---Healthcare_Inoculating-Health-Systems-from-Ransomware-Attacks.pdf

Gavin Publishers. (2023). *Barriers that Affect the Use of Patient Portals.* https://www.gavinpublishers.com/article/view/barriers-that-affect-the-use-of-patient-portals

Gibson, C. (1991). A concept analysis of empowerment. *Journal of Advanced Nursing, 16(3),* 354–361. Retrieved from https://doi.org/10.1111/j.1365-2648.1991.tb01660.x

Greene, J., & Hibbard, J. H. (2011). Why does patient activation matter? An examination of the relationships between patient activation and health-related outcomes. *Journal of General Internal Medicine, 27*(5), 520–526. https://doi.org/10.1007/s11606-011-1931-2

Gunawan, J., Aungsuroch, Y., & Marzilli, C. (2023). Beyond the classics: A comprehensive look at concept analysis methods in nursing education and research. *Belitung nursing journal, 9*(5), 406–410. https://doi.org/10.33546/bnj.2544

Hägglund, M., McMillan, B., Whittaker, R., & Blease, C. (2022). Patient empowerment through online access to health records. *BMJ (Clinical research ed.), 378,* e071531. https://doi.org/10.1136/bmj-2022-071531

Hosseini, N., Fakhar, F., Kiani, B., & Eslami, S. (2019). Enhancing the security of patients' portals and websites by detecting malicious web crawlers using machine learning techniques. *International Journal of Medical Informatics, 132,* 103976. https://doi.org/10.1016/j.ijmedinf.2019.103976

Johnson, K. B., Ibrahim, S. A., & Rosenbloom, S. T. (2023). Ensuring Equitable Access to Patient Portals-Closing the "Techquity" Gap. *JAMA health forum, 4*(11), e233406. https://doi.org/10.1001/jamahealthforum.2023.3406

Kelly, M., Thurber, A., Coller, R. J., Khan, A., Dean, S. M., Smith, W., & Hoonakker, P. (2019). Parent perceptions of real-time access to their hospitalized child's medical records using an inpatient portal: A qualitative study. *Hospital Pediatrics, 9*(4), 273–280. https://doi.org/10.1542/hpeds.2018-0166

Kruse, C. S., Bolton, K., & Freriks, G. (2015). The effect of patient portals on quality outcomes and its implications to meaningful use: A systematic review. *Journal of Medical Internet Research, 17*(2), e44. https://doi.org/10.2196/jmir.3171

Latulipe, C., Mazumder, S. F., Wilson, R. K. W., Talton, J. W., Bertoni, A. G., Quandt, S. A., Arcury, T. A., & Miller, D. P., Jr (2020). Security and privacy risks associated with adult patient portal accounts in US hospitals. *JAMA Internal Medicine*, *180*(6), 845–849. https://doi.org/10.1001/jamainternmed.2020.0515

Lyles, C. R., Fruchterman, J., Youdelman, M., & Schillinger, D. (2017). Legal, practical, and ethical considerations for making online patient portals accessible for all. *American Journal of Public Health*, *107*(10), 1608–1611. https://doi.org/10.2105/AJPH.2017.303933

McAlearney, A. S., Sieck, C. J., Gaughan, A., Fareed, N., Volney, J., & Huerta, T. R. (2019). Portal use across care settings: Qualitative study. *Journal of Medical Internet Research*, *21*(6), e13126.

McAlearney, A. S., Sieck, C. J., Gaughan, A., Fareed, N., Volney, J., & Huerta, T. R. Patients' perceptions of Next Avenue. (2024). *Hidden Costs Lurk Behind Patient Portals.* https://www.nextavenue.org/hidden-costs-behind-patient-portals/

Medline. (2018). Patient portals: An online tool for your health. Retrieved from https://medlineplus.gov/ency/patientinstructions/000880.htm

Nahm, E. S., Son, H., & Yoon, J. M. (2020). Older adults' use of patient portals: Experiences, challenges, and suggestions shared through discussion board forums. *Geriatric Nursing*, *41*(4), 387–393. https://doi.org/10.1016/j.gerinurse.2019.12.001

Nishii, A., Campos-Castillo, C., & Anthony, D. (2022). Disparities in patient portal access by US adults before and during the COVID-19 pandemic. *JAMIA Open*, *5*(4), ooac104. https://doi.org/10.1093/jamiaopen/ooac104

Oest, S., Hightower, M., & Krasowski, M. D. (2018). Activation and utilization of an electronic health record patient portal at an academic medical center: Impact of patient demographics and geographic location. *Academic Pathology*, *5*(2), 25–30. https://doi.org/10.1177/2374289518797573

Office of the National Coordinator for Health Information Technology. (2017). What is a patient portal? Retrieved from https://www.healthit.gov/faq/what-patient-portal

Powell, K. & Myers, C. (2018). Electronic patient portals: Patient and provider perceptions. *Online Journal of Nursing Informatics (OJNI)*, *22*(1), Retrieved from http://www.himss.org/ojni

ReferralMD. (2024). *Best Practices for Data Security: Protecting Patient Privacy.* https://getreferralmd.com/patient-portals-best-practices-for-protecting-data/

Risling, T., Martinez, J., Young, J., & Thorp-Froslie, N. (2017). Evaluating patient empowerment in association with ehealth technology: Scoping review. *Journal of Medical Internet Research*, *19*(9), e329. https://doi.org/10.2196/jmir.7809

Risling, T., Martinez, J., Young, J., & Thorp-Froslie, N. (2018). Defining empowerment and supporting engagement using patient views from the citizen health information portal: Qualitative study. *JMIR medical informatics*, *6*(3), e43. https://doi.org/10.2196/medinform.8828

Sorondo, B., Allen, A., Fathima, S., Bayleran, J., & Sabbagh, I. (2017). Patient portal as a tool for enhancing patient experience and improving quality of care in primary care practices. *EGEMS: Generating Evidence and Methods to Improve Patient Outcomes*, *4*(1), 1262. https://doi.org/10.13063/2327-9214.1262

U.S. Department of Health and Human Services. (2020, August 25). *Promoting interoperability: Provide patients electronic access to their health information: Guidance portal.* Promoting Interoperability: Provide Patients Electronic Access to Their Health Information|Guidance Portal. https://www.hhs.gov/guidance/document/promoting-interoperability-provide-patients-electronic-access-their-health-information

Wood, K. E., Pham, H. T., Carter, K. D., Nepple, K. G., Blum, J. M., & Krasowski, M. D. (2023). Impact of a switch to immediate release on the patient viewing of diagnostic test results in an online portal at an academic medical center. *Journal of pathology informatics*, *14*, 100323. https://doi.org/10.1016/j.jpi.2023.100323

# Chapter 4

# Addressing Clinical Documentation Burden

Elaine Hui-Martinez

## Introduction

Clinical documentation burden represents a significant challenge in modern healthcare, impacting clinicians across various disciplines. This burden is primarily linked to the extensive time and effort required for managing electronic health records (EHRs) and has been associated with increased stress and burnout among healthcare professionals (Moy et al., 2021). According to the American Medical Informatics Association (AMIA), documentation burden is defined as "work that does not add value" or work that exceeds what is required for good clinical care (AMIA, 2024). This burden can arise from organizational, state, and federal sources.

Documentation forms a cornerstone of patient care, ensuring safety and adherence to regulatory standards through the meticulous recording of patient interactions, treatment strategies, and their resulting outcomes. Building upon the foundational Quadruple Aim, which emphasized enhancing patient experience, improving population health, reducing per capita cost, and bolstering clinician well-being (Bodenheimer & Sinsky, 2014), the healthcare landscape has evolved to recognize the critical importance of health equity. This evolution has culminated in the Quintuple Aim, which explicitly adds the advancement of health equity as a core objective (Berwick et al., 2022). The profound impact of the COVID-19 pandemic further underscored the need to prioritize the well-being and resilience of healthcare professionals, highlighting the urgency of fostering joy in clinical practice alongside equitable care delivery (Medeiros, 2021). Consequently, the imperative to strike a balance between comprehensive documentation requirements and the practical usability of EHR systems has become even more critical. Effectively navigating this balance is essential not only for alleviating the documentation burden experienced by clinicians but also for simultaneously enhancing the quality of patient care and advancing health equity across all populations. This chapter delves into the historical progression of these aims, examines interventions designed to reduce documentation burden, and presents relevant case studies, with the overarching goal of providing a thorough understanding of


DOI: 10.4324/9781003464457-4

this multifaceted issue and exploring potential pathways toward sustainable solutions that support both clinicians and patients.

## Historical Overview

The transition from paper-based to electronic documentation in healthcare was significantly influenced by legislative measures aimed at improving healthcare delivery through better data management. The Health Information Technology for Economic and Clinical Health (HITECH) Act of 2009 marked a pivotal shift by incentivizing the adoption of EHRs. While this transition aimed to enhance data accuracy and accessibility, it also introduced new challenges, including increased documentation demands and the complexity of integrating diverse EHR systems (Englebright et al., 2021).

The introduction of EHRs was driven by the promise of streamlined documentation, enhanced patient care coordination, and improved clinical decision-making. Paradoxically, the transition from paper-based to electronic systems has, in many instances, resulted in an unintended consequence: an increase in the time clinicians spend on documentation. This shift has been identified as a significant factor contributing to heightened levels of clinician burnout and dissatisfaction. Recognizing this challenge, the 21st Century Cures Act of 2016 mandated that the US Department of Health and Human Services develop strategies to mitigate documentation burden. In response, the Office of the National Coordinator for Health Information Technology (ONC) released a final report in 2020, which proposed various strategies, including the reduction of regulatory demands, the promotion of best practices in documentation, and the strategic use of technology to standardize data and workflows (ONC, 2020). The intricate nature of current documentation requirements and the considerable time investment in record-keeping frequently detract from the time available for direct patient interaction and erode clinician satisfaction. Consequently, while initiatives aim to alleviate these burdens, their actual impact on reducing clinician burnout and enhancing the quality of patient care remains an area of continuous assessment, evaluation, and discussion.

## Interventions to Reduce Clinical Documentation Burden

Addressing clinical documentation burden requires a multipronged approach that includes optimizing EHR systems, implementing innovative technologies, and employing targeted interventions. Several frameworks and toolkits have been developed to guide organizations in these efforts.

### *Documentation Burden Reduction Toolkit*

The AMIA 25×5 Documentation Burden Reduction Toolkit is designed to help healthcare organizations minimize the excessive documentation demands of EHRs and improve clinician efficiency (AMIA, 2024). It advocates for focusing on value-added documentation, standardizing practices, and enhancing EHR usability. The toolkit outlines strategies such as establishing effective governance, streamlining processes, and providing clinician training. It emphasizes the need for a thorough assessment of current practices, stakeholder engagement in implementing changes, and ongoing monitoring of improvements. By offering practical resources and guidelines, the toolkit aims to create a more efficient documentation environment that supports clinician well-being and enhances patient care.

### *Six Domains of Burden*

The American Nursing Informatics Association's position paper on *The Six Domains of Burden* provides a framework for addressing the multifaceted challenges associated with EHR documentation. It identifies six key areas of documentation burden: reimbursement, regulatory, quality, usability, interoperability, and self-imposed burden. The paper underscores the need for targeted interventions to alleviate these burdens, such as simplifying documentation processes, improving EHR usability, and enhancing system integration. By addressing these domains, the paper aims to reduce the administrative load on clinicians, improve documentation practices, and ultimately enhance patient care and clinician satisfaction (Sengstack et al., 2020).

### *EHR Vendor Efficiency Programs*

The ONC (2020) recommends EHR vendors to provide solutions aimed at improving usability and reducing documentation burden. Clinician efficiency programs developed by EHR vendors include checklists of solutions, metrics for targeting time-consuming areas, and best practices derived from vendor client communities. These programs help organizations focus on optimizing the most burdensome aspects of EHR use and facilitate the sharing of successful implementation strategies.

### *Innovative Technologies*

Innovative technologies, such as voice recognition and artificial intelligence (AI), have been explored as potential solutions to documentation burden. Voice dictation and voice assistants can automate the process of recording clinical notes and navigating the EHR, reducing the time clinicians spend on administrative tasks (Kumah-Crystal et al., 2018). Similarly, AI tools can assist with predictive analytics, automating routine tasks, and enhancing decision-making processes (Gandhi et al., 2023). These technologies offer promising avenues for alleviating documentation burden and improving clinical efficiency.

## Case Studies

**CASE STUDY 1 REDUCTION OF TIME SPENT IN FLOWSHEET OPTIMIZATION**

Flowsheets, used for recording patient data such as vital signs and assessments, can be a major source of documentation burden. Surveys, EHR metrics, and time motion studies have revealed that nurses spent a significant portion of their time on these tasks, approximately between 19 and 35% of time and can equate to entering one data point per minute or an average of 23 clicks per minute (Collins et al., 2018; Khan et al., 2022).

To address this issue, a large healthcare system established a workgroup consisting of frontline nurses, nursing leaders, and informatics experts. This group focused on optimization of flowsheets by simplifying picklists, reducing redundant entries, and incorporating automated data entry features, such as device interface, copy forward, and flowsheet macros. Charting by exception was introduced to document only deviations from predefined standards, significantly decreasing the volume of required documentation. In addition, nursing documentation policy updates were made to include guidance on these predefined standards, allowing streamlined documentation practices and reducing redundant charting. Alignment of flowsheet redesign with documentation practices can benefit staff by decreasing workload, improving quality, and satisfaction (Lindsay and Lytle, 2022). As a result, the time spent by nurses on flowsheet documentation was reduced by over 15%, allowing more time for patient care and improving overall job satisfaction. This case study highlights the effectiveness of targeted interventions in alleviating documentation burden, such as flowsheet optimizations to enhance clinician efficiency.

## CASE STUDY 2 USE OF DICTATION AND VOICE ASSISTANTS TO AUTOMATE DOCUMENTATION

EHR integration of dictation and voice assistant technologies aimed to modernize clinical documentation methods. Instead of data entry using keyboard and mouse, dictation tools enable clinicians to record clinical notes more efficiently using speech recognition, while voice assistants facilitate the quick retrieval of patient information and navigation of the EHR. Adoption of dictation and voice assistants has demonstrated the potential for technology to alleviate documentation burden and enhance clinical workflow (Kumah-Crystal et al., 2018). At an acute care facility, implementation of these technologies included requirements to address patient privacy, ensure accurate speech recognition in a noisy environment with frequent clinical alarms, and seamless integration of tools with the EHR and mobile technology. Despite these challenges, the use of voice-assisted technologies successfully reduced the time clinicians spent on documentation and navigation tasks. Initial evaluations showed that these tools improved clinician efficiency and satisfaction by minimizing administrative workload.

However, dictation tools operate as speech-to-text and are used primarily for narrative notes. The solution is not optimal for use with structured documentation, such as flowsheets and admission screens. The acute care facility is seeking other innovative solutions to support the nursing staff who primarily document in structured documentation in the EHR. Nurses are vulnerable to burnout related to documentation burden and the correlation of poor usability implies the need for more work on improving the usability of EHR for nursing documentation (Gesner et al., 2022). Voice-activated macroinstructions (macros) may be an available solution, with potential 9% savings in documentation time on shift assessments and approximately 10–40 clicks saved with each use (Everett et al., 2022). This case study underscores the impact of innovative technologies on reducing the burden of documentation across clinical teams in an acute care setting.

### CASE STUDY 3 AMBIENT TECHNOLOGY IN CLINICAL SETTINGS

A private practice implemented an AI scribe using ambient technology to address the issue of after-hours documentation, also known as "pajama time." This technology captures real-time conversations during patient visits and converts them into clinical notes, reducing the need for physicians to spend additional time on documentation after hours. The AI scribe supports physicians and allows more focus on patient interactions by automatically documenting conversations. Physicians can review and edit the captured notes between patient appointments, streamlining the documentation process and reducing the burden associated with end-of-day documentation. Privacy concerns and informed consent were integral parts of the implementation process. The use of ambient technology resulted in reduced after-hours documentation and allowed physicians to concentrate on patient care during office hours. Feedback from physicians was optimistic and enabled more personal engagement with patients, leading to an increase in work satisfaction. Patient responses were also positive, with many reporting improved interactions. Evaluation metrics showed that while the AI scribe produced high-quality documentation, ongoing enhancements are needed, including direct EHR integration and improved language support. These challenges highlight the necessity for adaptive strategies in implementing these emerging technologies (Tierney et al., 2024). This case study highlights the potential of ambient technology and AI scribes to improve clinician efficiency and increase valuable patient care interactions.

### CASE STUDY 4 STREAMLINE INDIVIDUALIZED CARE PLANNING IN THE EHR

Nurses at a large health system faced challenges in developing and documenting individualized nursing care plans within the EHR. Care planning was a cumbersome process, involving multiple steps across several activity tabs within the EHR. A study on EHR nursing assessment data and the association with North American Nursing Diagnosis Association-International (NANDA-I), Nursing Interventions Classification (NIC), and Nursing Outcomes Classification (NOC), standardized classifications of nursing interventions and nursing-sensitive patient outcomes, found significant challenges in documenting nurse-focused assessments effectively and a lack of alignment between nursing assessments and care plans (Rossi et al., 2023). To address these challenges, the health system formed a workgroup to review and optimize the care planning module. The focus was on streamlining workflows, aligning care plans with nursing policies, and reducing burden when navigating the EHR. The workgroup integrated documentation practices with the care planning redesign by improving the connection between assessments and care plans, reducing the amount of navigation in the EHR. Discussions with the EHR vendor concluded that the "out-of-the-box" available care plans are not based on NANDA-I, NIC, and NOC, but there are options to purchase additional third-party content for consideration at this time. The workgroup opted to build standardized care plans for different patient groups based on the health system's policies and standards of care, while additional care plan goals and intervention options are available to supplement individualized patient care. The optimized care planning process led to more efficient documentation, reduction of burden on nurses, and support for better patient outcomes. This case study emphasizes the importance of workflow optimization, targeted interventions such as care plan updates, and enhancement of EHR usability to reduce documentation burden.

### CASE STUDY 5 ARTIFICIAL INTELLIGENCE (AI) IN EHRS

A large healthcare system explored the use of AI tools to enhance EHR functionality and reduce documentation burden. AI solutions offered by the EHR vendor include predictive analytic models and generative AI tools. Predictive analytics provided risk scores for conditions such as falls and sepsis, while generative AI tools automated tasks like patient message responses and clinical notes. The use of AI tools is aimed at streamlining documentation processes and improving clinical decision-making. Initial evaluations demonstrated that AI tools effectively reduced documentation strain, cognitive and work burden, and enhanced overall efficiency for frontline healthcare providers (Gandhi et al., 2023). The implementation of AI tools requires thorough validation of model accuracy and equity to ensure reliability and trust. Key issues to address may include user engagement, trust in using AI, model bias reduction, and the integration of AI tools into existing workflows. A collaborative approach between technology developers, clinical informaticists, and clinicians is critical in the design and successful use of AI in diverse settings within a large healthcare system. Continuous monitoring and validation of AI models are essential to maintain effectiveness and address any emerging issues. This case study discussed the potential of AI to transform documentation practices, improve efficiency, and reduce the burden on clinicians.

## Conclusion

Reducing clinical documentation burden requires a comprehensive and multifaceted approach that includes optimization of EHR systems, integration of innovative technologies, and implementation of targeted interventions. By addressing the various dimensions of documentation burden, healthcare organizations can improve clinician satisfaction, reduce burnout, and enhance patient care outcomes. The case studies presented in this chapter illustrate several strategies to mitigate documentation burden, including flowsheet optimization, voice-assisted documentation, ambient technology, streamlined care planning, and AI integration with EHRs. Each approach offers valuable insights into effective methods for alleviating the documentation burden and enhancing clinical efficiency. Ongoing evaluation and feedback from clinicians is crucial to ensure that documentation systems remain responsive to evolving needs. Healthcare organizations must prioritize these efforts to create a more balanced and efficient documentation environment. By systematically addressing documentation burden, organizations can foster a supportive work environment, improve clinician well-being, and ultimately enhance the quality of patient care.

## References

American Medical Informatics Association (AMIA). (2024). Documentation burden reduction toolkit. Retrieved from https://amia.org/about-amia/amia-25x5/25x5-documentation-burden-reduction-toolkit

Berwick, D. M., Feeley, D., & Feeley, T. W. (2022). Crossing the chasm: Improving health care for all. *JAMA*, *327*(10), 925–927.

Bodenheimer, T., & Sinsky, C. (2014). From triple to quadruple aim: Care of the patient requires care of the provider. *Annals of Family Medicine*, *12*(6), 573–576. https://doi.org/10.1370/afm.1713

Collins, S., Couture, B., Kang, M. J., Dykes, P., Schnock, K., Knaplund, C., Chang, F., & Cato, K. (2018). Quantifying and visualizing nursing flowsheet documentation burden in acute and critical care. *AMIA Annual Symposium Proceedings. AMIA Symposium, 2018*, 348–357. https://www.ncbi.nlm.nih.gov/pmc/articles/PMC6371331/

Englebright, J., Michel, S., Boyd, D. L., & Hulett, S. L. (2021). A framework for national collaboration to reduce documentation burden and design for usable and reusable data. *The Journal of Nursing Administration, 51*(3), 162–167. https://doi.org/10.1097/NNA.0000000000000988

Everett, M., Redner, J., Kalenscher, A., Durso, D. & Nguyen, S. (2022). Speech recognition technology for increasing nursing documentation efficiency. *Online Journal of Nursing Informatics (OJNI), 26* (2), https://www.himss.org/resources/online-journal-nursing-informatics

Gandhi, T. K., Classen, D., Sinsky, C. A., Rhew, D. C., Vande Garde, N., Roberts, A., & Federico, F. (2023). How can artificial intelligence decrease cognitive and work burden for front-line practitioners? *JAMIA Open, 6*(3). https://doi.org/10.1093/jamiaopen/ooad079

Gesner, E., Dykes, P. C., Zhang, L., & Gazarian, P. (2022). Documentation burden in nursing and its role in clinician burnout syndrome. *Applied Clinical Informatics, 13*(5), 983–990. https://doi.org/10.1055/s-0042-1757157

Khan, A., Rosenthal, C., Ternes, K., Sing, R., & Sachdev, G. (2022). Time spent by intensive care unit nurses on the electronic health record. *Critical Care Nurse, 42*(5), 44–50. https://doi.org/10.4037/ccn2022518

Kumah-Crystal, Y. A., Pirtle, C. J., Whyte, H. M., Goode, E. S., Anders, S. H., & Lehmann, C. U. (2018). Electronic health record interactions through voice: a review. *Applied Clinical Informatics, 9*(3), 541–552. https://doi.org/10.1055/s-0038-1666844

Lindsay, M. R., & Lytle, K. (2022). Implementing best practices to redesign workflow and optimize nursing documentation in the electronic health record. *Applied Clinical Informatics, 13*(3), 711–719. https://doi.org/10.1055/a-1868-6431

Medeiros, F. A. (2021). Joy in work during the COVID-19 pandemic. *Ophthalmic Surgery, Lasers and Imaging Retina, 52*(Suppl 1), S4–S5.

Moy, A. J., Schwartz, J. M., Chen, R., Sadri, S., Lucas, E., Cato, K. D., & Rossetti, S. C. (2021). Measurement of clinical documentation burden among physicians and nurses using electronic health records: a scoping review. *Journal of the American Medical Informatics Association, 28*(5), 998–1008. https://doi.org/10.1093/jamia/ocaa325

Office of the National Coordinator for Health Information Technology (ONC). (2020). Strategy on reducing regulatory and administrative burden relating to the use of health IT and EHRs. Retrieved from https://www.healthit.gov/sites/default/files/page/2020-02/BurdenReport_0.pdf

Rossi, L., Butler, S., Coakley, A., & Flanagan, J. (2023). Nursing knowledge captured in electronic health records. *International Journal of Nursing Knowledge, 34*(1), 72–84. https://doi.org/10.1111/2047-3095.12365

Sengstack, P., Adrian, B., Boyd, D., Davis, A., Hook, M., Hulett, S. L., Karp, E., Kennedy, R., Heermann Langford, L., & Niblett, T. A. (2020). The six domains of burden: a conceptual framework to address the burden of documentation in the electronic health record. *Position paper of the American Nursing Informatics Association board of directors*. Retrieved from https://www.ania.org/assets/documents/position/ehrBurdenPosition.pdf

Tierney, A. A., Gayre, G., Hoberman, B., Mattern, B., Ballesca, M., Kipnis, P., Liu, V., & Lee, K. (2024). Ambient artificial intelligence scribes to alleviate the burden of clinical documentation. *NEJM Catalyst: Innovations in Care Delivery, 5*(3). https://doi.org/10.1056/CAT.23.0404

# Chapter 5

# Leveraging Technology and Data in Driving Health Literacy and Health Equity

Mary Joy Garcia-Dia

## Introduction

This chapter systematically examines the transformative potential of Information Communication Technology (ICT) in advancing health literacy and culturally congruent care, driving significant progress toward health equity. It highlights that the successful implementation of digital health initiatives necessitates intentional design, robust ethical frameworks, and deep community engagement to overcome persistent disparities. The analysis reveals that while digital tools offer unprecedented opportunities to disseminate health information and facilitate care, their effectiveness is contingent upon addressing underlying issues of digital access, ensuring cultural relevance, and empowering individuals to critically appraise information. Healthcare systems can enhance engagement and equitable health outcomes by using multidimensional health literacy strategies and culturally sensitive digital solutions, guided by frameworks like the Digital Health Care Equity Framework (DHEF).

### *The Digital Imperative for Health Equity*

The global landscape of health disparities presents an enduring challenge, where socioeconomic factors such as income and educational attainment are intrinsically linked to access to essential health services and information. Within this context, the pervasive and increasing reliance on digital technologies, particularly mobile devices, has emerged as a primary channel for information access worldwide. The Pew Research Center (2024) report indicates that 15% of US adults identify as "smartphone-only" internet users, a demographic disproportionately represented among those with lower income and educational attainment. This statistic is crucial as it underscores a significant

DOI: 10.4324/9781003464457-5

existing digital dependency within vulnerable populations (Culli, 2025). The internet's established role as the most frequently utilized source of health information between 2008 and 2017 (Finney Rutten et al., 2019) is further amplified by the documented surge in online health information seeking observed during the COVID-19 pandemic (Mangono et al., 2021; Van Kessel et al., 2023). These trends collectively highlight the crucial necessity of digital platforms for modern health communication and management.

The reliance on smartphones among individuals with lower income and educational attainment presents a complex dynamic, often termed the "smartphone-only" phenomenon (Pew Research Center, 2024). While mobile devices offer unparalleled portability and convenience, enabling information access "anytime through cellular network" (Bouchrika, 2025), this very status often signifies a lack of home broadband service. This creates a situation where the tool offering flexibility and access (the smartphone) is simultaneously a marker of a deeper digital divide and potential digital exclusion (Culli, 2025; LexisNexis Risk Solutions, 2025). It is essential that digital health interventions are carefully designed to prioritize mobile accessibility, minimize data usage, and optimize performance for varying network conditions while ensuring compatibility with older devices. Failure to do so may result in the worsening of existing health disparities. The challenge extends beyond simply providing a device; it demands ensuring the quality and context of digital access are equitable. This highlights that digital dependency, if unchecked by broader infrastructure and design considerations, can become a barrier, widening the gap for disadvantaged communities.

The central objective of this chapter is to systematically examine how ICT can be strategically leveraged to enhance health literacy, facilitate culturally congruent care, and ultimately drive health equity. A critical gap persists despite the widespread proliferation of online health information and the increasing availability of ICT: the proportion of individuals easily seeking health-related services and educational materials remains below the Healthy People 2020 metric of 45% (Finney Rutten et al., 2019). This discrepancy points to a significant and persistent gap between the supply of digital health information and its effective utilization by the public. Developers of digital health technologies often create tools to engage patients, but understanding what motivates users remains underexplored (McGowan et al., 2022). This suggests that simply making health information available through ICT is insufficient for achieving desired public health outcomes. The core problem lies in translating this availability into meaningful engagement, comprehension, and actionable utilization. The failure to meet public health metrics indicates a systemic breakdown in user adoption and engagement, which could be attributed to a multitude of factors, including varying levels of health literacy, a lack of cultural relevance in content, or a fundamental misunderstanding of user motivations and barriers (Fitzpatrick, 2023). This implies that future efforts must pivot from a content-centric approach to a user-centric one, prioritizing user experience, building trust, and incorporating behavioral science principles to truly unlock the transformative potential of digital health.

## Conceptual Foundations: Defining Health Literacy, Culturally Congruent Care, and Health Equity

To effectively leverage ICT for health improvement, a clear understanding of the foundational concepts of health literacy, culturally congruent practice and care, and health equity is essential. These three concepts are deeply interconnected and form the theoretical bedrock for designing impactful digital health interventions.

## *Health Literacy*

Health literacy is defined as the cognitive and social skills that determine an individual's motivation and ability to understand and use health information (Nutbeam, 2010). It extends beyond mere reading or writing, encompassing a "constellation of skills including listening, analytical, and decision-making skills, and the ability to apply these skills to health situations" (Coughlin et al., 2020). The World Health Organization (WHO) (2024) provides a comprehensive definition, describing health literacy as

> representing the personal knowledge and competencies that accumulate through daily activities, social interactions and across generations… enabling people to access, understand, appraise, and use information and services in ways that promote and maintain good health and well-being for themselves and those around them.

Health literacy is often understood through Nutbeam's widely recognized three progressive levels (functional, interactive/communicative, and critical), where each level builds upon the preceding one, suggesting a hierarchical development of skills (2010).

## *Culturally Congruent Practice and Care*

Culturally congruent practice and care is defined as the provision of healthcare services that profoundly honor the cultural beliefs, values, and traditions of patients and their communities (Marion et al., 2016). This method requires personalizing care to each individual's background, rather than using a universal approach. As per the American Nurses Association (ANA), culturally congruent care involves respecting and integrating patients' cultural beliefs, traditions, and values into healthcare practices (Marion et al., 2016). Key principles include understanding diverse backgrounds, ensuring effective communication, involving patients in decisions, and tailoring care plans to align with cultural beliefs. This approach addresses cultural barriers while fostering trust and advocating for patients' needs.

## *Health Equity*

Health equity is defined as achieving the highest level of health standards for all by addressing inequalities, injustices, and health disparities (Hoyer et al., 2022). It is influenced by various societal factors, such as income, education, race, and access to healthcare, collectively known as social determinants of health (SDOH) (World Health Organization, 2024).

The "digital divide" is a major factor in health inequity, involving issues like broadband access, digital literacy, and cultural mismatches in technology design. It disproportionately impacts underserved populations, with policy-driven mechanisms like "digital redlining" further exacerbating disparities by limiting investment in broadband infrastructure in minority and low-income areas (McKoy, 2024).

The DHEF ensures that equity is embedded throughout the stages of developing and implementing digital healthcare technologies to enhance patient outcomes and promote healthcare equity (Hatef, et al., 2024). The development of the DHEF is based on six principles: addressing inequities, ensuring person-centered solutions, promoting inclusivity and participatory design, supporting diverse implementations, considering policy impacts, and focusing on outcomes for patients, health systems, and communities.

The framework addresses "digital determinants of health" and emphasizes participatory design, community engagement, and collaboration among diverse stakeholders. It ensures tools are both culturally relevant and accessible, particularly for underserved populations, by incorporating inclusive strategies like offering alternatives to digital services (Johns Hopkins Bloomberg School of Public Health, 2025). The DHEF spans various phases, including planning, development, implementation, and equity assessment, to promote equitable health outcomes.

Table 5.1 outlines the dimensions of health literacy—Functional, Interactive/Communicative, and Critical—and explains how ICT enhances each. ICT supports learning through multimedia, tailors advice to individual needs, enables digital communication, and fosters informed decision-making via apps, telehealth, and real-time tools like a clinical decision support system (CDSS).

**Table 5.1 Dimensions of Health Literacy and ICT Enhancement Mechanisms**

| *Health Literacy Dimension* | *Definition/Key Characteristics* | *Application of ICT* |
|---|---|---|
| **Functional Health Literacy** | Basic reading and writing skills are needed to understand key health information, such as prescription and nutrition labels. | Delivers spoken information via interactive voice response systems; Tailors advice and support to individual needs; Uses multimedia (audio, video) for education; Supports patient education and self-management through mobile apps, telemedicine, and online resources (Fitzpatrick, 2023; Tahsin et al., 2023). |
| **Interactive/ Communicative Health Literacy** | The text highlights the ability to interpret and use health-related communication effectively, adapt to new information, and engage in discussions with healthcare providers. | Telehealth and mobile health platforms enhance digital communication and care delivery, improving patient satisfaction. Social networks and interactive tools like chat rooms and online discussion boards facilitate health-related activities, while video conferencing supports remote communication and connectivity (Choy, 2021; Chirumamilla and Gulati, 2021). |
| **Critical Health Literacy** | The ability to evaluate health information, think critically about health issues, and articulate needs for health promotion, such as identifying biases and understanding complex concepts. | Mobile apps, digital platforms, and multimedia channels offer real-time campaigns; Consultations can break barriers to health education; Online health records, metrics, and alerts via CDSS enable informed decisions. Wearables and telemedicine for early detection promote preventive care. |

## *The Role of Data in Driving Health Literacy and Health-Promoting Behaviors*

In today's digitally connected world, data serves as a foundational asset in shaping effective health literacy strategies and promoting behavior change, particularly among populations disproportionately impacted by health inequities. Health data—when disaggregated by race, ethnicity, geography, and language—provides the granular insights needed to tailor interventions that are culturally, linguistically, and contextually appropriate (Oronce, Adia, & Ponce, 2021). The COVID-19 pandemic highlighted this need. For example, Filipinos in the United States represent only 1% of the population, but account for a disproportionate 30% of COVID-19 deaths among Asian Americans (AAs) in California and 80% of deaths among AA healthcare workers in the state (National COVID-19 Resiliency Network, 2021). These alarming disparities only became apparent through the collection and disaggregation of demographic and occupational health data—underscoring how data is not only a measurement tool but also a driver for equity-focused action and policy development.

## *Challenges and Ethical Considerations*

While ICT offers immense potential for advancing health literacy and equity, its implementation is fraught with significant challenges and ethical considerations that must be proactively addressed.

### *Digital Divide and Access*

The digital divide significantly hampers equitable healthcare access, particularly in underserved communities. Key barriers include inadequate broadband infrastructure, a lack of affordable devices, and low digital literacy rates. Rural and low-income populations face barriers to using telehealth and digital health tools effectively. Moreover, "digital redlining" exacerbates the problem by deliberately excluding certain areas from broadband investments (McKoy, 2024). Globally, 2.6 billion individuals lack high-speed internet access, and cost-prohibitive technology further hinders small organizations and providers from implementing necessary digital health solutions (Aguiar, 2023).

### *Data Privacy and Security*

Concerns about privacy and security remain critical as vulnerable populations often distrust digital health and AI technologies due to historical and recent issues. Building ethical AI that prioritizes patient data security and includes diverse datasets is essential to foster trust and improve effectiveness in healthcare (LexisNexis Risk Solutions, 2025).

### *Algorithmic Bias*

Algorithmic bias in AI healthcare tools can perpetuate health inequities, particularly for underserved groups. This bias arises from underrepresented data in AI training, leading to inaccurate results (Turner Lee et al., 2025). For example, pulse oximeters may overestimate oxygen levels in darker-skinned patients, and some AI models require patients of color to display more severe symptoms for equivalent care. Furthermore, AI models relying on large language models can widen disparities if underserved communities are excluded from their development or application.

### *Misinformation and Health Literacy*

Gaps in digital literacy hinder the effective use of healthcare tools and exacerbate misinformation. Educating the public about AI and involving underrepresented communities in its design is essential. The public health workforce plays a crucial role in addressing disparities but needs proper training and infrastructure to leverage AI effectively (Turner Lee et al., 2025).

### *Provider Burnout and Data Silos*

Provider burnout and administrative burdens limit effective patient care, particularly in underserved areas. Nearly 45% of physicians experience burnout, costing $4.6 billion each year. Data silos and reliance on self-reported SDOH data further hinder collaborative care and intervention effectiveness (LexisNexis Risk Solutions, 2025).

### *Ethical Principles in Health Promotion*

Health promotion and communication interventions inherently involve ethical considerations because their purpose is to influence people's views and lifestyles (Guttman, 2017). Potential harms and unintended consequences include:

- Privacy and Autonomy: Health interventions may affect individual freedom and autonomy, particularly through certain techniques or materials.
- Equity Concerns: Programs can unintentionally benefit wealthier populations, potentially affecting social inequalities.
- Psychological Impact: Efforts to influence behavior may impact individuals' or groups' mental health and self-perception.
- Cultural Sensitivity: Interventions may interact with cultural practices or focus on personal health, rather than broader social issues.
- Consent and Democracy: Lack of informed consent in government-endorsed interventions presents ethical considerations.
- Advertising Tactics: Emotional appeals and messaging can affect autonomy and cause discomfort.
- Digital Divide: Digital health tools may not reach underserved populations and present privacy risks.
- Denial of Enjoyment: Asking individuals to forgo valued practices without alternatives may affect disadvantaged groups.
- Collaborations and Sponsorships: Partnerships with corporations may prioritize certain messages over practical health advice.

## Case Example: Community-based Health Literacy Campaigns Using ICT and Persuasive Technology

During the COVID-19 pandemic, community organizations across the United States demonstrated the power of ICT to strengthen health literacy in underserved AA, Native Hawaiian, and Pacific Islander (AA and NH/PI) communities. Through the "Forging Partnerships" initiative, over 100 culturally tailored educational products—ranging from videos and infographics to

**Figure 5.1 Forging partnerships.**

multilingual brochures—were created in 26 languages. These tools addressed critical topics, including COVID-19 symptoms, vaccine safety, mental health, and anti-bullying. Dissemination through in-person events, social media, and community health workers allowed real-time, trusted engagement with the public (Figure 5.1).

The Philippine Nurses Association of America (PNAA), a professional nursing organization, developed Tagalog to English-language translation video guides on self-testing for COVID-19, distributed through YouTube, Facebook, and national conventions. The NICOS Chinese Health Coalition used WeChat to engage Chinese-speaking parents in San Francisco, helping to increase childhood vaccination rates. These efforts illustrate the importance of language accessibility and community-driven content in digital health literacy efforts (Figure 5.2).

Beyond traditional ICT tools, organizations can harness persuasive technology to influence positive health behaviors. Persuasive technology involves the ethical use of design features—like nudges, rewards, and storytelling—to change attitudes or behaviors (Aldenaini et al., 2020). In community health settings, this might include mobile health apps that provide vaccination reminders, testimonials from community leaders, or gamified education modules that reward users for completing learning tasks. Tailored digital interventions like these have proven more effective than one-size-fits-all approaches.

By combining real-time data collection, culturally relevant messaging, and ethically designed persuasive technologies, organizations can transform health literacy campaigns into dynamic tools for empowerment. Ensuring digital content is co-designed with community members, visually accessible, and accompanied by digital literacy support is essential for equitable impact.

These examples reinforce that ICT, when grounded in trust, equity, and cultural resonance, can be a transformative force in closing health information gaps and promoting long-term community health resilience.

## *Conclusion and Future Directions*

To achieve health equity through technology, it is essential to ensure digital health solutions are accessible, culturally relevant, and ethical. Bridging the digital divide can be addressed through

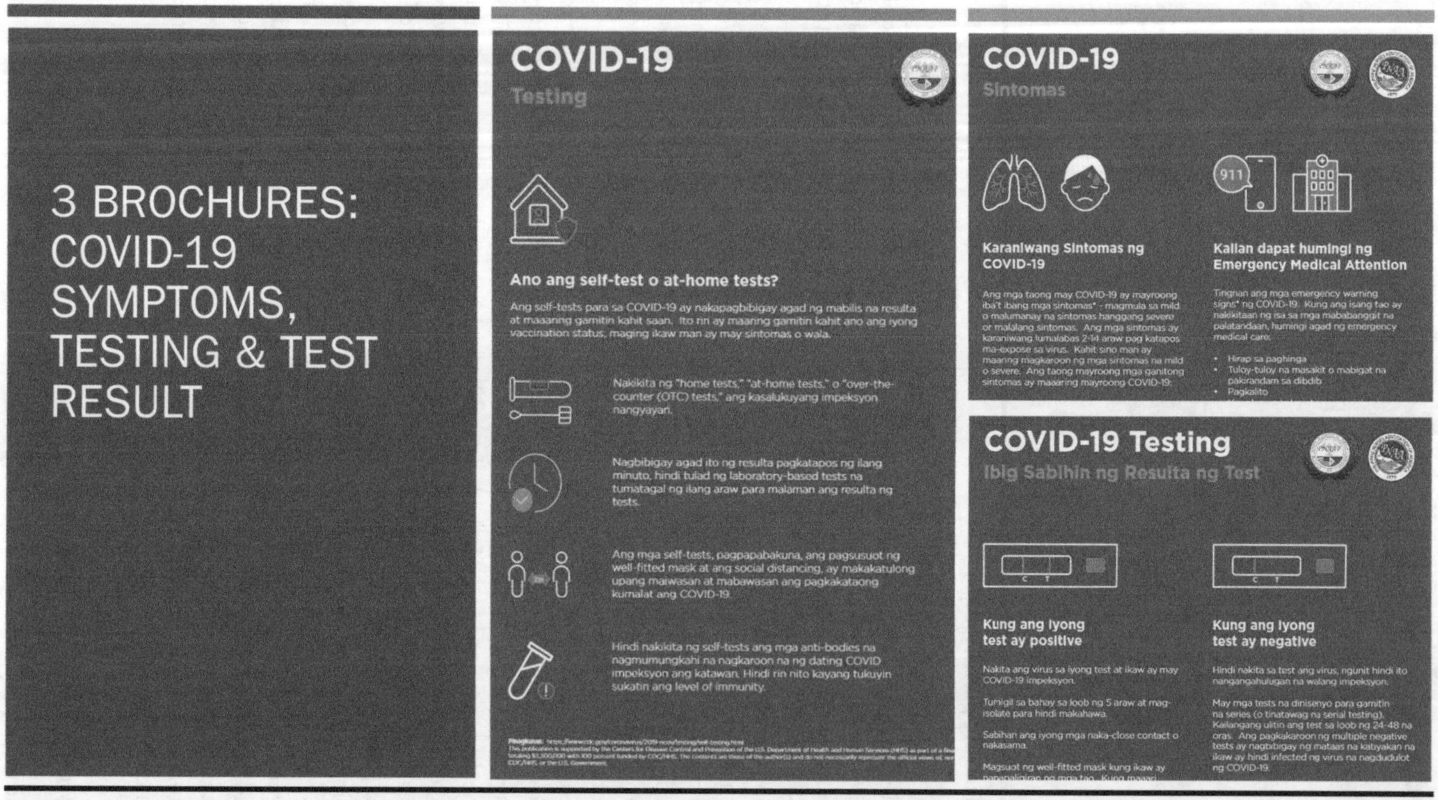


**Figure 5.2 COVID-19 brochures in Tagalog–English translation.**

targeted literacy programs and subsidized technology. AI-driven solutions should be ethical, diverse, and user-focused, offering opportunities to improve health outcomes while combating misinformation and bias. Collaboration between technology, data, and human-centered design is key to empowering communities and fostering equitable healthcare.

## References

Aguiar, J. (2023, December 6). *One-third of the global population remains offline*. Internet Society. https://pulse.internetsociety.org/blog/one-third-of-the-global-population-remains-offline

Aldenaini, N., Alqahtani, F., Orji, R. &, Sampalli, S. (2020). Trends in persuasive technologies for physical activity and sedentary behavior: A systematic review. *Frontiers in Artificial Intelligence*, 3. https://www.frontiersin.org/journals/artificial-intelligence/articles/10.3389/frai.2020.00007. https://doi.org/10.3389/frai.2020.00007

Bouchrika, I. (2025, May 22). *Mobile vs Desktop Usage Statistics for 2025*. Research.com. https://research.com/software/guides/mobile-vs-desktop-usage

Chirumamilla, S., & Gulati, M. (2021). Patient education and engagement through social media. *Current Cardiology Reviews*, *17*(2), 137–143. https://doi.org/10.2174/1573403X15666191120115107

Choy, V. (2021, March 31). *How to improve health literacy through communication*. Artera. https://artera.io/blog/how-to-improve-health-literacy/

Coughlin, S. S., Vernon, M., Hatzigeorgiou, C., & George, V. (2020). Health literacy, social determinants of health, and disease prevention and control. *Journal of Environment and Health Sciences*, *6*(1), 3061.

Culli, L. (2025, January 16). *Bridging the digital divide in health care: A new framework for equity*. Johns Hopkins Bloomberg School of Public Health.

Finney Rutten, L. J., Blake, K. D., Greenberg-Worisek, A. J., Allen, S. V., Moser, R. P., & Hesse, B. W. (2019). Online health information seeking among US adults: Measuring progress toward a healthy people 2020 objective. *Public Health Reports*, *134*(6), 617–625.

Fitzpatrick P. J. (2023). Improving health literacy using the power of digital communications to achieve better health outcomes for patients and practitioners. *Frontiers in Digital Health*, *5*, 1264780. https://www.frontiersin.org/journals/digital-health/articles/10.3389/fdgth.2023.1264780/full

Guttman, N. (2017, February 27). Ethical Issues in Health Promotion and Communication Interventions. *Oxford Research Encyclopedia of Communication*. Retrieved 3 Jun. 2025, from https://oxfordre.com/communication/view/10.1093/acrefore/9780190228613.001.0001/acrefore-9780190228613-e-118

Hatef, E., Hudson Scholle, S., Buckley, B., Weiner, J.P., & Austin, J. M. (2024). Development of an evidence- and consensus-based Digital Healthcare Equity Framework, *JAMIA Open*, *7*(4), ooae136, https://doi.org/10.1093/jamiaopen/ooae136

Hoyer, D., Dee, E., O'Leary, M. S., Heffernan, M., Gelfand, K., Kappel, R., & Fromknecht, C. Q. (2022). How do we define and measure health equity? The state of current practice and tools to advance health equity. *Journal of Public Health Management and Practice: JPHMP*, *28*(5), 570–577. https://doi.org/10.1097/PHH.0000000000001603

Johns Hopkins Bloomberg School of Public Health. (2025). *Bridging the Digital Divide in Health Care: A New Framework for Equity*. https://publichealth.jhu.edu/2025/bridging-the-digital-divide-in-health-care-a-new-framework-for-equity

LexisNexis Risk Solutions. (2025). *Health equity predictions 2025: Addressing provider burnout and digital divides*. https://risk.lexisnexis.com/insights-resources/blog-post/health-equity-trends

Mangono, T., Smittenaar, P., Caplan, Y., Huang, V., Sutermaster, S., Kemp, H., & Sgaier, S. (2021). Information-seeking patterns during the COVID-19 pandemic across the United States: Longitudinal analysis of Google Trends data. *Journal of Medical Internet Research*, *23*(5), e22933.

Marion, L., Douglas, M., Lavin, M., Barr, N., Gazaway, S., Thomas, L., Bickford, C., (2016). Implementing the new ANA standard 8: Culturally congruent practice. *OJIN: The Online Journal of Issues in Nursing*, 22(1), 9. https://doi.org/10.3912/OJIN.Vol22No01PPT20

McGowan, A., Sittig, S., Bourrie, D., Benton, R., & Iyengar, S. (2022). The intersection of persuasive system design and personalization in mobile health: Statistical evaluation. *Journal of Medical Internet and Research*, *10*(9), e40576. https://pubmed.ncbi.nlm.nih.gov/36103226/

McKoy, J. (2024, March 21). *Combating digital redlining is imperative for advancing health equity*. Boston University School of Public Health. https://www.bu.edu/sph/news/articles/2024/combating-digital-redlining-is-imperative-for-advancing-health-equity/

National COVID-19 Resiliency Network. (2021). *Filipinos profile report*. Morehouse School of Medicine.

Nutbeam, D. (2010, October). *The evolving concept of health literacy*. [PowerPoint]. https://www.bumc.bu.edu/healthliteracyconference/files/2010/04/Don-Nutbeam.pdf

Oronce, C. I., Adia, A. C., & Ponce, N. A. (2021). US health care relies on Filipinxs while ignoring their health needs: Disguised disparities and the COVID-19 pandemic. *JAMA Health Forum*. 2021;2(7):e211489. https://doi.org/10.1001/jamahealthforum.2021.1489

Pew Research Center. (2024, November 13). *Internet, Broadband Fact Sheet*. https://www.pewresearch.org/internet/fact-sheet/internet-broadband/

Tahsin, F., Armas, A., Kirakalaprathapan, A., Kadu, M., Sritharan, J., & Steele Gray, C. (2023). Information and communications technologies enabling integrated primary care for patients with complex care needs: Scoping review. *Journal of Medical Internet Research*, *25*, e44035.

Turner Lee, N., Simmons, M. & Crawford, M. (2025, March 3). *Health and AI: Advancing responsible and ethical AI for all communities*. Brookings. (2025). https://www.brookings.edu/articles/health-and-ai-advancing-responsible-and-ethical-ai-for-all-communities/

Van Kessel, R., Kyriopoulos, I., Mastylak, A., & Mossialos, E. (2023). Changes in digital healthcare search behavior during the early months of the COVID-19 pandemic: A study of six English-speaking countries. *PLOS Digital Health*, *2*(5), e0000241.

World Health Organization. (2024, August 5). *Health literacy*. https://www.who.int/news-room/fact-sheets/detail/health-literacy

# Chapter 6

# Social Determinants of Health and Health Equity

Anna Schoenbaum

## Introduction

Health equity signifies that every individual possesses an equitable opportunity to lead a health equity requires addressing disparate treatment within healthcare systems and tackling the unequal outcomes and burdens of disease faced by various demographic groups. Regardless of race/ethnicity, socioeconomic status, gender identity, disability status, religion, primary language, or sexual orientation, everyone should have access to optimal care and opportunities for attaining optimal health. However, historical discrimination, structural oppression, and provider unconscious bias continue to undermine efforts to achieve health equity. For example, Black women are disproportionately affected by maternal mortality, highlighting the pervasive impact of structural racism and discrimination (Hoyert, 2023).

In the dynamic realm of healthcare, the intricate interplay between Social Determinants of Health (SDOH) and health equity assumes paramount importance. Earlier studies underscore that SDOH significantly influence health outcomes, accounting for approximately 30% to 55% of health disparities (Marmot, 2005; Braveman & Gottlieb, 2014). Recent research highlighted that SDOH were responsible for as much as 80% of health outcomes prior to the COVID-19 pandemic, and the pandemic may have heightened the potential effects of SDOH on patient health and well-being (Hood et al., 2016). With these findings, organizations are integrating strategies to address social drivers of health into their plans to improve the health and well-being of people in their communities, regions, and globally. Addressing SDOH is also key to value-based performance improvement, underscoring its critical role in achieving better health outcomes and reducing disparities.

Nurse informaticists, positioned at the intersection of healthcare and technology, possess the tools and insights to mitigate health disparities rooted in SDOH (National Academies of

DOI: 10.4324/9781003464457-6

Sciences, Engineering, and Medicine, 2021). Beyond managing data, nurse informaticists leverage health IT systems to revolutionize healthcare delivery and advocate for equitable outcomes for all. By integrating comprehensive data analysis and patient-centered care strategies, they can significantly contribute to reducing health disparities and promoting health equity (Schoenbaum et al., 2023).

## Frameworks for Guiding Action

Frameworks like the World Health Organization's (WHO) SDOH (2021) and the Social Determinants of Health and Social Needs Model of Castrucci and Auerbach (2019) provide strategies for combating health disparities and promoting health equity. By integrating these frameworks into health IT systems, targeted interventions can be developed to address the underlying social determinants contributing to health disparities. The WHO's SDOH framework sheds light on the nonmedical determinants, ranging from economic policies to social norms, that significantly influence health outcomes (WHO, 2021). Similarly, the Social Determinants of Health and Social Needs Model of Castrucci and Auerbach (2019) addresses upstream factors like low education levels, midstream factors such as homelessness and food insecurity, and downstream strategies like disease treatment to enhance individual and population health. By integrating these frameworks into our health IT systems, we can develop targeted interventions to address the underlying social determinants contributing to health disparities.

Nurse informaticists must be aware of the variability of Electronic Health Record (EHR) data in clinical settings and the challenges of interoperability. It is important to advocate for the inclusion of United States Core Data for Interoperability (USCDI) data elements to facilitate the seamless sharing of electronic health information across different platforms. This includes integrating social determinants into core clinical activities like assessments, diagnoses, interventions, and outcomes. By ensuring the incorporation of these standardized elements into health IT systems, nurse informaticists contribute significantly to improving health outcomes and advancing health equity (Office of the National Coordinator for Health Information Technology, 2021; The Gravity Project, n.d.).

## Navigating Policy Changes and Regulatory Mandates

In the rapidly evolving healthcare policy landscape, nurse informaticists must remain vigilant about changes and regulations concerning SDOH. Understanding regulatory mandates is crucial for guiding practice and advocating for initiatives that advance health equity. Recent policy changes necessitate requirements for technology developers and provider organizations related to the implementation and use of certified Health Information Technology (Health IT), including standardized data elements held in health IT systems. These changes include the integration of social determinants screening tools into health IT systems for the inpatient care setting, with expansion plans beyond.

Table 6.1 displays the regulatory requirements related to health technology and health data for SDOH (OASH, n.d., HIMSS, 2021; AHIMA, 2024). The mandatory screening of social drivers

**Table 6.1 SDOH Regulatory Requirements Reporting**

| **Centers for Medicare and Medicaid Services (CMS)** | | |
|---|---|---|
| Hospitals – Admitted Patients | Screen for Social Drivers of Health-Related Social Needs (HRSNs):<br>■ Food Insecurity<br>■ Housing Instability<br>■ Transportation Needs<br>■ Utility Difficulties<br>■ Interpersonal Safety<br><br>Report the number of patients screened for all five HSRNs that have a need in one of the five HRSNs. Each need is calculated and reported separately | Informatics considerations:<br>■ Configure data classes and elements needed for SDOH, including individual data elements and coding requirements for documentation<br>■ Design different workflows for data collection, risk assessment, consultation of care manager, coding, etc.<br>■ Develop education and training content for nurses, physicians, care managers, coders, and other disciplines<br>■ Develop patient education for community resources<br>■ Create regulatory report(s).<br>■ Test transmission of report(s)<br><br>Review compliance of data collection. |
| Medicare Advantage and Part D Plans | Requires special needs plans to include one or more questions on housing stability, food security, and access to transportation in health risk assessments | |
| FY 2024 Inpatient Prospective Payment Rule | Designation of the ICD-10-CM codes describing homelessness as a complication/comorbidity under the hospital IPPS | |
| FY 2025 Inpatient Prospective Payment Rule (proposed) – Long-term care hospital (LTCH) | Screen for Social Drivers of Health-Related Social Needs (HRSNs) in LTCH Settings | |
| CY 2024 Physician Fee Schedule | Establish code for a SDOH risk assessment that is furnished in conjunction with an evaluation and management (E/M) visit. Consider the additional element of the Medicare Annual Wellness Visit (AWV) | |

(*Continued*)

**Table 6.1 (*Continued*)**

| **Office of the National Coordinator for Health IT (ONC)** | | |
|---|---|---|
| ONC's Health Data, Technology, and Interoperability: Certification Program Updates, Algorithm Transparency, and Information Sharing (HTI-1) | Proposed rule includes mandating the inclusion of the United States Core Data for Interoperability Version 3 (USCDI v3) in all Certified Electronic Health Record Technology (CEHRT) by January 1, 2025 | Informatics considerations:<br>USCDI v3 contains multiple standardized data elements relating to SDOH that must adopt including:<br>■ Assessment and Plan of Treatment: SDOH Assessment<br>■ Goals: SDOH Goals<br>■ Problems: SDOH Problems/ Health Concerns<br>■ Procedures: SDOH Interventions. |
| **The Joint Commission** | | |
| The Joint Commission Quality and Safety Standards for the healthcare equity certification program. | Accredited organizations must show they have a solid plan for gathering SDOH data.<br>■ **Leadership:** Form an organizational committee to address SDOH<br>■ **Assessment:** Use appropriate SDOH screening tools<br>■ **Identification:** Identify patients with unmet social needs and prioritize those who require intervention<br>■ **Intervention:** Develop actionable plans to address the identified SDOH and provide necessary support and resources to patients<br>■ **Evaluation:** Regularly evaluate the effectiveness of the SDOH program<br>■ **Communication:** Ensure effective communication among stakeholders involved in addressing SDOH, including patients, healthcare providers, and community organizations | ■ Informatics considerations:Develop education and training on health equity priorities and technology implementations. Configure self-reported patient data across the care spectrum.<br>■ Configure SDOH assessment to generate a consult.<br>■ Configure data transmission to community resources |

of health measures and the integration of screened Health-Related Social Needs (HRSNs) are critical. The five HRSNs patients should be screened for include:

- Food Insecurity
- Housing Instability
- Transportation Needs
- Utility Difficulties
- Interpersonal Safety

However, organizations may add other social drivers in their assessments, such as health behaviors, diet and exercise, smoking, and substance abuse.

## The Role of Nurse Informaticists in Advancing Health Equity

Nurse informaticists play a pivotal role in ensuring compliance by advocating for standardized screening tools and facilitating their consistent use across the continuum of care. Drawing from their extensive experiences engaging with healthcare leaders, frontline staff, and community agencies, nurse informaticists are uniquely positioned to confront historical discrimination and inequality that underpin health disparities (National Academies of Sciences, Engineering, and Medicine, 2021). Understanding cultural nuances and diversity enables nurse informaticists to approach health disparities with sensitivity and effectiveness. For instance, when implementing SDOH screenings, cultural factors must be considered to tailor health IT systems to meet the diverse needs of patients and communities.

Additionally, nurse informaticists can assist in establishing protocols for reviewing collected data, creating workflows to identify at-risk patients, and understanding the interoperability requirements needed for downstream systems used by different clinicians in various healthcare settings. By understanding the spectrum of care with the patients' drivers of health, nurse informaticists can enforce a more comprehensive approach in care delivery across the home, outpatient, emergency department, and acute care settings.

Furthermore, nurse informaticists are integral to advancing precision health, which aims to tailor healthcare treatments to individual characteristics, including genetics, environment, and lifestyle. By integrating SDOH data with clinical and genetic information, nurse informaticists can help develop more personalized and effective care plans. This integration ensures that precision health initiatives consider the broader context of patients' lives, thereby enhancing the ability to address and reduce health disparities.

## Examples From the Field: Driving Change in Practice Settings

### *Healthcare System/Hospital Setting*

In a hospital setting, nurse informaticists should spearhead efforts to integrate SDOH considerations into clinical workflows. By staying abreast of policy mandates, organizational initiatives, and resource constraints, informatics leaders strategically prioritize projects aimed at seamlessly incorporating SDOH data collection, visualization, and reporting tools into the EHR. Advocating for standardized SDOH data elements, such as social and behavioral drivers, food insecurity, housing instability, interpersonal safety, transportation needs, and utility difficulties (Centers for Medicare & Medicaid Services, n.d.), informatics leaders facilitate a shift toward a more comprehensive approach to patient care. This holistic approach acknowledges not only medical needs but also the significant impact of social and environmental factors on health outcomes. Nurse informaticists need to understand available screening tools and how other data will be visualized for clinicians, including administrative claims data, clinical data, and patient-reported data. These tools prompt clinicians to document various social determinants, ensuring comprehensive data collection.

Advocating for SDOH screening tools that identify patients facing any or all the social drivers within existing workflows is crucial. When patients are flagged as experiencing these challenges during the screening process, the information should automatically trigger a notification for a case manager, facilitating coordinated care. This enables hospitals to collaborate with community organizations to provide housing assistance and support services, effectively addressing critical social determinants impacting patient health. Additionally, consider leveraging predictive analytics algorithms that can help identify at-risk populations and prioritize interventions, while population health management platforms facilitate targeted outreach and resource allocation to address specific social determinants.

Acknowledging potential budget and resource constraints that may arise as these programs expand, conducting regular impact assessments becomes imperative to evaluate the effectiveness of interventions aimed at addressing SDOH and ensuring efficient resource allocation to maximize positive patient outcomes. Moreover, it is essential for operational leaders and informatics to monitor the compliance of SDOH documentation, track the number of patients with positive screening results and consults, and ensure coding is completed.

## Key Takeaways

- Implement using standardized SDOH screening tools across the care continuum.
- Ensure SDOH data can be exchanged with other systems. Must work together as a community.
- Clarify roles and responsibilities for completing the screening and establish a clear schedule for screening frequency.
- Provide clinicians with adequate training and support for sensitive conversations about SDOH topics during data collection.
- Establish protocols for action when a patient's needs are identified and ensure that relevant resources are readily available for referrals and assistance.
- Monitor compliance of SDOH documentation and track patient screening results for ongoing improvement.

## Industry Setting

In the healthcare technology industry, nurse informaticists collaborate closely with product development teams to design health IT systems that encompass both clinical and SDOH data elements. It is crucial for nurse informaticists to advocate for the incorporation of standardized SDOH data elements and prioritize features that cater to the diverse needs of patient populations. Moreover, these systems must be designed with sensitivity to the culture, background, and practices of the communities they serve. Through robust partnerships with community organizations and a continuous feedback loop from end users, innovative solutions can be developed to effectively support healthcare organizations in addressing health disparities and promoting health equity.

Designing health IT systems that prompt clinicians to document social drivers, food insecurity, housing instability, interpersonal safety, transportation needs, and utility difficulties is paramount. Prioritizing the integration of SDOH considerations and facilitating seamless data exchange between health IT systems is essential. Thoroughly assess for bias, fairness, and accuracy to uphold the effectiveness and integrity of the solution. Lastly, implement robust security measures to safeguard patient confidentiality and trust when collecting and exchanging sensitive SDOH information.

## Key Takeaways

- Avoid making assumptions about patients when designing solutions. Be aware that social factors impact health outcomes and design health IT systems with that in mind.
- Implement standardized SDOH elements that can be exchanged securely from one system to another to promote interoperability.
- Configure health IT systems to undergo testing for bias, fairness, and accuracy to ensure their effectiveness and integrity.

## Public Health Agencies

In public health, nursing informaticists play a vital role in advocating for policy changes aimed at improving health equity by integrating standardized SDOH data elements into systems and population health management platforms. This advocacy prioritizes interoperability, ensuring seamless data exchange between health systems and community agencies/organizations for effective and secure sharing across platforms (The Gravity Project, n.d.). By fostering collaboration between healthcare entities and community organizations, public health agencies contribute to a more holistic approach to healthcare delivery that addresses the underlying social determinants impacting health outcomes.

Utilizing data analytics to identify disparities in access to preventive care services among different demographic groups is essential. Analysis of population health data may reveal lower rates of cancer screenings in certain communities compared to others. To address this disparity, the agency should consider implementing targeted outreach programs in collaboration with local clinics and community organizations to increase access to screenings in underserved areas. Through their informatics expertise, nurse informaticists play a pivotal role in promoting health equity and improving health outcomes for vulnerable populations by advocating for policy changes and implementing effective interventions based on data-driven insights.

## Key Takeaways

- Prioritize policy advocacy for integrating standardized SDOH data elements into health IT systems and population health management platforms.
- Foster collaboration across sectors (i.e., local clinics, community organizations) is essential for implementing targeted interventions aimed at promoting health equity.
- Utilize data analytics and population health data, public health informaticists can identify disparities in access to preventive care services and other healthcare interventions.

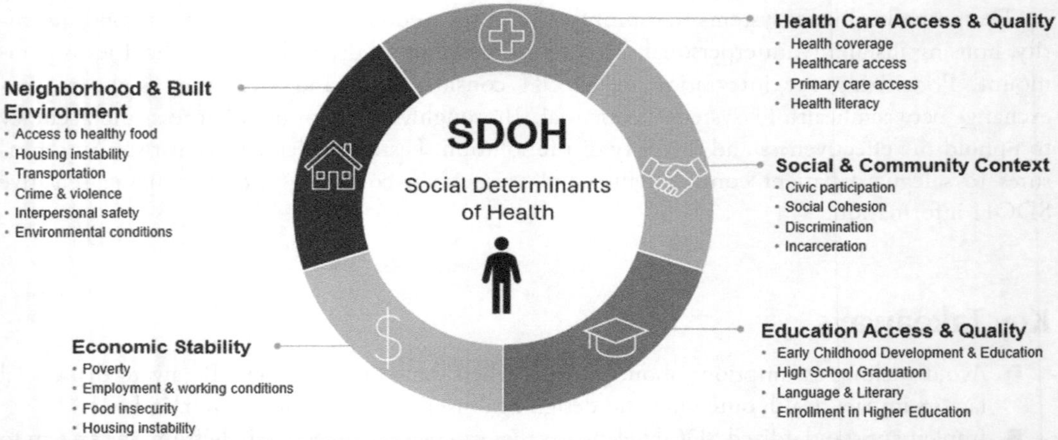


**Figure 6.1 Social drivers of health that influence health and well-being.**

In the pursuit of health equity, nurse informaticists serve as catalysts for driving initiatives that address disparities and promote equitable healthcare delivery. Through their expertise in leveraging technology, advocating for policy changes, and collaborating across sectors, nurse informaticists play a pivotal role in advancing health equity in various settings, including healthcare systems, industry, and public health agencies. Their involvement extends beyond addressing SDOH to encompass the realm of precision health—tailoring healthcare treatments to individual characteristics, including genetics, environment, and lifestyle.

Nurse informaticists contribute to these initiatives by integrating SDOH data with clinical and genetic information, thereby developing more personalized and effective care plans. This comprehensive approach ensures that healthcare delivery is not only equitable but also tailored to the specific needs and circumstances of each patient, regardless of social or demographic factors. However, it is imperative to conduct impact assessments of these implementations, particularly regarding SDOH and health equity. Nurse informaticists must evaluate the effectiveness of interventions aimed at addressing SDOH, monitoring outcomes, and assessing their impact on health equity. By gathering and analyzing data, informaticists can inform future strategies and ensure that initiatives are both effective and equitable.

By embracing standardized approaches to integrating SDOH considerations, ensuring interoperability, and advocating for the needs of diverse patient populations, nurse informaticists can contribute to creating a future where healthcare is truly equitable for all. Together, we can continue to innovate, advocate, and implement solutions that address the root causes of health disparities, ultimately leading to improved health outcomes and a more just society for everyone (Figure 6.1).

## References

American Health Information Management Association (2024). *Data for Better Health.* https://www.ahima.org/advocacy/data-for-better-health/

Braveman, P., & Gottlieb, L. (2014). The social determinants of health: It's time to consider the causes of the causes. *Public Health Reports, 129*(Suppl 2), 19–31. https://doi.org/10.1177/00333549141291S206

Castrucci, B., & Auerbach, J. (2019). Meeting individual social needs falls short of addressing social determinants of health. *Health Affairs Blog.* https://doi.org/10.1377/forefront.20190115.234942

Centers for Medicare & Medicaid Services. (n.d.). Addressing social determinants of health through Medicare and Medicaid. Retrieved from https://www.cms.gov/Medicare/Quality-Initiatives-Patient-Assessment-Instruments/Value-Based-Programs/Value-Based-Programs

HIMSS (2021). Social Determinants of Health Guide

Hood, C. M., Gennuso, K. P., Swain, G. R., & Catlin, B. B. (2016). County health rankings: Relationships between determinant factors and health outcomes. *American Journal of Preventive Medicine* 50(2):129–135

Hoyert, D.L. (2023). Maternal mortality rates in the United States, 2021. *NCHS Health E-Stats.* https://doi.org/10.15620/cdc:124678

Marmot, M. (2005). Social determinants of health inequalities. *Lancet, 365*(9464), 1099–1104. https://doi.org/10.1016/S0140-6736(05)71146-6

National Academies of Sciences, Engineering, and Medicine. (2021). *The Future of Nursing 2020–2030: Charting a Path to Achieve Health Equity.* Washington, DC: The National Academies Press.

Office of Disease Prevention and Health Promotion. (n.d.). *Healthy People 2030.* U.S. Department of Health and Human Services.

Office of the National Coordinator for Health Information Technology (ONC) (2021). *United States Core Data for Interoperability (USCDI) - July 2021 - Version 2.* Retrieved from https://www.healthit.gov/isa/united-states-core-data-interoperability-uscdi.

Schoenbaum, A., Stephenson, L., & Evans, J. (2023). *Health Equity and Social Determinants of Health, Part 2.* Addressing Social Determinants of Health (SDOH) in Healthcare Part 2|HIMSS.

The Gravity Project. (n.d.). Retrieved from https://thegravityproject.net/

World Health Organization. (2021). Social determinants of health. Retrieved from https://www.who.int/health-topics/social-determinants-of-health#tab=tab_1

# Chapter 7

# Ethical Use of Emerging Technologies in Healthcare

Lilly Mathew

## Introduction

Emerging common technologies in healthcare today include Artificial Intelligence, Robotics, Telemedicine, Wearables, 3D Bioprinting, Blockchain, Nanomedicine, Augmented Reality, Virtual Reality, Remote Patient Monitoring, and Virtual Care. This chapter focuses on the ethical use of such technologies in general, using key concepts to consider with a few case studies. The key ethical concepts (Figure 7.1) that are integrated in the content of this chapter and case studies include the following:

1) Patient-Centered Concepts: Patient Consent, Patient Autonomy, Patient Privacy, Patient Confidentiality, and Patient Education.
2) Data-Centered Concepts: Data Access, Data Storage, Data Sharing, Data Security, and Data Use.
3) Health Equity–Centered Concepts: Bias in Programming, Availability, and Use.
4) Workforce-Centered Concepts: Healthcare Staff Education/Training, Staff Privacy, and Professional Liability.

## Significance

The application of automation and intelligent systems in healthcare is known to be efficient; it can reduce costs and minimize errors with improved workflows (Sripathi & Leelavati, 2024). However, with the increasing use of emerging new technologies, ethical concerns also arise. Diverse patient populations and the healthcare workforce are key stakeholders and are directly impacted by the use of emerging technologies. Regarding the patient population groups, the ethical concerns surround topics related to patient informed consent, patient autonomy, patient privacy, confidentiality, and

 DOI: 10.4324/9781003464457-7

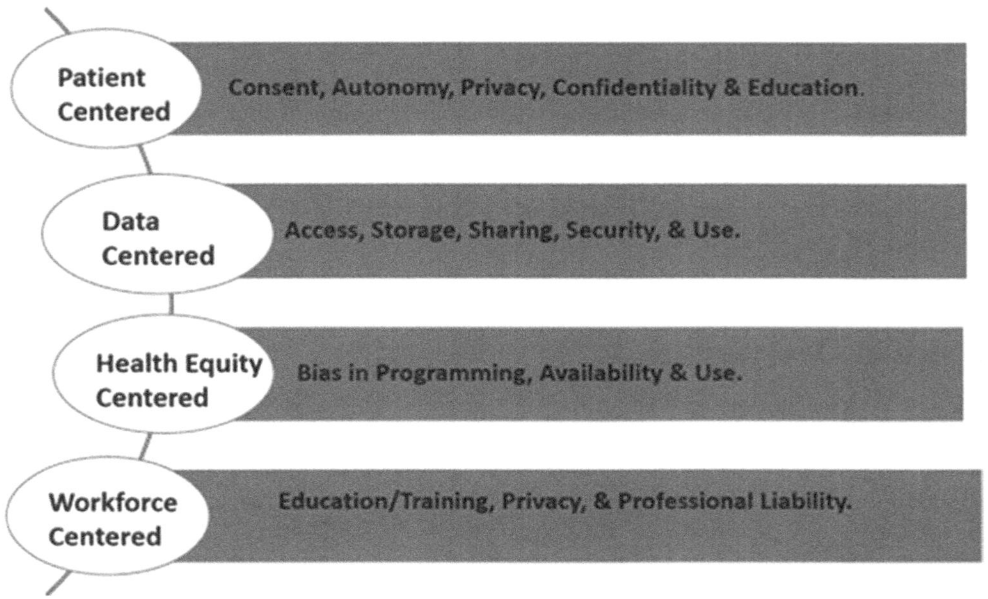


**Figure 7.1 Ethical concepts for emerging technology adoptions.**

patient education. There are data-related ethical concerns that revolve around the topics of data access, data storage, data sharing, data security, and data use. Additionally, ethical concerns also include bias in the programming and design of emerging technologies, especially those that use automation with machine learning and artificial intelligent algorithms. The availability of robust technologies and access to their use also raises ethical concerns as these may not be affordable by all healthcare institutions and could be available only for a privileged few. Regarding the healthcare workforce, ethical concerns arise around adequate staff education regarding the capabilities of emerging technologies, staff privacy, and professional liability risks.

The concerns regarding safe and ethical use of emerging technologies are real, and it is important to examine how their use will impact patients, providers, populations, and the overall healthcare industry. Traditionally, healthcare decisions were made by healthcare professionals based upon their education, experience, skills, intellect, and expertise, which is now being augmented with artificially intelligent algorithms, automation, and machine learning. Therefore, it is critical to consider if the policies developed around the use of emerging technologies are inclusive and that provisions are made for stakeholder involvement in all phases of technology development and continuous evaluation of their use and effectiveness for positive patient outcomes.

With newer technology implementations, it is essential to assess patients' consent to the use of the technology, provision of patient autonomy in decision-making, and protection of patients' private health information. Additionally, opportunities for patient education in understanding the capabilities and functions of the technology, including ways it might impact their health and treatment decisions are essential. When thinking about the ethical use of technology, it is extremely critical to discuss the data that these systems generate. It is essential to develop knowledge about system-produced patient data, access control, data storage, data sharing, data security, and data usage policies of both vendors and healthcare institutions. Healthcare institutions' ethical experts should have the capability to examine bias in the programming to determine factors that might contribute to health disparities among certain population groups and assess if the use of a particular technology enhances health equity. Healthcare workforce can be directly impacted by technology such as the use of tracking systems; therefore, it is important that they are engaged as stakeholders in each stage of technology development and have the opportunity to educate themselves on understanding the functions and capabilities of new technologies and how they impact their daily workflows. Additionally, it is also ethical to consider the protection of healthcare workforce information generated by the new systems and examine any professional liability risks that are associated with the use of the new systems.

## Historical Overview

Healthcare ethics is an existing field of study that encompasses both practical applications in clinical settings and is also based upon scholarly works from the fields of philosophy, history, and sociology. The history of healthcare ethics dates back to thousands of years, when the first code of medical ethics was published in the 5th century, which is widely known as the Hippocratic Oath (Riddick, 2003). The Declaration of Helsinki (1964), which is a set of ethical principles regarding human experimentation developed for the medical community by the World Medical Association (General Assembly of the World Medical Association, 2014), and the Nuremberg Code (1947), a set of ethical principles governing human experimentation, are well-known documents that contribute to medical ethics (Lopes, 2014; Schuster, 1997). In 2005, a universal declaration on Human Rights and Biomedicine was adopted, which highlighted and broadened the scope of bioethics by integrating international human rights law into biomedicine, with consideration of the environmental biosphere and biodiversity (Magnus, 2016).

The four core ethical principles in healthcare are respect for autonomy, beneficence, non-maleficence, and justice (Moskop, 2016). Autonomy is about enabling individuals to make their own healthcare decisions and recognizing patients' capability of making informed decisions, and the right to refuse any treatments. Beneficence is to ensure that healthcare actions and decisions are in the best interest of the patients. Non-maleficence is to do no harm, and justice is to practice what is right with full integrity and disclosure.

## Key Ethical Principles

The four-core healthcare ethical principles in the context of emerging technologies are discussed, which include autonomy, beneficence, non-maleficence, and justice. With emerging technologies that include tracking systems, it is essential to evaluate if "autonomy" is being enabled. For example, when tracking systems are used as an intervention, it is important to question whether they will interfere with the autonomy of both patients and providers. Fall prevention systems that use a patient tracker to monitor for high-risk activities can interfere with patient autonomy of free movement. Likewise, using a tracker on the workforce to monitor for hand hygiene compliance and answering call lights in a timely manner can increase the risk of professional liability. In the light of emerging automated systems, it is essential to make patients and providers aware of how their information is tracked, collected, analyzed, and used, as doing this will support the ethical principle of beneficence, which is to examine the benefit of using the system and how it brings positive outcomes.

Safe design of the systems is essential, including strong data security to prevent data breaches so that patient information is not misused inadvertently causing patient harm, doing this supports the ethical principle of non-maleficence. Justice is about being transparent to the patients and providers about system-generated sensitive patient data and its use. It is important to assure the providers that system-generated data will not be used to evaluate providers' individual performance; however, it can be used as a mode to base new educational activities to improve compliance with the use of the new system. An example is using bar code medication administration compliance reports to seek educational opportunities for staff education and improvement. Additionally, it is also important to include here the fact that healthcare ethics is also connected to human culture, as different cultures view ethical values differently, with some placing more emphasis on family values and downplaying the importance of autonomy. Cultural sensitivity is an essential skill for the healthcare workforce to have in order to understand the application of healthcare ethical principles in certain patient population groups.

## Case Studies

Presented here are five different case studies that apply key concepts and ethical principles.

### CASE STUDY 1 ETHICAL DECISION-MAKING IN HEALTHCARE TECHNOLOGY DEVELOPMENT AND IMPLEMENTATION

A healthcare technology firm developed an artificial intelligence (AI) diagnostic tool to improve the accuracy and speed of disease diagnosis using electronic health records (EHR). The tool uses machine learning algorithms to analyze patient history, labs, and radiology data to provide diagnostic recommendations and treatment options. A large healthcare institution wants to purchase the tool to be used with its EHR system. During the procurement, it is noted that the diagnostic tool was developed with the assistance of a few technology consultants and large patient data sets, and there was no evidence of any members representing patients nor providers being directly involved in the development process. In this situation, the ethical concern was of trustworthiness in the use of the diagnostic AI tool and potential for algorithmic bias. The vendor also did not disclose the origin of the large patient data sets. As a solution, a proposal was developed by the leadership team to establish a multidisciplinary team of providers, patients, and diagnostic experts to examine for any potential bias and test the tool with rigor and caution. The team was entrusted with the responsibility to conduct a thorough analysis to understand the root cause of the bias, if present, and its potential impact on patient care. The team was entrusted to cross-examine the four core ethical principles to detect any violations. The team opted to treat if bias is detected by retraining the algorithms, adding diverse data sets, and adding diverse stakeholders representing both the patient and provider groups in collaboration with the vendor. Post changes the team wants to conduct rigorous testing to ensure the tools safety and efficacy. The team will also establish a continuous monitoring process to detect and address any potential bias and ethical concerns. In conclusion, ethical decision-making is crucial in the healthcare technology development stage. Identification and addressing of bias and ethical concerns are essential, collaborations between diverse stakeholders are vital, and continuous monitoring and evaluation ensure the safety and efficacy of healthcare technologies.

## CASE STUDY 2 EXAMINATION OF EQUITY ISSUES RELATED TO THE ADOPTION OF EMERGING HEALTHCARE TECHNOLOGIES

A large healthcare organization implemented telemedicine services to expand access to care for a rural and underserved population group. However, ethical concerns were noted regarding equity issues in access, quality, and outcomes. Limited internet connectivity and poor internet bandwidth caused poor video quality, frequent disconnections, and patient difficulty with timely login for appointments were noted. It was important to address these issues to improve patient engagement and health outcomes. Additionally, patients with limited English proficiency had to have translators available, as the system lacked the incorporation of live translators. The ethical concern in this situation was health equity issues among those who could not afford internet connectivity and had language barriers. It was clear that barriers like computer literacy, internet access, and language barrier impacted patient engagement. A team of experts in telemedicine examined equity issues when using telemedicine services and discussed engaging patients as stakeholders to improve equity-related issues. The team measured the outcomes of the use of telemedicine in this rural community. They analyzed patient demographics, technology access, and health outcomes. Their recommendations included significant investment in infrastructure development in rural areas, implementing language access services and health literacy programs, providing culturally competent training for providers, and developing targeted outreach and education programs. Additional recommendations included engaging stakeholders by conducting interviews with patients, providers, and community leaders. To also examine organizational policies and state regulations related to telemedicine. In conclusion, emerging healthcare technologies offering telemedicine care can exacerbate existing equity issues. Proactive approaches to examining and addressing equity concerns and collaboration with diverse stakeholders are essential for developing effective solutions. Ongoing monitoring and evaluation of equitable access and outcomes are essential.

## CASE STUDY 3 INFORMED CONSENT AND PATIENT AUTONOMY IN HEALTHCARE DECISION-MAKING

A large healthcare facility implemented a new EHR system and patient portal to improve patient engagement and to streamline care. However, ethical concerns arose regarding informed consent and patient autonomy in healthcare decision-making as patients were not fully informed about data sharing, privacy, and the use of patient portals. An interdisciplinary committee was established to address the issue, and they focused on collecting data to analyze the current ethical concern and to discuss the process of engaging stakeholders and the essential steps to address the identified ethical concern. This committee decided to survey patients on satisfaction with portal use, assess portal use by examining access logs, and review consent forms for adequate information about data sharing and privacy written at a sixth to eighth grade reading level, in clear and simple language, avoiding any technical terms and complex medical terminologies. A decision was made to conduct interviews with stakeholders, including patients, providers, and IT staff. Interviews were planned to include questions regarding portal access and use, and their engagement in decision-making. The team also decided to examine organization policies and state and federal regulations regarding EHR use and patient portals.

Upon examination, the committee found that the patients were not fully informed about the data-sharing and privacy policies, and patients faced barriers in accessing and managing their health information, as they had received no formal training on how to effectively use the patient portal. The committee recommendations included implementing a transparent and patient-centered consent process, enhancing patient portal user experience and accessibility, and providing education and support for patients managing their health information. In conclusion, technology can both enhance or hinder informed consent and patient autonomy. Patient-centered approaches will ensure transparency, accessibility, and patient engagement. Ongoing monitoring and evaluation are crucial for maintaining ethical standards. Collaboration between patients, providers, and IT staff is essential for successful technology implementations and better patient outcomes.

## CASE STUDY 4 ETHICAL LEADERSHIP AND GOVERNANCE IN HEALTHCARE TECHNOLOGY ADOPTION

A cutting-edge healthcare organization is looking to adopt technologies that enable precision medicine to enhance patient care and outcomes using patient genomic data in the EHR to improve the field of pharmacogenomics in practice. The organization's first step was to establish ethical leadership and governance to ensure responsible adoption of the innovation. They successfully implemented a multidisciplinary governance committee to oversee ethical considerations. The committee was entrusted with many responsibilities, which included establishing an ethical framework that would guide technology adoption and use to foster a culture of transparency and accountability, engaging patients, providers, and communities to regularly assess for ethical implications and processing any claims of ethical violations. Such a committee is needed with a clear vision and commitment to innovation, a governance structure ensuring accountability and oversight, and a culture of transparency, trust, and mutual respect. The expected outcomes were to create a strong reputation for ethical leadership and governance and improve stakeholder trust and engagement.

In conclusion, ethical leadership and governance are crucial in healthcare technology adoption; a robust institutional framework for ethical technology adoption is needed, and continuous monitoring and evaluation are essential for improved patient outcomes. Patient involvement is crucial when testing precision technologies. Patient consent for using their genomic data and storing it in the EHR is essential, and it is equally important to disclose the use of such data. The committee was also entrusted to review laws that protect patient genomic data like the Genetic Information Nondiscrimination Act (GINA), which prohibits genetic discrimination and restricts access to individuals' genetic information (Slaughter, 2013), and the National Institutes of Health (NIH) Genomic data sharing policies that set the guidelines for protecting research participants' privacy while enabling access to valuable research data (Martone & Nakamura, 2022). The committee was also entrusted to review any State laws and regulations, as many US states have genomic privacy laws in effect to provide additional protection of the genetic data of individuals.

**CASE STUDY 5 ETHICAL DILEMMAS FACED BY HEALTHCARE PROFESSIONALS IN THE ADOPTION OF NEW TECHNOLOGIES**

A radiology department of a large healthcare institution adopted AI-powered imaging tools to enhance diagnostic accuracy and efficiency. However, healthcare professionals faced ethical dilemmas as they were concerned about bias in AI algorithmic decision-making, expressed difficulty in understanding AI-driven diagnostic processes and results, data privacy and security, as they were concerned about data breaches and data sharing. Also, many questions were posed about the human–AI relationship and about the role of human radiologists in AI-driven imaging, accountability, and liability for AI-driven diagnostic errors. A technology adoption team was appointed to address the concerns raised by healthcare professionals. The team researched literature on AI-driven imaging and ethical considerations research, conducted interviews with radiologists, ethicists, and patients, and also examined organizational policies along with industry regulations. They recommended that the developer of the radiology diagnostic tool to be transparent about the AI algorithms and the source of data sets, to implement features that explain and interpret how the algorithm works, to establish and share robust data privacy and security protocols, to be open to algorithmic auditing and testing, and obtain consent from patients regarding data sharing. In conclusion, healthcare professionals face ethical dilemmas in adopting new AI technologies, and it is crucial that healthcare leadership is proactive in addressing ethical concerns and developing collaboration between stakeholders, and developing an ongoing monitoring and evaluation plan for newly adopted technologies.

## Call to Action

With the growing use of new technologies that are efficient in diagnostic and clinical decision capacity, it is becoming essential to develop an interdisciplinary governance to oversee all potential ethical concerns and to prioritize ethics in the adoption of advanced healthcare technologies. AI systems require vast amounts of data to operate, which raises questions about privacy and data security. To address these concerns, AI systems must be designed and implemented with robust data security measures (Potočnik et al., 2023). Obtaining informed consent from patients and giving them control over their data use is crucial. Another challenge is the potential for AI systems to exhibit bias and discrimination, especially if they are trained on datasets that do not represent the diversity of the population. It is therefore essential to ensure that AI systems are trained on diverse datasets to avoid any potential biases (Koohi-Moghadam & Bae 2023).

To address potential biases and discrimination, it is crucial to create AI systems that are trained on datasets that are representative of the population, and before deploying AI systems in clinical practice, it is essential to assess for any potential biases or discrimination. In addition to these concerns, other challenges must be sorted out before AI can be widely used in healthcare, including issues related to data privacy and data protection (Van Leeuwen et al., 2022). Healthcare professionals need to be knowledgeable and physically trained in the use of AI systems responsibly, which includes understanding how AI systems work, how to interpret their results, and how to mitigate the risks of bias and discrimination. Developing and deploying AI systems can be expensive, and this may make it difficult for some healthcare organizations to adopt AI, which can be of disadvantage to many (Hosny et al., 2018).

AI system malfunction is a possibility as well. One of the documented concerns is "dataset shift" with AI systems. Dataset shift can occur when the systems underperform due to a mismatch situation when the training data differs from the actual data (Finlayson et al., 2021). Clinicians must validate any AI-driven clinical decisions for clinical relevance. Clinicians require adequate preparation in understanding how the AI systems generate information so that they can immediately identify and report AI system malfunctions and failures.

## Conclusion

In conclusion, it is important to think ethically when adopting new advanced technologies. The future of ethical use of emerging technologies is a priority to protect patients, providers, and the community at large. Every technology that is adopted must be thoroughly tested and studied before implementation, and research should occur on an ongoing basis to assess how the technology has improved patient care and outcomes. Establishing ethical governance and oversight is essential for successful adoption, including all stakeholders. The four key concepts to include when considering ethical adoption of emerging new technologies are first patient-centered concepts, which include obtaining patient consent, maintaining patient autonomy in decision-making, maintaining patient privacy and confidentiality, and providing an opportunity for patient education. The second key concept is data-centered, and it is to ensure that data collected can be accessed for audits, and information on data storage, sharing, security, and use is available to stakeholders. The third is to ensure that health equity–centered concepts are addressed, and the ability to examine for bias in programming, availability, and use is possible upon request by the ethical governing body of a healthcare institution. Lastly, incorporation of workforce-centered concepts like opportunity for healthcare staff education/training, staff privacy, and professional liability in technology adoption is essential.

## References

Finlayson, S. G., Subbaswamy, A., Singh, K., Bowers, J., Kupke, A., Zittrain, J., ... & Saria, S. (2021). The clinician and dataset shift in artificial intelligence. *New England Journal of Medicine*, *385*(3), 283–286.

General Assembly of the World Medical Association. (2014). World Medical Association Declaration of Helsinki: ethical principles for medical research involving human subjects. *The Journal of the American College of Dentists*, *81*(3), 14–18.

Hosny, A., Parmar, C., Quackenbush, J., Schwartz, L. H., & Aerts, H. J. (2018). Artificial intelligence in radiology. *Nature Reviews Cancer*, *18*(8), 500–510.

Koohi-Moghadam, M., & Bae, K. T. (2023). Generative AI in medical imaging: applications, challenges, and ethics. *Journal of Medical Systems*, *47*(1), 94.

Lopes, J. A. (2014). Bioethics–a brief history: From the Nuremberg code (1947) to the Belmont report (1979). *Revista Médica de Minas Gerais*, *24*(2), 253–264.

Magnus, R. (2016). The universality of the UNESCO universal declaration on bioethics and human rights. In *Global bioethics: The impact of the UNESCO international bioethics committee* (pp. 29–42). Cham: Springer International Publishing.

Martone, M. E., & Nakamura, R. (2022). *Changing the culture on data management and sharing: Getting ready for the new NIH data sharing policy*. Harvard Data Science Review.

Moskop, J. C. (2016). *Ethics and health care: an introduction*. Cambridge University Press.

Potočnik, J., Foley, S., & Thomas, E. (2023). Current and potential applications of artificial intelligence in medical imaging practice: A narrative review. *Journal of Medical Imaging and Radiation Sciences, 54*(2), 376–385.

Riddick, F. A. (2003). The code of medical ethics of the American Medical Association. *Ochsner Journal, 5*(2), 6–10.

Shuster, E. (1997). Fifty years later: The significance of the Nuremberg Code. *New England Journal of Medicine, 337*(20), 1436–1440.

Slaughter, L. (2013). Genetic information non-discrimination act. *Harvard Law Journal on Legislation, 50,* 41.

Sripathi, M., & Leelavati, T. S. (2024). The Fourth Industrial Revolution: A paradigm shift in healthcare delivery and management. *Digital Transformation in Healthcare 5.0: Volume 1: IoT, AI and Digital Twin, 67.*

Van Leeuwen, K. G., de Rooij, M., Schalekamp, S., van Ginneken, B., & Rutten, M. J. (2022). How does artificial intelligence in radiology improve efficiency and health outcomes? *Pediatric Radiology,* 1–7.

# Chapter 8

# Healthcare Interoperability

Virginia Lorenzi

## Introduction

"Imagine a world where your medical records are just where they need to be when you show up with the provider and you don't have to do any work" (Forbes Business Council, 2024). This vision, articulated by Micky Tripathi, US National Coordinator for Health IT, encapsulates the essence of interoperability in healthcare. According to the US 21st Century Cures Act, interoperability is defined as:

Health information technology that:

(A) enables the secure exchange of electronic health information with, and use of electronic health information from, other health information technology without special effort on the part of the user.
(B) allows for complete access, exchange, and use of all electronically accessible health information for authorized use under (U.S. House. H.R.34, 21st Century Cures Act, 2016) applicable State or Federal law.
(C) does not constitute information blocking (Health Insurance Portability and Accountability Act, 1996).

The 21st Century Cures Act's overall purpose is to accelerate the development of cures for disease, yet an entire subtitle of the rule has a focus on interoperability. Imagine having an interoperable health IT infrastructure, nationwide, such that the health information needed to enable the best treatment, efficient and accurate payment, streamlined operations, patient access, public health, and research was accessible when and where it was needed. To understand why 21st Century Cures has a focus on interoperability, we need to look back in time.

DOI: 10.4324/9781003464457-8

# History of US Healthcare Interoperability

## *HIPAA*

The Health Insurance Portability and Accountability Act (HIPAA) of 1996 (Health Insurance Portability and Accountability Act, 1996) is widely known for its role in protecting patient privacy and enforcing security of Health IT. However, HIPAA also laid the groundwork for permitted sharing. In particular, health information can be shared:

- For treatment purposes
- For operational purposes
- For payment purposes
- With the patient or their legal proxy
- With public health
- Other purposes with appropriate patient consent.

## *An Office for Healthcare IT*

In 2004, the US Office of the National Coordinator of Health IT (the ONC) was created by an executive order. The executive order stated that "the work of the National Coordinator shall be consistent with a vision of developing a nationwide interoperable health information technology infrastructure that:

- Ensures that appropriate information to guide medical decisions is available at the time and place of care.
- Improves healthcare quality, reduces medical errors, and advances the delivery of appropriate, evidence-based medical care.
- Reduces healthcare costs resulting from inefficiency, medical errors, inappropriate care, and incomplete information.
- Promotes a more effective marketplace, greater competition, and increased choice through the wider availability of accurate information on healthcare costs, quality, and outcomes.
- Improves the coordination of care and information among hospitals, laboratories, physician offices, and other ambulatory care providers through an effective infrastructure for the secure and authorized exchange of healthcare information (e-Patient Dave, n.d.).
- Ensures that patients' individually identifiable health information is secure and protected" (Executive Order No. 13335, 2004).

This executive order also called for a National Health IT infrastructure so that the right data was available when and where it was needed. The ONC was created and began efforts to build consensus on standards for information sharing between systems, and for the voluntary certification of Electronic Health Records (EHRs) (Executive Order No. 13335, 2004).

The new office convened standards developers to create standards, worked to develop interoperability policy, and developed a voluntary certification program. The National Health Information Network (NHIN) was also created with the goal of sharing health information nationwide built from voluntary participants. Despite these efforts, very little interoperability was occurring. Studies were published citing the value of EHRs and interoperability to improve healthcare, and the public called for a more concerted effort.

## The Patient Advocacy Movement

One important set of voices were end users of the healthcare system, patients, and their personal caregivers, as well as their advocates. As the nation turned its focus on the potential of health IT, end users of the system began advocating for access to their records so they could be more active in their own care and the care of loved ones. Two important patient advocates in this "free the data" movement were Dave DeBronkart (known as E-Patient Dave) (e-Patient Dave, n.d.), who collaborated with his doctor in his kidney cancer treatment and identified the importance of patient access and sharing of healthcare information. Dave had a partnership with his doctor, Dr. Danny Sands (Society for Participatory Medicine, n.d.), who fully supported Dave's engagement in his care. Dave gave a TED talk in 2012 describing this idea, entitled "Let Patients Help." He also collaborated with doctor, musician, and songwriter Ross Martin in creating the song "Gimme My DAM Data" (DAM means Data About Me) (YouTube, 2012) to raise awareness of the importance of empowering patients with easy access to their medical records. Dave is still championing the cause: he co-founded HL7's Patient Empowerment workgroup in 2021 and still speaks across the world about the importance of the patient voice.

The OpenNotes (OpenNotes, n.d.) movement, started at Harvard Medical School and Beth Israel Deaconess Hospital, began with a large research study in which 20,000 patients were invited to read their notes. The results showed that little impact on clinician burden occurred, and the patients overwhelmingly approved (Delbanco et al., 2012). The OpenNotes foundation advocates for the open sharing of clinical notes with patients. It partners with patient advocates in all of its work. Another activist, Casey Quinlan (aka Mighty Casey), who unfortunately succumbed to her illness, tattooed a QR code to her chest, which when scanned, gave access to her records. Regina Holliday, an artist, uses her art in her advocacy for patients. Her story is a sad one, and it spurred her to advocacy through art. Her husband passed away after a difficult journey through the US healthcare system – a journey in which patient and caregiver access to medical records would have helped. On this journey, she found Dave on social media and asked for help. In 2009, she painted a mural in DC entitled "73 cents," named after the price she had to pay for each printed page of her husband's record (Holliday, 2015). Later, she started the Walking Gallery of Healthcare (Holliday, 2011), in which she and other artists painted the backs of business jackets with paintings depicting personal healthcare stories and the need to improve the system. The owners of the jackets (the walkers) represent a community committed to the cause, and each agrees to wear their jackets to healthcare conferences and policy events to raise awareness of the need for interoperability and patient electronic access to their records. There are over 700 jacket wearers of the Walking Gallery of Healthcare, many of them patient activists and allies like the ones mentioned here.

## HITECH and Meaningful Use

In 2009, the ARRA (American Recovery and Reinvestment Act, 2009) was passed, which included a whole section of health information technology called Health Information Technology for Economic and Clinical Health (HITECH). The HITECH Act codified the ONC and included significant funding for EHR adoption, Health IT training, and establishment of local networks.

Numerous regulations followed as part of the HITECH Act, which implemented the adoption of health IT interoperability standards, the certification criteria for EHRs, and provider incentives (and later penalties) for the meaningful use of certified EHRs. The dreams were for providers to have access to information electronically and share information with other providers, for electronic transmission of prescriptions to pharmacies, for public health to have access to information, for information to be shared for quality improvement of healthcare, and for patients themselves to have access to their data. Data sharing was a key component of the EHR Incentive program. Interoperability standards such as HL7 V2, HL7 CDA, LOINC, NCPDP-Script, SNOMED-CT, RxNorm, the DIRECT protocol, and IHE XDS were critical enablers to accomplish sharing across diverse systems. Standards development organizations such as HL7 worked to advance standards and implementation guides for this purpose.

## Sharing between Providers

A critical standards artifact that was produced through these efforts was the HL7 CCDA – Consolidated Clinical Document Architecture (H.R.34, 2016; HL7 CDA, n.d.) – which integrated terminology standards such as LOINC for labs and RxNorm for medications – to provide a fully encoded, standardized XML-formatted document containing patient data that could be exchanged at transition of care or during referrals. The dream of an NHIN was still there, but now the concept was to start small and build a network of networks. Local providers in a region were connected to each other for data sharing through a Regional Health Information Exchange or RHIO. For example, a RHIO might include small providers, larger clinics, nursing homes, hospitals, payors, public health authorities, and community-based organizations. RHIOs would then be connected to other networks across a state forming a state network, and then the states could be connected to form a national network.

Another mechanism for data sharing built into EHRs as a certification requirement included the ability to share electronic care summaries (formatted as CCDAs) on referrals and transitions of care using the Direct Protocol, analogous to a secure email for healthcare. Each of these solutions had difficulty scaling, since the RHIOs needed to connect each provider to their network, and the Direct protocol provided point-to-point connectivity between providers and provided the sender to have the destination provider's direct address. An alternative standard sharing mechanism for document exchange was created by Integrating the Healthcare Enterprise (IHE) called IHE Cross Domain Sharing (XDS). IHE XDS did not have the point-to-point limitations of direct, but required more technical infrastructure. A newer network architecture emerged that leveraged IHE XDS. EHR vendors and other stakeholders determined how to share data between their respective systems, each following the same standards and trust frameworks.

Examples of these newer networks include Carequality and CommonWell. This simplified sharing for the provider because the EHR vendor established the connections, and there was no need to keep track of direct addresses. Each type of network has pros and cons to its architecture as well as challenges in business sustainability. Also, without comprehensive participation in these networks across the US healthcare system, and with limitations of what data is made available and when, none of the networks or sharing mechanisms were complete. As a result, a clinician querying for information on a new patient might get some but not all of the information based on which EHRs or providers were connected, what data they made accessible, and in some cases, whether appropriate consents were provided.

## Sharing with Patients

In addition to data sharing about providers, data sharing with patients is an important goal in our country. The EHR Incentive program required that patients could View, Download, and Transmit their data. Other requirements included the ability for patients to message their providers and receive electronic reminders. The EHR vendors primarily solved the patient-facing certification requirements by creating tethered patient portals to their software. A patient got their window into the EHR and could download and transmit the information if they chose.

A proposed requirement in the Meaningful Use program that was never finalized was for the ability to share patient-generated data with providers.

## Limitations to Interoperability Identified

There was progress in interoperability across the country – adoption of EHRs equipped with standards-based interoperability capabilities, providers incentivized or penalized if they did not use these features to share data, patients able to access some of their data electronically, and a proliferation of health information exchanges. However, actual interoperability was still sparse. The 2013 JASON Report on a Robust Health Data Infrastructure (Office of the National Coordinator for Health Information Technology, 2014) seriously criticized the progress and strategy and concluded that Meaningful Use had not successfully achieved meaningful interoperability in healthcare. It recommended an alternative design that used standards-based APIs. "Advancing Interoperability, Information Sharing, and Data Access: Improving Health and Healthcare for Americans" recommended clear actions on how to achieve robust interoperability, including improving the business case, advancing the technical infrastructure, improving public policy, and strengthening leadership (Bipartisan Policy Center & Healthcare Leadership Council, 2019).

There were also numerous accounts of incidents where data was not shared when requested, or not shared in an electronic format, and in a timely manner. The term "information blocking" was created to describe this problem. Vendors, HIEs, and providers were all identified as potential information blockers in a report written for Congress by the ONC in 2015. Information blocking is defined as the act of preventing or delaying the access, exchange, or use of electronic health data. The report expressed a concern that providers and developers were engaging in information blocking to "lock in" providers and consumers (Office of the National Coordinator for Health Information Technology, 2015).

In addition, payers, key stakeholders in the healthcare system, had limited interoperability capabilities. Perhaps this was because payers were not included in the incentives/disincentives of the Meaningful Use program. It was difficult for patients to access data electronically from payers, for patient information to be portable between payers, and there were inefficiencies in payer/provider communication for key workflows such as prior authorization.

And while patients had access to some of their information via patient portals, the data was a limited subset of their medical record, was not always accessible in a timely manner, and patients who chose to use clinicians at distinct organizations found they needed multiple portals (one for each organization), a problem some managing complicated illnesses referred to as "portalitus."

## Addressing Limitations with 21st Century Cures

In 2016, the 21st Century Cures Act was passed. The law (U.S. House. H.R.34, 21st Century Cures Act, 2016) included a focus on fixing the limitations in interoperability previously identified. This law required that the United States have "interoperability" in healthcare "without special effort" and called for a national trusted exchange framework to support interoperability across the country. Numerous regulations were published that implemented the interoperability requirements of the 21st Century Cures. This included the renaming and refocusing of the EHR Incentive program to Promoting Interoperability, emphasizing the key focus and need. The certification program was enhanced to include criteria for API access, as recommended by the JASON Report, as well as other interoperability requirements as a condition of maintenance for their certifications. Providers eligible for the Promoting Interoperability were given a new objective to enable API access for patients.

EHR vendors, providers, government standards experts, and other key stakeholders worked collaboratively with the Health Level Seven standards development community to create a standardized API format that used the HL7 Fast Healthcare Interoperability Resources (FHIR) standard (HL7 International, n.d.), a standard that is very amenable to the RESTful API paradigm of the web. As a consequence, many EHRs implemented the same API, making it easy for patient-facing applications to access information from different EHRs. This enabled an alternative model for patient records access where a patient could connect and download information from multiple EHRs to a Personal Health Record (PHR) untethered to any particular EHR. The PHR centralized patient information from disparate sources in one place, and patients could potentially add their own information, such as home blood pressure readings, symptom logs, etc. The certified EHR capability for patients to connect PHR apps and download their data was added in 2019 and has continued to be enhanced from that point forward with FHIR and other standards for terminology, authentication, and authorization required. In addition, a process was established to continually expand and enhance the data elements required to be shared. The ever-expanding set of data elements is referred to as the United States Core Data Set for Interoperability (USCDI).

One of the most significant data elements included was clinical notes across the full spectrum of healthcare. The addition of notes sharing as a regulatory requirement was a huge milestone for data transparency for patients and caregivers and the OpenNotes initiative.

Regulations were also passed that required payers to support standards-based interoperability for the following data flows:

- Payer to patient to support data access and directory access
- Payer to payer
- Provider to payer to support prior authorization

Two HL7 Accelerators, DaVinci and the CARIN Alliance, convened stakeholders and created HL7 FHIR implementation guides to support the needed use cases.

To ensure that actors across the health IT spectrum were not an obstacle to interoperability, the 21st Century Cures Act banned the practice of information blocking. Information blocking was further defined in the regulation "21st Century Cures Act: Interoperability, Information Blocking, and the ONC Health IT Certification Program" (U.S. House. H.R.34, 21st Century Cures Act, 2016) to include:

- What constituted information blocking?
- Who were the actors who could be subject to information blocking? Actors included a wide breadth of healthcare participants, including any form of provider, vendors of certified Health IT, and Health Information Exchanges.
- What exceptions were allowed? Exceptions allowed information blocking in limited circumstances, such as to protect a patient's privacy or to prevent imminent physical harm to the patient.
- How complaints of information blocking would be received and managed?
- How would actors be penalized?

As a result of these new requirements, vendors openly published their APIs and other interoperability specifications and simplified access to interoperability capabilities for applications and other external parties. Providers created new workflows to support requests for electronic health information and reconfigured their systems for the timely release of electronic health information to patients and external parties using standards-based interoperability technology. HIEs also provided access to information for patients.

Finally, 21st Century Cures called for the creation of a single national "Trusted Exchange Framework" for healthcare interoperability. The network would have a single Recognized Coordinating Entity (RCE). The Sequoia Project was chosen for this role. Sequoia had deep experience in managing these frameworks, since they coordinated Care Quality and EHealth Exchange. The backbone nodes of the network are called Qualified Health Information Networks (QHINs). Organizations interested in being QHINs have to apply and must meet rigorous requirements in terms of functionality, performance, and security. Connected to each QHIN are participants and sub-participants, which could be other networks, providers, payers, etc. Trust is established with all the exchange partners through each node in the network through adherence to a "Common Agreement." For example, the Common Agreement specifies that the network can only be used for permitted purposes such as treatment and operations. Collectively, this is referred to as the Trusted Exchange Framework and Common Agreement (TEFCA). TEFCA went live at the end of 2023 with six QHINs and a multitude of participants. More participants are joining and additional QHINs are being established. The technical infrastructure of the trusted exchange initially used HIS XDS and is moving toward the use of HL7 FHIR. The FHIR at Scale Task Force (FAST) HL7 accelerator is working on developing FHIR implementation guides to support this level of national exchange. As the network becomes more robust, there will be less need for organizations to connect to multiple networks, and the information available to all participants, including patients, will be much more comprehensive. As of 2024, participation is voluntary, but it is expected that regulatory agencies will encourage participation in the future through penalties and incentives.

## Challenges of Implementing Interoperability

Implementing interoperability has numerous complexities and special cases that need to be considered. Several of these challenges are described here, but the list is not inclusive.

## Moving to Transparency

The change to sharing data with patients in real time requires workflow and culture changes. One of the challenges of sharing notes in near real time with patients is that the authors need to be mindful of their wording in notes. For example, the clinician has to be mindful of condescending language or using abbreviations or expressions that could be misinterpreted (e.g., SOB for shortness of breath) or writing text in notes that the patient was not told. There could also be certain situations in which holding back the note is warranted and satisfies a valid information blocking exception – however, the process of holding back a note is a new workflow step. A clinician could decide to hold back a note if sharing could cause the patient imminent physical harm or if the patient requested that it not be shared. One example might be a contentious home situation in which the portal would be viewable by someone other than the patient. There are also concerns with a patient being upset when seeing a life-changing result prior to the doctor reviewing and/or contacting them. This is exasperated by false positives or intermediate findings, especially on screening tests (e.g., a concern on a mammogram does not mean the patient has breast cancer – it just means more testing is warranted). To mitigate this concern, pre-counseling as well as explanatory notices on the portal can help a patient not overreact to a result.

## Sharing of Information for Behavioral Health Patients

Behavioral health notes are also required to be shared with patients. Some worry about negative impacts on patients, but studies show that it increases patient trust. Psychotherapy notes should not be shared, but regular behavioral health progress notes need to be shared. There might be reasons to hold back various information from behavioral health patients to prevent imminent physical harm, such as the toxicology report on an overdose attempt or weight and BMI for a patient with anorexia. Also, when sharing with other providers, a patient may request limitations on sharing for privacy reasons. They might be comfortable sharing some information but not other information. This is referred to as data segmentation. For example, a patient might not want a mental illness diagnosis shared with another provider, but would like the rest of their record shared. Much work has gone into the area of data segmentation, but a robust solution has not been implemented in a widespread manner. Finally, there are state and federal regulations that offer additional privacy beyond HIPAA for certain behavioral health issues – one example is special privacy protections for substance disorder patients.

## Sharing of Information for Pediatric Patients

Sharing of clinical information for pediatric patients also has challenges (Elias et al., 2023). First, it is important that the parents or legal guardians have robust access to pediatric patient information. Occasionally, there might be an issue with one spouse seeing information about the other or about a newborn's health that implies the health of the mother (e.g., baby born with HIV). When adolescents come of age to consent for specific healthcare without parental permission, that information needs to be protected from the parents or legal guardians unless the adolescent provides permission. The adolescents should have the ability to view their chart as well. In addition, the parents still have a right to see much of the adolescent's record so they can advocate for their child's care. This requires the ability to carefully segment parts of the record when sharing with parents. This problem becomes more unwieldy when parents use their own emails to create adolescent portals. Sharing data across state lines that have different rules for care for children could also be problematic. For example, if a 12-year-old adolescent has care they are allowed to seek without parental consent in one state, and then the record is shared with a state that requires parental consent at age 12, the parents may now be able to access records they were not able to access before. Another example would be the sharing of information across state lines with differing laws for patients who have abortions or gender-affirming care.

## Sharing with Caregivers

In addition to sharing with both patients and caregivers in the pediatric space, there is also a need for caregivers of adults to have access to their loved ones' records. This could be a many-to-one or one-to-many relationship – a caregiver may care for multiple people, and a patient may have multiple caregivers. At any point in time, a patient may want to remove or limit (segment) the access of a caregiver, and as children age, the parents' access needs to change to better reflect the patient's consent. Each caregiver may also have information to share as part of the patient's story. This complexity of caregiver and patient relationships and access may not be supportable in today's systems.

## *Errors in the Records*

While interoperability holds great promise, it can also proliferate errors. Unfortunately, errors are made in the documentation of medical records (Bell et al., 2020). Examples include wrong diagnosis, wrong gender, even the patient could be wrong (patient matching error). If a patient or another party sees an error, correcting it is often difficult. Current processes are manual and opaque, and even when corrections are made, they might not be automatically shared across all the places that have received the incorrect information.

## *Sharing of Images*

Images – radiology, cardiology, scanned documents, and more – are a valuable part of a patient's medical record. Much success has been made in the sharing of images between disparate systems within an organization, such as the sharing between the imaging machines, the EHR, the Radiology Information System, and the Picture Archiving and Communications System (PACS) due to the work of ACR/NEMA and IHE who made standards-based sharing using Digital Imaging and Communications in Medicine (DICOM) a success within organizations. However, sharing images across the healthcare ecosystem is more difficult due to the size of the images.

## *Patient Contributed Data*

Finally, while there are instances of patients sharing the data they collect on themselves, this is not widespread, and there is a great opportunity to share more. To get a full picture of a patient, one needs to understand what is happening outside the healthcare environment. Patients (and their personal caregivers) are obtaining and collecting information on themselves more than ever before. Patients are tracking their symptoms, environmental data, data from health devices, self admin of prescription and over-the-counter meds and food intake. Yet the workflows, standards, and interoperability infrastructure have yet to evolve so that the patient's perspective and data are fully shared. The HL7 Patient Empowerment workgroup published a white paper entitled "Patient Contributed Data" (HL7 International, 2023), which defines Patient Contributed Data and the opportunities it brings.

## *Compliance with Terminology Standards*

To truly make clinical data types groupable and comparable, proper use of terminology standards is critical. Terminology standards are a detailed nuance of interoperability that provides a computable way to know that two meds or two tests are both the same kind or that a certain med is used to treat a certain diagnosis. When healthcare concepts are not coded and shared using appropriate terminologies and value sets, true interoperability cannot be achieved. For example, if a CCDA is shared but there is no validation that the information inside the CCDA is coded properly, the receiving system might not be able to reconcile the information or do other computational work with it.

## Summary

> One of the most powerful levers we have to improve health outcomes and reduce health care costs is the seamless sharing of clinical data with consumers and providers, regardless of technology systems. To realize the potential of the digital health era, we must empower individuals with information to engage in their own health, while creating pathways to ensure the right information is available at the right place and time for high-quality, cost-efficient care delivery.
>
> (Shafer, 2015)

This statement from Brent Shafer, former chairman and CEO of Cerner Corporation, underscores the importance of interoperability.

The 21st Century Cures Act represents a significant milestone in advancing healthcare interoperability in the United States and realizing this vision. By mandating interoperability "without special effort" and addressing information blocking, the Act aims to ensure that healthcare providers and patients have timely access to critical health information. Interoperability standards such as HL7 FHIR enable widespread data exchange between disparate systems. However, opportunities for improvement remain, including the ability to segment data and provide other fine-grained privacy controls for patients, data sharing that is truly ubiquitous and comprehensive, and integrating patient-contributed data. Looking forward, achieving the full aspirations of the 21st Century Cures Act will require continued collaboration among stakeholders, robust regulatory support, and ongoing innovation in health IT. This is a worthy goal – achieving interoperability will mean providers and patients will be less burdened and more empowered. Efficiencies across the system will streamline the care and payment process and reduce costs. And each stakeholder in the healthcare system will have the right data at the right time in the right format so they can make data-driven decisions leading to higher quality care.

## References

American Recovery and Reinvestment Act of 2009, 111th Congress (2009). https://www.congress.gov/bill/111th-congress/house-bill/1/text

Bell, S. K., Delbanco, T., Elmore, J. G., Fitzgerald, P. S., Fossa, A., Harcourt, K., Leveille, S. G., Payne, T. H., Stametz, R. A., Walker, J., & DesRoches, C. M. (2020). Frequency and types of patient-reported errors in electronic health record ambulatory care notes. *JAMA Network Open*.

Bipartisan Policy Center & Healthcare Leadership Council. (2019, February). Advancing interoperability information sharing and data access: Improving health and healthcare for Americans. https://bipartisanpolicy.org/download/?file=/wp-content/uploads/2019/03/Advancing-Interoperability-Information-Sharing-and-Data-Access-Improving-Health-and-Healthcare-for-Americans.pdf

Delbanco, T., Walker, J., Bell, S. K., Darer, J. D., Elmore, J. G., Farag, N., Feldman, H. J., Mejilla, R., Ngo, L., Ralston, J. D., Ross, S. E., Trivedi, N., Vodicka, E., & Leveille, S. G. (2012). Inviting patients to read their doctors' notes: A quasi-experimental study and a look ahead. *Annals of Internal Medicine*, *157*(7), 461–470. https://www.acpjournals.org/doi/10.7326/0003-4819-157-7-201210020-00002

Elias, J., Gossey, J. T., Xi, W., Sharko, M., Robbins, L., Bostwick, S., Chang, J., Lorenzi, V., Giatzikis, V., Scofi, J., Trepp, R., & Lewis, R. (2023). Sharing clinical notes while protecting adolescent confidentiality and maintaining parental insight. *Applied Clinical Informatics*, *14*(3), 555–565.

e-Patient Dave. (n.d.). Retrieved from https://www.epatientdave.com/

Executive Order No. 13335, 3 C.F.R. § 702 (2004). https://www.govinfo.gov/content/pkg/WCPD-2004-05-03/pdf/WCPD-2004-05-03-Pg702.pdf

Forbes Business Council. (2024, April 15). Why healthcare interoperability shouldn't force professionals to choose sides. *Forbes*. https://www.forbes.com/sites/forbesbusinesscouncil/2024/04/15/why-healthcare-interoperability-shouldnt-force-professionals-to-choose-sides/?sh=1d453141a7dc

Health Insurance Portability and Accountability Act of 1996, Pub. L. No. 104-191, 110 Stat. 1936 (1996). https://www.congress.gov/bill/104th-congress/house-bill/3103/text

HL7 CDA® R2 Implementation Guide: Consolidated CDA Templates for Clinical Notes Edition 3 - US Realm. (n.d.). Retrieved from https://www.hl7.org/implement/standards/product_brief.cfm?product_id=492

HL7 International. (2023, November 16). *Patient Contributed Data*. Retrieved from https://www.hl7.org/implement/standards/product_brief.cfm?product_id=638

HL7 International. (n.d.). *FHIR specification*. Retrieved from https://hl7.org/fhir/index.html

Holliday, R. (2011, April). The Walking Gallery. *Regina Holliday's Medical Advocacy Blog*. https://reginaholliday.blogspot.com/2011/04/walking-gallery.html

Holliday, R. (2015). *The Writing on The Wall*. CreateSpace Independent Publishing Platform.

Office of the National Coordinator for Health Information Technology. (2014). *A robust health data infrastructure*. https://digital.ahrq.gov/sites/default/files/docs/publication/a-robust-health-data-infrastructure.pdf

Office of the National Coordinator for Health Information Technology. (2015). *Report to Congress on Health Information Blocking*. U.S. Department of Health and Human Services.

OpenNotes. (n.d.). Retrieved from https://www.opennotes.org/

Shafer, B. (2015). *Advancing Interoperability, Information Sharing, and Data Access: Improving Health and Healthcare for Americans*. Healthcare Leadership Council. https://bipartisanpolicy.org/download/?file=/wp-content/uploads/2019/03/Advancing-Interoperability-Information-Sharing-and-Data-Access-Improving-Health-and-Healthcare-for-Americans.pdf

Society for Participatory Medicine. (n.d.). Retrieved from https://participatorymedicine.org/

U.S. House. H.R.34 - 21st Century Cures Act, 114th Congress (2015–2016). https://www.congress.gov/bill/114th-congress/house-bill/34/text

YouTube. (2012). *Gimme My DAM Data*. https://www.youtube.com/watch?v=0gpk-fbfg4Y

# Chapter 9

# HIPAA Revisited, Privacy and Confidentiality, and Cybercrimes

Young-Shin Park

## Introduction

In the digital era, there has been an exponential adoption of the Internet of Things (IoT) devices and Internet of Medical Things (IoMT) devices, which have been used daily in the healthcare environment (Cartwright, 2023). Clinical staff utilize mobile phones, iPads, or tablets not only to communicate with other clinical team members but also to view patients' health records, check real-time lab results, document clinical information, or capture images and attach electronic clinical documentation. Artificial Intelligent (AI)–based solutions have been increasingly deployed and embedded in daily clinical workflows (Shah et al., 2023). As digital transformation occurs in healthcare, confidentiality and privacy must be protected and strengthened because there are more chances that hackers can invade healthcare information systems and steal protected health information (PHI).

There are numerous instances where PHI has been exposed purposefully or unintentionally. One medical center in New York City reported that one of the employees inappropriately accessed electronic patient records and sold 12,517 patients' PHI to an identity theft ring in 2013. This resulted in the hospital paying $4.75 million (Office for Civil Rights [OCR], 2024b). Hospital employees could take a picture that includes sensitive patient data in the background and post it on social media without realizing the Health Insurance Portability and Accountability Act (HIPAA) violation. Hospital workers might share admitted patient information via hands-free open communication devices in a hospital public area without realizing the exposure of the patient's specific health condition. There have been multiple incidents where hospital employees have opened other celebrities' Electronic Medical Records (EMRs) out of curiosity, which resulted in disciplinary actions for tens of employees, financial charges, or termination (Ornstein, 2015). An insurance company, Excellus Health Plan, has reported a compromised PHI incidence in 2015 because of hacking, compromising over 9.3 million individuals' data, including their names, addresses, dates of

 DOI: 10.4324/9781003464457-9

birth, email addresses, Social Security numbers, bank account information, health plan claims, and clinical treatment information, and paying $5.1 million settlement fees (HHS Press Office, 2021). All of these incidents lead to a HIPAA violation, which ultimately impacts patient privacy and becomes a financial burden to healthcare facilities. It is imperative that hospital employees adhere to HIPAA regulations, carefully handle patients' PHI, and prevent potential security breaches.

Vendors and software developers take security seriously. A vulnerability is a specific weakness in an information system, including design flaws, gaps in security procedures, or broken internal controls that may cause potential threats (Spitzer, 2017). Organizational information technology cybersecurity team, network team, and vendors proactively monitor vulnerabilities that reside in the hardware, software, database, and networking side, as well as provide vulnerability scanning results, remediation plans, and appropriate steps to their customers. Affected areas could be on the server, operating systems, networking, and/or vendor-specific software. Proper remediation plans should be executed regularly depending on the vulnerability reports.

One instance where this has been effective is in patient-facing audio-visual devices that can be installed in the hospital for remote patient monitoring, tele-consult, or virtual nursing programs. Hackers have invaded these devices through the connected hospital network. This may also be available due to specific camera models or software versions used within the hospital. The vendor has the responsibility to report to the hospital IT department about these potential security concerns. Then, proper software patches or camera firmware can be applied to prevent these cyberattacks. Establishing a secure hospital network environment along with continuous staff education and proactive vulnerability monitoring with remediation plans is a common strategy to protect sensitive health information (Ibrahim et al., 2024).

In this chapter, we will go over HIPAA updates and changes, different types of cyber threats, and preventable strategies to protect patients' confidentiality.

## HIPAA Modifications

As discussed in the previous chapters, the initial HIPAA of 1996, Public Law 104-191, has been modified and reinforced several times (OCR, 2024c).

- The final Privacy Rule was published in 2000, modified in 2002, and mandated in 2003 to "*set national standards for the protection of individually identifiable health information*"
- The final Security Rule was published in 2003 and mandated in 2005 to protect "the confidentiality, integrity, and availability" of electronic PHI
- The HIPAA Enforcement Rule was proposed in 2005 and finalized in 2006 to provide standards for compliance, investigations, penalties for all the HIPAA Administrative Simplification Rules and hearing procedures
- The original HIPAA Security Rules have been strengthened and reformed by the Health Information Technology for Economic and Clinical Health (HITECH) Act in 2009. Under the HITECH Security Rule, the original HIPAA compliance should be audited periodically by the HHS, with the responsibilities extended to the Business Associates (Shah et al., 2023)
- The HIPAA Omnibus Rulemaking was released in 2013 and reinforced patient health data security in the digital health environment by finalizing the Breach Notification Rule. A breach is defined as "an impermissible use or disclosure under the Privacy Rule that compromises the security or privacy" of the PHI. HIPAA-covered organizations or business associates should report any PHI breach cases via the Web Breach Portal. Figure 9.1 is an example of the Breach Report Portal

| | A | B | C | D | E | F | G |
|---|---|---|---|---|---|---|---|
| 1 | Name of Covered Entity | State | Covered Entity Type | Individuals Affected | Breach Submission Date | Type of Breach | Location of Breached Information |
| 2 | Change Healthcare, Inc. | MN | Business Associate | 190000000 | 7/19/2024 | Hacking/IT Incident | Network Server |
| 3 | Anthem Inc. | IN | Health Plan | 78800000 | 2/13/2015 | Hacking/IT Incident | Network Server |
| 4 | Welltok, Inc. | CO | Business Associate | 14782887 | 11/6/2023 | Hacking/IT Incident | Network Server |
| 5 | Kaiser Foundation Health Plan, Inc. | CA | Health Plan | 13400000 | 4/12/2024 | Unauthorized Access/Disclosure | Network Server |
| 6 | Optum360, LLC | MN | Business Associate | 11500000 | 7/1/2019 | Hacking/IT Incident | Network Server |
| 7 | HCA Healthcare | TN | Business Associate | 11270000 | 7/31/2023 | Hacking/IT Incident | Network Server |
| 8 | Premera Blue Cross | WA | Health Plan | 11000000 | 3/17/2015 | Hacking/IT Incident | Network Server |
| 9 | Laboratory Corporation of America Holdings dba LabCorp | NC | Healthcare Provider | 10251784 | 7/13/2019 | Hacking/IT Incident | Network Server |
| 10 | Excellus Health Plan, Inc. | NY | Health Plan | 9358891 | 9/9/2015 | Hacking/IT Incident | Network Server |
| 11 | Perry Johnson & Associates, Inc. dba PJ&A | NV | Business Associate | 9302588 | 11/3/2023 | Hacking/IT Incident | Network Server |
| 12 | Maximus, Inc. | VA | Business Associate | 9179390 | 8/4/2023 | Hacking/IT Incident | Network Server |
| 13 | Managed Care of North America | GA | Business Associate | 8627242 | 5/26/2023 | Hacking/IT Incident | Network Server |
| 14 | Community Health Systems Professional Services Corporations | TN | Healthcare Provider | 6121158 | 8/21/2014 | Hacking/IT Incident | Network Server |
| 15 | PharMerica Corporation | KY | Healthcare Provider | 5815591 | 5/12/2023 | Hacking/IT Incident | Network Server |
| 16 | Ascension Health | MO | Healthcare Provider | 5466931 | 7/3/2024 | Hacking/IT Incident | Network Server |
| 17 | HealthEC LLC | NJ | Business Associate | 4656293 | 12/21/2023 | Hacking/IT Incident | Network Server |
| 18 | University of California, Los Angeles Health | CA | Healthcare Provider | 4500000 | 7/17/2015 | Hacking/IT Incident | Network Server |

**Figure 9.1 A sample of the breach of unsecured PHI report – HHS OCR (n.d.-b).**

- In 2014, patients were able to access their test results via the Clinical Laboratory Improvement Amendment (Alder, 2024a)
- The HIPAA rule was changed in 2016, "*2016 Privacy Rule*", allowing covered entities to disclose PHI to the National Instant Criminal Background Check System (NICS)

In public health emergency cases such as the COVID-19 pandemic, the Office for Civil Rights (OCR) has announced flexibilities in Good Faith and provided guidance, clarification, and justification to these regulatory rules (Alder, 2024b). For instance, the Coronavirus Aid, Relief, and Economic Security (CARES) Act was enacted in 2020 during the COVID-19 pandemic and modified some of the existing rules. The "*Notices of Enforcement Discretion*" allowed healthcare providers to share COVID-19 test results, patient information, or Substance Use Disorder (SUD) information in order to provide proper patient care. Additionally, a "Notification of Enforcement Discretion for Telehealth Remote Communications (also known as Telehealth Notification)" was implemented and allowed the use of audio-only telehealth services in specific cases (Alder, 2024a, 2024b). Based on the CARES Act, the "*Telehealth Notification*" covered that healthcare providers could use non-public-facing audio or video remote communication technology, and that it might not be fully compliant with HIPAA Rules (OCR, 2022). This temporary modified Rule ended on May 11, 2023 as the COVID-19 pandemic crisis ended officially.

Another example of a public health emergency is the substance use crisis. As the National Center for Health Statistics announced, there has been a continual rise in drug overdose deaths in the United States over the past few decades (Spencer et al., 2024). The SUD information used to be covered by the "*Confidentiality of Substance Use Disorder (SUD) Patient Records*" regulation to protect patients' privacy. Later, SUD or mental health information was treated under the same HIPAA regulations. Under the CARES Act, the SUD information could be shared with public health professionals if patient information is de-identified and adheres to the HIPAA Rules (Alder, 2024b).

On the other hand, there were concerns that patients may avoid treatment due to discrimination or fear of PHI disclosure (Alder, 2024a; Department of Health and Human Services [HHS], 2024). In this context, a Privacy Notice of Proposed Rulemaking (NPRM), also known as "*2022 Part 2 NPRM*" was proposed in 2022 to protect patients from this concern. The regulations at 42 Code of Federal Regulations (CFR) part 2, also referred to as "*Part 2*" protect

> records of the identity, diagnosis, prognosis, or treatment of any patient which are maintained in connection with the performance of any program or activity relating to substance abuse education prevention, training, treatment, rehabilitation, or research, which is conducted, regulated or directory or indirectly assisted by any department of the United States.
>
> (OCR, 2024a)

Subsequently, the "*2023 Privacy Rule NPRM*" was issued to revise the regulations in Part 2 (HHS, 2024). The Final Rule "2024 Privacy Rule" was announced, effective on June 25, 2024, and amended provisions to reinforce highly sensitive PHI about the reproductive healthcare of Security Rule standards (Alder, 2024a; HHS, 2024; Kutak Rock Client Alert, 2024).

Since the initial HIPAA Privacy and Security Rules have been deployed over the last 25 years, there have been increasing demands to ease the administrative burden and to remove certain provisions. As a result, the HIPAA Safe Haber Bill, HR7898, was amended to the HITECH Act in 2022 to reduce burdens from the HIPAA-regulated healthcare facilities (HHS, 2024). This helped reduce the penalties and shorten the length of investigation of data breaches as long as the facilities had adopted security practices 12 months prior. Additionally, the OCR (2024b) issued a Request for Information (RFI) in 2021 and received comments on the HIPAA Privacy rules. The Final Rule will update both HIPAA Privacy and Security Rules, which is effective from July 8, 2024, and was enforced to be applied within a short 180-day compliance period, January 1, 2025, by HIPAA-regulated facilities (Alder, 2024b; HHS, 2024).

The Updated HIPAA Privacy Rule includes that (Alder, 2024a, 2024b; HHS, 2024):

- Patients can inspect their PHI in person and take notes or photographs of their PHI
- The maximum time to provide access to PHI will be changed from 30 days to 15 days
- Requests by individuals to transfer ePHI to a third party will be limited to the ePHI maintained in an EHR via e-signature
- Individuals will be permitted to request their PHI be transferred to a personal health application and the ePHI will be at no cost
- Covered entities will be required to inform individuals that they have the right to obtain or direct copies of their PHI to a third party when a summary of PHI is offered instead of a copy
- HIPAA-covered entities will be required to post estimated fee schedules on their websites for PHI access and disclosures and to provide an individualized fee estimation for providing an individual with a copy of their own PHI
- Pathways created for individuals to direct the sharing of PHI will be maintained in an EHR among covered entities
- Healthcare providers and health plans will be required to respond to certain record requests from other covered healthcare providers and health plans, in cases when an individual directs those entities to do so under the HIPAA Right of Access.
- The requirement for HIPAA-covered entities to obtain written confirmation that a Notice of Privacy Practices has been provided will be dropped
- Covered entities will be allowed to disclose PHI to avert a threat to health or safety when harm is "*seriously and reasonably foreseeable*" and to make certain uses and disclosures of PHI based on their good faith belief that it is in the best interest of the individual
- There will be an addition of a minimum necessary standard exception for individual-level care coordination and case management uses and disclosures, regardless of whether the activities constitute treatment or healthcare operations.
- The definition of healthcare operations will be broadened to cover care coordination and case management.
- The Armed Forces' permission to use or disclose PHI to all uniformed services will be expanded

The HIPAA Privacy Rule will strengthen reproductive healthcare privacy that was recently introduced in the Part 2 change (Alder, 2024b; HHS, 2024). The details are as follows:

- A definition of "reproductive health care" for EHR is added to HIPAA and covers terminations, contraception, fertility, and miscarriage healthcare

- New limitations are imposed on the uses and disclosures of PHI relating to reproductive healthcare that cannot be bypassed by obtaining consent or an authorization
- A request for reproductive healthcare information must be accompanied by an attestation that the information will not be used or disclosed for an out-of-state judicial or administrative proceeding
- Clarification that providing or facilitating reproductive healthcare is not abuse, neglect, or domestic violence
- Patient reassurance that PHI relating to reproductive healthcare will not be used or disclosed, and a new section must be added to the existing Notices of Privacy Practices, with the compliance date of February 16, 2026

Regarding the HIPAA Security Rule changes, the following concurrent steps will improve cybersecurity resiliency and patient safety (Alder, 2024b; HHS, 2024):

- Establishing voluntary cybersecurity goals for the healthcare sector
- Providing resources to incentivize and implement cybersecurity practices
- Implementing an HHS-wide strategy to support greater enforcement and accountability
- Expanding and maturing the one-stop shop within HHS for healthcare sector cybersecurity

Another change in the new 2024 HIPAA Rules involves establishing tiers with different penalty values in order to alleviate financial burdens in healthcare organizations caused by security breaches ( Alder, 2024b; HHS, 2024). The details are indicated in Table 9.1.

These changes will require updating HIPAA policies and procedures in each organization, developing new staff training materials, communication strategies, provisioning of attestations related to reproductive healthcare, and revising Business Associate Agreement documents (Alder, 2024b; Kutak Rock, 2024). Time and effort will be required to fully provide an individual's right to access their healthcare information, including their billing statements, within the specified time constraints. Nurses work with multiple care providers, so it is critical to adhere to patient privacy and confidentiality and be familiar with new regulatory changes and institutional policies

**Table 9.1 Penalty Values Published in Federal Register (HHS, 2024)**

| *Annual Penalty Limit* | *Minimum Penalty per Violation* | *Maximum Penalty per Violation* | *Annual Penalty Cap* |
|---|---|---|---|
| Tier 1 – Lack of Knowledge | $ 137 | $34,464 | $34,464 |
| Tier 2 – Reasonable Cause | $ 1,379 | $68,928 | $137,886 |
| Tier 3 – Willful Neglect | $13,785 | $68,928 | $344,638 |
| Tier 4 – Willful Neglect (not corrected within 30 days) | $68,928 | $68,928 | $2,067,813 |

(Ibrahim et al., 2024). As the HIPAA Privacy and Security Rules reinforce PHI protection, it is important to understand the different types of cybercrimes, preventive strategies, and remediation plans.

## Types of Cybercrimes in the Healthcare Environment

The increased use of technology and telehealth could contribute to the increased number of cyberattacks and data breaches (Lieneck et al., 2023). Cyberattack refers to compromises caused by people with malevolent intent, whereas breach refers to unintentional data compromises caused by mistake, negligence, or other unintentional reasons (Spitzer, 2017). The number of cybersecurity attacks in 2021 during the pandemic has increased to four times higher than the previous year, compromising 40 million patient records (Freeman, 2023). The breaches of unsecured PHI are posted on the breach portal (as seen in Figure 9.1) and reveal that there were over 13 million breach incidents as of March 5, 2024 (HHS OCR, n.d.-a).

The OCR under the HHS has shared Health Industry Cybersecurity Practice (HICP) guidelines and identified five main threats of cybersecurity (Healthcare & Public Health Sector Coordinating Council [HPHSCC], 2023a). Ransomware is a type of malicious software that limits or prevents a user's access to their system, usually through data encryption (Spitzer, 2017). Hackers access the organization's information system and encrypt it so users in the organization cannot access their computer systems without an encryption key. Ransomware attacks, which have become more common, pose significant threats to the confidentiality, integrity, and availability of private information. Kuchno (2024) has reported the most recent ransomware attack that occurred on August 6, 2024, at the Michigan-based McLaren Health Care, which consisted of 13 hospitals, clinics, and cancer and surgical centers. This cybercrime caused not only a delay in patient care but also forced staff to revert back to paper records for the first time in 20 years.

Social engineering is another type of cybercrime (HPHSCC, 2023a). Hackers attempt to trick users into disclosing sensitive personal information or infect individual users' devices via malicious links or attachments. E-mail phishing is a common type of social engineering. Smishing via Social Media SMS text messages and vishing via phone are other examples (Freeman, 2023). Regular security awareness staff training is a key to impeding phishing attempts (HIMSS, n.d.).

Cyberattacks may occur against the network through connected medical devices (HPHSCC, 2023a). Hackers could connect to a hospital network via an e-mail phishing attack, affect a file server, and take control of multiple IoT devices. If hackers control devices, such as powering off or continuously rebooting heart monitoring or imaging devices in the Cardiac Intensive Care Unit (CICU), for instance, this would not only compromise hospital information systems but also place patient safety at risk. Figure 9.2 includes some of the medical or IoT devices.

A fourth type of security threat is loss or theft of equipment or data (National Institute of Standards and Technology and Office for Civil Rights [NIST OCR], 2023). Equipment such as hospital-issued laptops, mobile phones, or USB drives, containing patient data, could be lost or stolen. For example, OCR charged the University of Texas MD Anderson Cancer Center $4,348,000 because approximately 35,000 individual PHI were compromised, caused by the theft of an unencrypted laptop and two flash drives (Alder, 2024b). To prevent equipment-associated

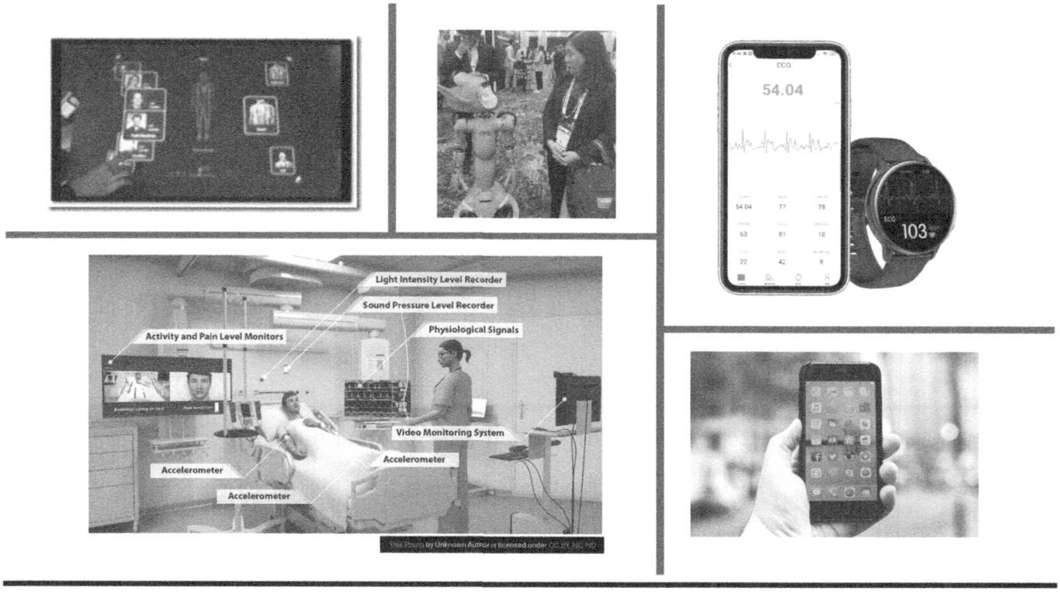


**Figure 9.2 Examples of Internet of Things (IoT) medical devices.**

data breaches, it is important to increase device security including data encryption or biometric authentication (HPHSCC, 2023b). Encryption refers to the use of an algorithm to convert plaintext into ciphertext – data scrambled to the point it becomes unreadable – to set up additional security to sensitive data, auditability, and secure healthcare transactions (Spitzer, 2017; Kelly et al., 2023).

Lastly, cybersecurity is related to the human part. Insider accidental or intentional data loss is the last type of main cybersecurity threats (NIST OCR, 2023). Data loss may occur unintentionally by internal employees, contractors, or other users who have access to the organizational infrastructure, network, or database. Hackers could use deep fake audio-video makers through advanced AI technologies, imitate hospital C-suites or leadership from social media, launch their scams through hospital users' e-mails or phones, and steal sensitive data. A structured, continuous user training and awareness of the latest cybersecurity tactics are essential prevention strategies (HPHSCC, 2023a).

Legacy end-of-life (EOL) systems that are no longer supported by the manufacturer increase IT vulnerability concerns because there is a lack of applying most recent security patches or software updates (HIMSS, n.d.). Security patches are defined as any updates to an operating system, application, or software that directly address particular vulnerabilities (Spitzer, 2017). The United Kingdom National Health Services (NHS) "WannaCry" ransomware attack is a well-known cybercrime example for using EOL software (Kelly et al., 2023). As you see in Figure 9.3, PHI breaches, hacking incidences, and unauthorized access or disclosure have drastically increased in the last ten years (Cartwright, 2023). Moreover, the incidences keep growing, although various security remediation plans are actively applied in the healthcare industry.

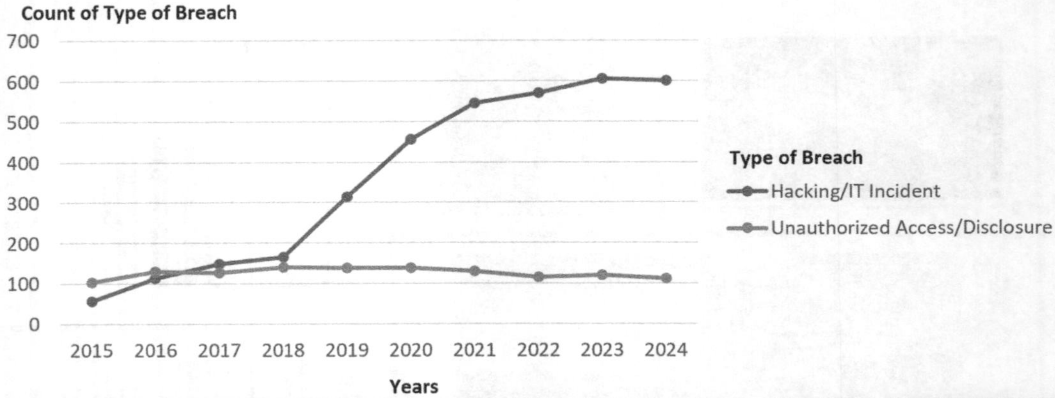


**Figure 9.3 Types of PHI breaches, hacking incidences, and unauthorized access.**

# Case studies

## *Case Study: Security Scanning and IT Vulnerability Remediation*

Various software, listed below, have become an integral part of our daily lives.

- Microsoft Office applications – MS Word, MS Excel, MS PowerPoint, MS Visio, MS Project, .Net MS development framework, etc.
- Various clinical applications and clinical decision support systems – EHR vendor applications such as Epic, Allscripts, Cerner, etc.
- Communication tools – Zoom, WebEx, Google Meet, MS Teams, Tele-health applications
- Data analytics and visualizations – SPSS, SAS, SAP Crystal Report, Tableau, etc.
- Programming languages – SQL, Python, etc.
- Mobile applications either on iOS or Android – Epic MyChart, Haiku, Rover, Patient Portal
- Web-based applications – Google, Hospital Intranet, Healthcare Website, Java, etc.
- Communication tools, protocols, or rules on a network – .Net, Secure Socket Layer (SSL), Transport Layer Security (TLS), etc.

Frequently, IT vulnerabilities are related to an operating system running on outdated software. This enables hackers to gain control of hospital information systems, so it is critical to put regular patches before vulnerabilities are taken advantage of by hackers (Cartwright, 2023; HHS, 2023; Kelly et al. 2023). Outdated software examples include SQL 2008 on Microsoft 2008 database servers, Microsoft Windows XP 2003 or 2008 versions on desktop PCs, Java 5.0, SSL versions 1.0, 2.0, 3.0, and TLS 1.0.

The vendor community such as Microsoft releases new patches to remediate security vulnerabilities frequently. So, hospital security operations scan the servers that reside in the hospital network routinely and plan to remove unauthorized software applications once detected. It is important that the hospital IT department follows best practices to remediate vulnerability files. IT operations should collect monthly patch information, check with the vendor on the compatibility concerns, conduct appropriate regression tests to ensure that patches do not negatively impact operations, and implement the changes during the approved time period (HPHSCC, 2023b).

For example, if applications were running on the Microsoft servers, hospital IT application owners should confirm with vendors whether the newly released Microsoft patches would impact system functionalities or not. Once confirmed, the removed vulnerability files and/or applied patches should be done in the application TEST environment first, so application analysts can conduct functional and regression testing to ensure no major system impact. Thorough integration testing in the TEST environment is essential to check general system functionalities. If applicable, device integration testing should be conducted, such as printing, barcode scanning, image capture, video recording, etc. After testing is completed, IT should plan monthly server patches or vulnerability remediation plans on the application production environment with an IT change management approval.

This can have an impact on the clinical operational side. For instance, there were multiple help desk tickets opened because perioperative staff could not print out post-op discharge summary reports. This issue delayed patient discharge because Post Acute Care Unit (PACU) staff could not provide patients' discharge instructions. After a full investigation, the root cause was identified to be that one of the removed vulnerability files caused an application printing issue. Although the regression testing was performed successfully in the TEST environment, device integration testing was omitted in this case. The IT support team had to revert the changes and request the vendor to develop a hotfix/software update to be able to reapply the patches.

## *Case Study: Remote Patient Monitoring and Medical Devices*

A security vulnerability was identified on Dahua's Open Network Video Interface Forum (ONVIF) products (Lakshmanan, 2022): Dahua A model, version prior to v1, Dahua B model, version prior to v2, and Dahua C model, version prior to v3. The identified vulnerability made it possible for hackers to compromise network cameras and add a malicious administrator account to obtain unrestricted access, including watching live camera feeds from affected cameras or making the devices unresponsive. A discovery of similar types of IoT devices led to remediation plans, such as firmware updates or security patches, which were issued by the US Cybersecurity and Infrastructure Security Agency to prevent potential cyberattacks.

During the COVID-19 pandemic, new types of care models have been adapted to supplement the bedside team (Ball, n.d.). Using advanced technology, patients can be monitored remotely, even in the ICU. Several tertiary hospitals such as UMass Memorial System have launched a real-time intensive eICU monitoring program to detect subtle changes in patients' vital signs before patients' conditions deteriorate. Clinical outcomes of the eICU program reported include faster recovery, 27% reduction in mortality rate, and reduced medical costs related to shorter hospital stay (UMass Memorial health, 2024). Similarly, a virtual nursing program allows patients to easily connect to virtual nurses via TV monitors by pressing a specifically designed button. Virtual nurses positively impact both the bedside team and patient experience by covering admission and discharge instructions to patients, secondarily verifying nurses' medication administration, and even receiving nurse calls from patients (Bell, n.d.).

There are various types of IoT in healthcare, where sensors or other identifiable devices are added to the Internet through a communication network to collect, send, store, and receive health-related data (Kelly et al., 2020). Countless IoTs are adapted in healthcare aside from the physiologic monitoring devices at the patient bedsides, wearable vital signs devices, two-way audio-video cameras, portable insulin pumps, smart infusion pumps and smart patient rooms, etc. IoT-based applications can be vulnerable to cyberattacks because of their easily accessible wireless nature along with the inability to implement complex security schemes (Kelly et al., 2020). Emerging technologies significantly improve patient care quality and clinical outcomes; however, it is equally important to secure patient data access and hospital information systems to protect patient privacy (Kasoju et al., 2023). PHI access via IoT devices should be protected from unauthorized identification.

To protect against unexpected security breaches, vendors regularly monitor security vulnerabilities at the device level as well as those available through software versions. Vendors provide a list of vulnerabilities, with severities based on the Common Vulnerability Scoring System – V3.0 scale and remediation plans. For instance, if the vulnerabilities reside on the remote monitoring cameras, the latest firmware upgrade may be required in older camera models. In some cases, vendors need to develop a new software version, which may take longer to remediate IT vulnerabilities.

## Case Study: Firewall Rules and Network Security

There are multiple unsecured "Public" or "Guest" network accesses in public areas. Connecting to these unsecured networks without proper user verification exposes unencrypted devices wide open to the public (Cartwright, 2023). Wireless devices such as hospital-issued laptops or mobile phones are remotely connected to hospital networks, so if a password or certification is not required, any unencrypted devices can be accessed through the hospital network. Moreover, other types of wired or wireless devices connected to the hospital network should be closely monitored and protected. This includes desktop PCs, Workstation On Wheels (WOWs), network printers, or any other medication devices. To protect organization information systems, each organization can set up a firewall network infrastructure. This can be a program or part of a computer system that controls the flows in network traffic and enables proper access inside and outside of the organization (HPHSCC, 2023b; Spitzer, 2017).

IT cybersecurity teams in each health organization should reinforce firewalls and protect server infrastructure. Otherwise, hackers can connect the networked unsecured devices and gain control of hospital networks and information systems (Cartwright, 2023). For instance, when servers or AI incidents are stored in a local hospital network, hospital IT groups closely monitor the network traffic flow to look out for any malfunctions or improper usage (Shah et al., 2023). If there is a large spike in network traffic, it could indicate a volumetric Denial of Service (DoS) attack (HHS, n.d.-b). It is critical that the hospital security team periodically reviews firewalls and ensures they are properly structured as required (HPHSCC, 2023b).

If vendor-hosted servers need to be connected to the hospital networked PCs or devices, a new firewall request should be submitted and reviewed by the hospital security team. Additionally, vendors may change their infrastructure settings from an on-prem server located in the hospital network to a vendor-hosted Cloud environment. In this case, the IT security team should obtain a firewall change approval form and review for modification with the following questions:

- How would information travel between the hospital and the vendor?
- Which ports should be opened to receive or send messages?

In the hospital IT department, network teams review and approve firewall change requests for new applications during a server refresh or Cloud migration or updating the existing protocol/port information.

Table 9.2 is an example of the firewall approval form.

Frequently, vendors may not be ready to develop applications to match the latest infrastructure. For example, though a patient-tracking application is not compatible with Windows 10 PCs and

**Table 9.2 Firewall Change Request Form**

<table>
<tr><td colspan="3">Requester Name:</td><td colspan="3">Date of Submission:</td></tr>
<tr><td colspan="3">Application Name:</td><td colspan="3">Contact information:</td></tr>
<tr><td colspan="3">Facility, Units, and Departments using the application</td><td colspan="3"></td></tr>
<tr><td colspan="3">Business Justification</td><td colspan="3">Outline the business function of the request</td></tr>
<tr><td colspan="3">Any medical device or industrial control system?</td><td colspan="3">Y/N</td></tr>
<tr><td colspan="3">New implementation?</td><td colspan="3">Y/N</td></tr>
<tr><td colspan="3">Any transmission and/or storage of high-risk data (i.e., PHI, finance, or hospital intellectual data)?</td><td colspan="3">Y/N</td></tr>
<tr><td>Number</td><td>Source Address</td><td>Destination Address</td><td>Destination Protocol/Port</td><td>Rule: Add/ Remove / Modify</td><td>Description</td></tr>
<tr><td>Example</td><td>10.10.10.43</td><td>10.10.12.15</td><td>http/80</td><td>Add</td><td>A brief description of the type of traffic taking place over the listed port(s)</td></tr>
</table>

operates only on Windows 8 PCs, the PC support team has plans to roll out Windows 10 PCs in the hospital. Another example is that the patient-tracking database server can only run the outdated SQL 2008 version on Windows 2008 servers, although the hospital infrastructure team has decided to move the entire server to Windows 2016 with SQL 2016. In this case, the hospital networking team must execute a network access control and set up a segregated network tunnel for the legacy application. By keeping the legacy systems isolated from the rest of the network, the application will not leave the entire hospital network vulnerable (HPHSCC, 2023b).

## *Case Study: ChatGPT and AI*

Since ChatGPT was released in November 2022, this Natural Language Processing (NLP)-based technology has been utilized in the industry exponentially. There were 100 million users in the first two months after launching ChatGPT (Li et al., 2024). It used deep learning techniques to produce text-based, human-like responses to end users based on training on a large dataset. Woo et al. (2024) have reported that applying ChatGPT technology to an unstructured radiology report provides fairly high accuracy and proficiency. Levin et al. (2024) found that sending automated real-time machine learning alerts directly to the Rapid Response Team (RRT) has reduced patient mortality. It is also an efficient time-saving method to set up predefined notes or recordings (ambient technology) automatically to ClinDoc or summary notes. Other examples that demonstrate ChatGPT use in healthcare include (1) generating accurate diagnosis, radiology reports, patient clinical letters, progress notes, or discharge summaries efficiently, (2) supporting clinical decision-making for patient care, (3) optimizing clinical decision support, and (4) providing insight for cancer-screening decisions or obtaining reliable information on diseases and medical queries (Liu et al., 2023).

However, AI tools should be used carefully because of the input and output risks. Data input in the Generative AI tool depends on the quality of the training data, but it could be vulnerable because the data is not secured and therefore can be extracted. On the other hand, public ChatGPT outputs may produce a biased or incorrect conclusion because they can be manipulated by users or obtained from misleading data from the Internet (Li et al., 2024). So, it is important to verify the contents of the public ChatGPT, and users should not post any sensitive data using the public Generative AI tools. There is a concern regarding entering sensitive patient data into a proprietary product as it might violate privacy regulations (Woo et al., 2024). Shah et al. (2023) addressed new digital security challenges to maintain patient's confidentiality and data integrity during the AI implementation in radiology practice. When used in healthcare, a HIPAA-compliant version of GPT-4 or HIPAA-compliant Microsoft Azure Cloud servers can be utilized to protect patient data.

Based on a systematic review of ChatGPT in the healthcare environment, researchers addressed concerns that it is still unreliable for actual clinical use (Li et al., 2024) and stressed the importance of oversight by active clinicians (Woo et al., 2024).

## *Case Study: User Access Control*

The number one reason for system breaches is user error and carelessness (Vukotich, 2023). Hospital workers, including clinical ancillary staff, administrators, staff in finance, and the information technology department, log in to the health information systems. Users can access systems remotely via the hospital virtual private network (VPN) tunnels. Vendors also regularly access servers in the hospital network to troubleshoot technical issues or implement software upgrades. Vendor access should be limited to only required information that is segmented from the main corporate network (HPHSCC, 2023b):

a. Virtual Private Network (VPN) provides an end-to-end wireless and wired encrypted connection for users. VPN must be enabled before vendors or the IT support team gets access to privileged servers in the organizational data center.
b. Multi-Factor Authentication (MFA) *is "the process of verifying a user's identity through more than one credential* (HPHSCC, 2023b)" such as a second credential on a mobile phone. It is an important layer of security that acts as a second checkpoint and should be implemented on remote-access technology or privileged accounts.
c. Biometric Authentication involves a physical system for login access. For instance, Pyxis, a medication dispenser where narcotics are stored, utilizes user authentication via fingerprint.

Although multifactor authentication is an important security method, it can still be a vulnerable point. Hackers can send a link to victims and send a clone MFA site with a look-alike webpage to get the MSA security code and access the hospital network. Hackers may also put scam files in an embedded advertisement on a trusted website. It is important to note that nothing is guaranteed to be protected, so end users should preview URLs by hovering over the advertisement or link and check the URLs before logging in to any accounts.

## Remediation Plans

Although cyberattacks cannot be fully prevented, proactive vulnerability remediation plans should be established to protect patients' privacy and confidentiality. HHS (2023b) provides ten practices to mitigate cybersecurity threats as described below:

- E-mail Protection Systems
- Endpoint Protection Systems
- Access Management
- Data Protection and Loss Prevention
- Asset Management
- Network Management
- Vulnerability Management
- Security Operation Centers and Incident Response
- Network Connected Medical Devices
- Cybersecurity Oversight and Governance

Bruce (2024) also provided ways that healthcare organizations could prevent cyberattacks including:

- Infrastructure upgrades and redundancy
- Regular security audits and patch management
- Distributed Denial-of-Service (DDoS) mitigation services
- Security Information and Event Management (SIEM) solutions
- Incident response plan and
- Monitoring network traffic

HIMSS (n.d.) has also recommended robust security controls, ranging from basic to advanced security controls. Basic security control includes:

> setting up anti-virus, back and restoration of files/data, data loss prevention, e-mail and Web gateway, data encryption for archival or transit, firewall, intrusion detection and prevention system, Mobile Device Management, vulnerability management program/ patch maintenance, policies and procedure, secure disposal, and security awareness training.

Advanced security control includes "anti-theft devices, business continuity and disaster recovery plan, digital forensics, multi-factor authentication, penetration testing, threat intelligence sharing and vulnerability scans". Robust cybersecurity protocols at both the device and the regulatory body levels are pivotal to safeguard collected patient data.

To reduce human errors, a whitelisting technique can be used to block unidentified e-mails to filter out hackers' phishing e-mails. Health organizations continuously educate staff to protect hospital information systems and adhere to HIPAA regulations. Most importantly, each organization should create a health policy for handling PHI and sensitive data. Through annual mandatory staff education, staff are provided information on how to identify and avoid phishing e-mails, malicious links, or attachments and report any suspicious activities. The training covers the importance of utilizing strong passwords and securing PCs, WOWs, mobile phones, IoT devices, and hospital networks. When users are outside the hospital network, they should use VPN tunnels via MFA as we learned earlier in this chapter.

During troubleshooting of technical issues with vendors, care should be taken so PHI is not shared with external users via emails. End-to-end encryption is the process of encrypting data while it is passed through a network (Spitzer, 2017). PHI details should be shared via "[Secure]" encrypted messages, and cases including PHI should be opened via vendor portals as these methods require user authentication. It is also important that the vendor supports encryption of PHI data in transit for device configuration and software upgrade for all database connections and Web applications (HPHSCC, 2023b). On the hospital infrastructure side, network traffic should be proactively monitored, and the application and database servers should be scanned to identify any vulnerability files. TLS 1.2 is used to secure .NET Framework applications on Windows servers that use the TLS protocol.

Many health organizations set up a Bring Your Own Devices (BYOD) policy to utilize staff's own mobile phones to see and document patient records. In these cases, Mobile Device Management (MDM) service along with a Mobile Application Management (MAM) would be beneficial for managing patient data on mobile devices (HPHSCC, 2023b). This containerization technology limits user access to specific applications, protects against maliciously downloaded applications, and easily wipes the container and clears business data when employees leave the organization (HHS, n.d.-b).

When a new vendor brings an application for the first time to the healthcare organization, hospital governance and legal teams review the Business Association Agreement (BAA) along with a cybersecurity amendment. The BAA covers HIPAA Security and HIPAA Privacy rules, which is modified along with new HIPAA changes. In addition, at the service level, vendors should present Systems and Organization Control (SOC 2) certification to secure client data in five areas: security, availability, processing integrity, confidentiality, and privacy (Shah et al., 2023).

To protect organizations from cyberattack, the Department of Defense [DoD] (2022) has provided a comprehensive approach known as Zero Trust (ZT) cybersecurity. The term ZT represents "an evolving set of cybersecurity paradigms that move defenses from static, network-based perimeters to focus on users, assets, and resources (DOD, 2022)." As seen in Figure 9.4, the ZT security model consists of seven pillars to ensure standardization of execution: (1) User, (2) Devices, (3) Application and Workloads, (4) Data, (5) Network and Environment, (6) Automation and Orchestration, and (7) Visibility and Analytics. The execution enablers are located at the bottom of the framework that are "crosscutting, non-technical capabilities and activities that address culture,

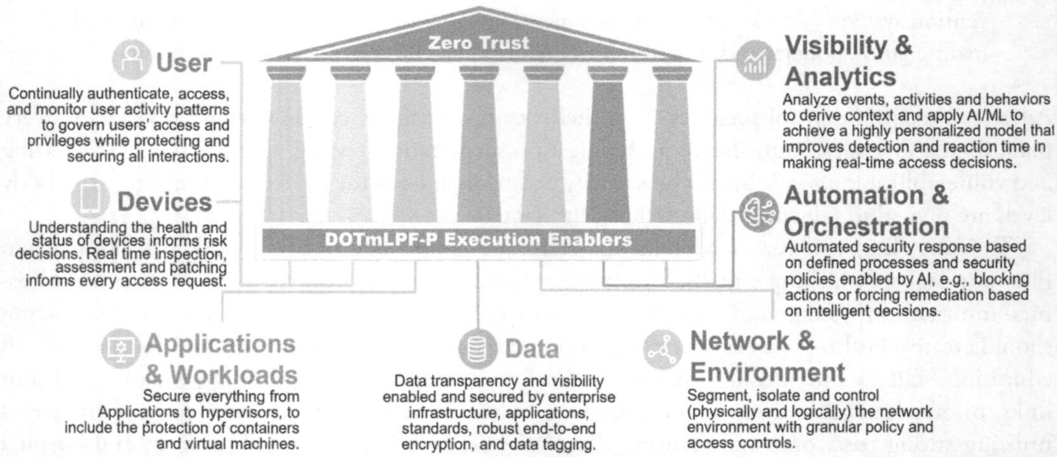


**Figure 9.4 Zero Trust (ZT) security model.**

governance, and elements" such as Zero Trust Training. All Enablers within the Pillars should work together to secure the "*Data Pillar*", which is central to the model.

AI can provide rapid insight to identify malicious activities or actual threats as well as reduce response time in remediating identified threats (Kelly et al., 2022; Vukotich, 2023). Shah et al. (2023) recommended best practices when AI technology was deployed in the radiology department: (1) to determine the minimum necessary PHI to minimize compromising data during data transit from or to servers, (2) to encrypt data transmission, and (3) to manage the minimum data retention time. Blockchain, in which digital information is stored in a distributed, shared ledger rather than copied, is another safe technology as it disaggregates the data (Abbing, 2020). Hacking one block in the chain is impossible without simultaneously hacking every other block in the chain's chronology. It passes information from A to B in a fully automated and safe manner.

## Conclusion

Protecting individuals' PHI and advocating for confidentiality based on the HIPAA Privacy and Security Rules are major roles of healthcare professionals. Since the revised HIPAA Rules have been issued and mandated, healthcare organizations should become familiar with the enforced changes, prepare to adapt practice changes into organizational policy and procedures, and establish staff education strategies. While sharing critical information among interdisciplinary teams, clinicians should be mindful to adhere to patient privacy and confidentiality (Ibrahim et al., 2024). At the same time, everyone should be alerted regarding the numerous cybercrimes and threats, as PHI breach incidents have increased in the recent digital healthcare environment. Hackers develop sophisticated tools and processes; so, some of the protective methodologies used today may become outdated in the near future (DOD, 2022).

Most importantly, it is pivotal to create an environment of organizational awareness to detect, monitor, and prevent cyberattacks and to establish requirements to protect healthcare systems (Nahm et al., 2019). Organizations should set up network policies, control user access, and proactively monitor aspects such as users' system access patterns, devices connected to the network, and data encryption. Advanced technologies such as AI should be used for early detection. These efforts should aim to produce quick responses to any threats. In order to prevent or recover from a potential cyberattack, organizations should create cross-functional incident response plans, involving IT, security, legal, public relations, and executive leadership (Freeman, 2023). Especially, nursing informaticists should be gatekeepers of protecting patient-sensitive data and healthcare infrastructure as they are frontline health information system users (Nahm et al., 2019).

## Reference

Abbing, H.R. (2020). Innovative Technologies in Healthcare, Beware of the Pitfalls, *European Journal of Health Law, 27*(1), 1–8. https://doi.org/10.1163/15718093-12271453

Alder, S. (2024a, January 2). HIPAA Updates and HIPAA Changes in 2024, *The HIPAA Journal*, https://www.hipaajournal.com/hipaa-updates-hipaa-changes/

Alder, S. (2024b, April 28). New HIPAA Regulations in 2023–2024, *The HIPAA Journal*, https://www.hipaajournal.com/new-hipaa-regulations/

Ball, J. (n.d.). Virtual Nursing: What is it?, American Nurses Association Innovation, Retrieved August 31, 2024, from https://www.nursingworld.org/practice-policy/innovation/blog/virtual-nursing-what-is-it/

Bruce, G. (2024, June 6). HHS Warns Hospitals of DDoS Cyberattacks, *Becker's Health IT*, https://www.beckershospitalreview.com/cybersecurity/hhs-warns-hospitals-of-ddos-cyberattacks.html?utm_campaign=bhr&utm_source=website&utm_content=latestarticles

Cartwright, A.J. (2023). The Elephant in the Room: Cybersecurity in Healthcare, *Journal of Clinical Monitoring and Computing*, *37*, 1123–1132 https://doi.org/10.1007/s10877-023-01013-5

Department of Defense Office of Publication and Security Review, (2022, October 21). DoD Zero Trust Strategy. https://dodcio.defense.gov/Portals/0/Documents/Library/DoD-ZTStrategy.pdf

Department of Health and Human Services. (2024, April 26). 45 CFR Parts 160 and 164 HIPAA Privacy Rule to Support Reproductive Health Care Privacy, *Federal Register*, *89*(82), 32976–33066.

Freeman, G. (2023). Common Spirit Ransomware Attack Holds Lessons for Cybersecurity, *Healthcare Risk Management*. *45*(1), 1–12. Relias LLC, Morrisville, NC.

Healthcare & Public Health Sector Coordinating Council, (2023a). 405(d) Health Industry Cybersecurity Practices: Managing Threats and Protecting Patients, *National Institute of Standards and Technology and Office for Civil Rights*, Retrieved August 26th 2024 from https://405d.hhs.gov/Documents/HICP-Main-508.pdf

Healthcare & Public Health Sector Coordinating Council, (2023b). Technical Volume 2: Cybersecurity Practices for Medium and Large Healthcare Organizations, *National Institute of Standards and Technology and Office for Civil Rights*, Retrieved August 26th 2024 from https://405d.hhs.gov/Documents/tech-vol2-508.pdf

HHS 405(d) Aligning Health Care Industry Security Approaches (n.d.-a). Cyber Safety is Patient Safety, *Department of Human and Health Services*. Retrieved August 26, 2024, from https://405d.hhs.gov/

HHS 405(d) Aligning Health Care Industry Security Approaches (n.d.-b). Have you heard about the top 5 threats facing the HPH sector? *Department of Human and Health Services*. Retrieved August 26, 2024, from https://405d.hhs.gov/cornerstone/hicp

HHS Press Office. (2021, January 15). Health Care Insurer Pays $5.1 Million to Settle Data Breach Affecting Over 9.3 Million People. *U.S. Department of Human and Health Services*, https://public3.pagefreezer.com/browse/HHS.gov/28-12-2022T07:11/https://www.hhs.gov/about/news/2021/01/15/health-insurer-pays-5-1-million-settle-data-breach.html

HIMSS. (n.d.), Cybersecurity in Healthcare, Retrieved August 14th 2024 from https://www.himss.org/resources/cybersecurity-healthcare

Ibrahim, A.M., Abdel-Aziz, H.R., Mohamed, H., Ai, H., Zaghamir, D.E.F., Wahba, N.M.I., Hassan, G.A., Shaban, M., El-Nablaway, M., Aldughmi, O.N., & Aboelola, T.H. (2024). Balancing Confidentiality and Care Coordination: Challenges in Patient Privacy, *BMC Nursing*, *23*, 564. https://doi.org/10.1186/s12912-024-02231-1

Kasoju, N., Remya, N.S., Sasi, R., Sujesh, S., Soman, B., Kesavadas, C., Muraleedharan, C.V., Varma, P.R., & Behari, S. (2023). Digital Health: Trends, Opportunities and Challenges in Medical Devices, Pharma and Bio-Technology, *CSIT*, *11*(1). 11–30. https://doi.org/10.1007/s40012-023-00380-3

Kelly, B., Quinn, C., Lawlor, A., Killeen, R., & Burrell, J. (2023). Cybersecurity in Healthcare. In H. Sakly, K. Yeom, K. Halibi, M. Said, J. Seekins & M. Tagina, *Trends of Artificial Intelligence and Big Data in E-Health* (pp. 213–231).

Kelly, J.T., Campbell, K.L., Gong, E., & Scuffham, P. (2020). The Internet of Thing: Impact and Implications for Health Care Delivery, *Journal of Medical Internet Research*, *22*(11), 1–11. E20135. https://doi.org/10.2196/20135

Kelley, B., Quinn, C., Lawlor, A., Killeen, R., & Burrell, J. (2022). Cybersecurity in Healthcare In Sakly, H., Yeom, K., Halabi, S., Said, M., Seekins, J., & Tagina, M. (Eds.), *Trends of Artificial Intelligence and Big Data for E-Health, Integrated Science 9* (pp. 213–232). Springer. https://doi.org/10.1007/978-3-031-11199-0_11

Kuchno, K. (2024, August 29). Cyberattack Forced Michigan Hospital to Use Paper Records for 1st Time in 20 years, CEO Says, *Becker's Health IT*, https://www.beckershospitalreview.com/cybersecurity/cyberattack-forced-michigan-hospital-to-use-paper-records-for-1st-time-in-20-years-ceo-says.html

Kutak Rock Client Alert. (2024, April 30). New HIPAA Rules Limit the Use and Disclosure of PHI Related to Reproductive Health Care and Revise Notice of Privacy Practices Requirements, Kutak Ruck LLC. https://www.kutakrock.com/newspublications/publications/2024/april/hipaa-privacy-rule-amendment

Lakshmanan, R. (2022, July 29). Dahua IP Camera Vulnerability Could Let Attackers Take Full Control Over Devices, *The Hacker News*, https://thehackernews.com/2022/07/dahua-ip-camera-vulnerability-could-let.html

Levin, M. A., Kia, A., Timsina, P., Cheng, F., Nguyen, K., Kohli-Seth, R., Lin, H., Ouyang, Y., Freeman, R., & Reich, D. L. (2024). Real-Time Machine Learning Alerts to Prevent Escalation of Care: A Nonrandomized Clustered Pragmatic Clinical Trial, *Critical Care Medicine*, *52*(7), 1007–1020. https://doi.org/10.1097/CCM.0000000000006243

Li, J., Dada, A., Puladi, B., Kleesiek, J., & Egger, J. (2024). ChatGPT in Healthcare: A Taxonomy and Systematic Review, *Computer Methods and Programs in Biomedicine*, *245*, https://doi.org/10.1016/j.cmpb.2024.108013

Lieneck, C., McLauchlin, M., & Phillips, S. (2023). Healthcare cybersecurity ethical concerns during the Covid-19 global pandemic: A rapid review, *Healthcare*, *11*, 2983. https://doi.org/10.3390/healthcare11222983

Liu, J., Wang, C, & Liu, S. (2023). Utilizing ChatGPT in Clinical Practice. *Journal of Medical Internet Research*, *25*, e48568.

Nahm, E., Poe, S., Lacey, D., Lardner, M., Van De Castle, B., & Powell, K. (2019). Cybersecurity Essentials for Nursing Informatics. *Computers, Informatics, Nursing*, *37*(8), 389–393.

National Institute of Standards and Technology and Office for Civil Rights, (2023). 405(d) Health Industry Cybersecurity Practices: Managing Threats and Protecting Patients (HICP), [Poster slides]. Retrieved on August 26, 2024, from https://www.nist.gov/system/files/documents/2019/10/16/1-4-hicp-405d-chua-decker-heesters.pdf

Office for Civil Rights. (2022, June 13). Guidance on How the HIPAA Rules Permit Covered Health Care Providers and Health Plans to Use Remote Communication Technologies for Audio-Only Telehealth, *Department of Health and Human Services*. https://www.hhs.gov/hipaa/for-professionals/privacy/guidance/hipaa-audio-telehealth/index.html

Office for Civil Rights. (2024a, April 16). HIPAA and Part 2, *Department of Health and Human Services*. https://www.hhs.gov/hipaa/for-professionals/special-topics/hipaa-part-2/index.html

Office for Civil Rights. (2024b, June 25). Voluntary Resolution Agreement Between the United States Department of Health and Human Services Office for Civil Rights ("HHS") and Montefiore. *U.S. Department of Health and Human Services*, https://www.hhs.gov/hipaa/for-professionals/compliance-enforcement/agreements/montiefore/index.html

Office for Civil Rights. (2024c, July 19). Health Information Privacy, HIPAA for Professional, *U.S. Department of Health and Human Services*, https://www.hhs.gov/hipaa/for-professionals/index.html

Ornstein, C. (2015, December 10). Celebrities' Medical Records Tempt Hospital Workers to Snoop, *NPR*, https://www.npr.org/sections/health-shots/2015/12/10/458939656/celebrities-medical-records-tempt-hospital-workers-to-snoop

Shah, C., Nachand, D., Wald, C., & Chen, P. (2023). Keeping Patient Data Secure in the Age of Radiology Artificial Intelligence: Cybersecurity Considerations and Future Directions, *Journal of the American College of Radiology*, *20*(9), 828–835. https://doi.org/10.1016/j.jacr.2023.06.023

Spencer, M.R. Garnett, M.F., & Minino A.M. (2024). Drug Overdose Deaths in the United States, 2002–2022, *National Center for Health Statistics Data Brief, 491*. https://doi.org/10.15620/cdc:135849

Spitzer, J. (2017, September 19). 11 Cybersecurity Terms to Know. *Becker's Health IT*, https://www.beckershospitalreview.com/cybersecurity/11-cybersecurity-terms-to-know.html

UMass Memorial health. (2024). Virtual Health Services, EICU, Retrieved August 31, 2024 from https://www.ummhealth.org/umass-memorial-health-all-hospitals/services-treatments/virtual-health-services/eicu

Vukotich, G. (2023). Healthcare and Cybersecurity: Taking a Zero Trust Approach, *Health Services Insights, 16.*

Woo, K., Simon, G.W., Akindutire, O., Aphinyanaphongs, Y., Austrian, J.S., Kim, J.G., Genes, N., Goldenring, J.A., Major, V.J., Pariente, C.S., Pineda, E.G., & Kang, S.K. (2024). Evaluation of GPT-4 Ability to Identify and Generate Patient Instructions for Actionable Incidental Radiology Findings, *Journal of the American Medical Informatics Association*, *31*(9). 1983–1993. https://doi.org/10.1093/jamia/ocae117

# Chapter 10

# Challenges with Integration, Access, and Security/ Global EMR

Young-Shin Park

## Introduction

There has been an exponential increase in healthcare information systems using emerging technologies over the decades. Software developers configure applications to meet the clinicians' needs in different care areas and services. 'Best of Breed' is a strategy where each department and service chooses the best electronic solution to meet the clinical workflows within the department. A challenge with this approach is that each patient care area has its own electronic documentation, but the segmented multiple clinical documentation does not provide a holistic view of the patient health record to the clinical team, which could negatively impact patient outcomes (Kasoju et al., 2023). It is hard to review the patients' clinical information from a continuity of care perspective. Let's imagine that a vendor A's product has been well known for an inpatient Electronic Health Record (EHR); however, vendor A's available modules are not sufficient for the Emergency Department (ED) or Intensive Care Units (ICUs) practice. The vendor also does not have any perioperative electronic clinical documentation modules. In this case, hospital administration leadership may have decided to adopt multiple vendor applications, such as the Inpatient module from vendor A, the Admission, Discharge and Transfer (ADT) system from vendor B, the perioperative and supply chain systems from vendor C, the ED and ICU modules from vendor D, and the Laboratory information system from vendor E, etc. This will result in a disconnected, redundant clinical information system.

In order to share patients' operating room (OR) records, OR nurses should print out intraoperative nursing documentation and attach it to the patients' charts so that Post Anesthesia Care Unit (PACU) nurses and inpatient nurses can review performed procedures, patients' condition, and special health issues or events that occurred in the OR. On the other side, if ICU patients need an emergency surgery, OR nurses need to go through paper or printed ICU charts. There may be potential transcription errors when the core information is copied over to another system. To minimize this redundant process and reduce human error, some of the core information, like ADT or


DOI: 10.4324/9781003464457-10

scheduling messages, can be shared via an interface engine among the multiple clinical applications. It can be shared as a real-time Health Level 7 (HL7) interface or as a batched file (i.e., send a charge file daily at midnight). Many hospitals may choose to switch over to a vendor that provides enterprise-integrated application modules within a single system.

Yet, there are exponential demands to establish integration between the new information system and the main EHR system. Emerging technology has introduced various medical device data integration with EHR, mobile, or wireless technology integrated with EHR (mHealth), and Robotics or AI technologies to bring precise, predictive patient care. Using AI technology, clinicians can improve patient care by predicting upcoming adverse events, reducing documentation time, and obtaining care-relevant data efficiently. According to Health Information Management Systems Society (HIMSS, n.d.), interoperability is defined as

> the ability of different information systems, devices and applications (systems) to access, exchange, integrate and cooperatively use data in a coordinated manner, within and across organizational, regional and national boundaries, to provide timely and seamless portability of information and optimize the health of individuals and populations globally.

Data sharing and exchange will greatly improve patient care, such as medication safety and reconciliation but also reduce patient safety events, data entry errors, or costs (Li et al., 2022). Epic Everywhere is a good example that patient data can be shared with other care providers who handle similar cases.

On the other hand, interoperability creates more cybersecurity risks for healthcare organizations (Freeman, 2023). While improving interoperability, it is crucial to adhere to privacy regulations (Medroa Inacio et al., 2024; Shrivastava et al., 2021). In this chapter, we will review some practical examples of the challenges with integration for accessing, sharing patient data, while improving continuity of patient care, patient safety, and quality improvement. We will discuss adhering to minimum need-based system access requirements while allowing the system open access for sharing EMR globally.

## Case Studies

### *Case Study: EHR Data Integration for Infection Prevention Surveillance*

National Healthcare Safety Network (NHSN) is the national healthcare infection tracking system, governed by the Center for Disease Control and Prevention (CDC, 2023). It is required for healthcare facilities to submit data on a monthly basis on Hospital Acquired Infections (HAIs): communicable diseases (*Clostridioides difficile* or methicillin-resistant *Staphylococcus aureus* (MRSA) infections), Central-Line Acquired Bloodstream Infection (CLABSI), Catheter-Associated Urinary Tract Infection (CAUTI), Surgical Site Infection (SSI), and Antimicrobial Use and Resistance (AUR). Figure 10.1 is an example of the NHSN CLABSI data report in 2022 by state (National Healthcare Safety Network (NHSN) (2024a, 2024b).

This data used to be queried from multiple complex data repositories based on an algorithm by the data analyst. Sometimes, this involved a manual process because the information systems were not fully integrated. It is very time-consuming and tedious work to retrieve NHSN data from clinical information systems. Data previously was pulled from multiple clinical ancillary systems, including patient ADT, Orders, Clinical Documentation (Vital Signs flowsheet, I/O flowsheet), Surgery information, Lab results, and Billing for diagnosis, surgery procedure codes.

As the monthly NHSN reporting process has been tedious, time-consuming, and labor-intensive, some of the vendors have developed reporting tools based on the keyword search from patient

**Table 1. Characteristics of NHSN Acute Care Hospitals reporting to NHSN by State[1], 2022:**
**1a. Central line-associated bloodstream infections (CLABSI)[2]**

| State | 2022 | | | | | | |
|---|---|---|---|---|---|---|---|
| | | | | Inpatient Locations | | | |
| | State NHSN Mandate[3] | Any Validation[4] | No. of Acute Care Hospitals Reporting[5] | Total | ICU | Wards[2] | NICU[6] |
| Alabama | Yes | Yes | 89 | 542 | 150 | 371 | 21 |
| Alaska | Yes | No | 10 | 53 | 10 | 40 | 3 |
| Arizona | No | No | 75 | 470 | 107 | 343 | 20 |
| Arkansas | Yes | Yes | 52 | 346 | 76 | 244 | 26 |
| California | Yes | YesA | 343 | 2,895 | 567 | 2,068 | 260 |
| Colorado | Yes | Yes | 59 | 398 | 72 | 292 | 34 |
| Connecticut | Yes | Yes | 33 | 362 | 60 | 287 | 15 |
| D.C. | Yes | No | 9 | 119 | 26 | 84 | 9 |
| Delaware | M | No | 10 | 109 | 15 | 88 | 6 |
| Florida | No | No | 228 | 2,096 | 437 | 1,567 | 92 |
| Georgia | Yes | YesA | 112 | 906 | 198 | 653 | 55 |
| Guam | No | No | 2 | . | . | . | . |
| Hawaii | No | Yes | 16 | 99 | 24 | 71 | 4 |
| Idaho | No | No | 18 | 119 | 22 | 83 | 14 |
| Illinois | Yes | Yes | 136 | 1,098 | 209 | 839 | 50 |
| Indiana | Yes | Yes | 95 | 637 | 115 | 483 | 39 |
| Iowa | No | Yes | 39 | 237 | 46 | 176 | 15 |
| Kansas | No | Yes | 63 | 314 | 64 | 236 | 14 |
| Kentucky | Yes | Yes | 71 | 548 | 117 | 400 | 31 |
| Louisiana | No | No | 109 | 566 | 131 | 399 | 36 |
| Maine | Yes | No | 21 | 107 | 23 | 79 | 5 |
| Maryland | Yes | Yes | 47 | 484 | 83 | 376 | 25 |
| Massachusetts | Yes | Yes | 68 | 607 | 124 | 464 | 19 |
| Michigan | No | Yes | 101 | 789 | 158 | 593 | 38 |
| Minnesota | Yes | Yes | 50 | 349 | 63 | 267 | 19 |
| Mississippi | Yes | No | 64 | 411 | 85 | 299 | 27 |
| Missouri | Yes | No | 80 | 711 | 135 | 530 | 46 |
| Montana | No | Yes | 13 | 80 | 13 | 57 | 10 |
| Nebraska | No | Yes | 29 | 175 | 30 | 131 | 14 |
| Nevada | Yes | No | 30 | 261 | 49 | 193 | 19 |
| New Hampshire | Yes | Yes | 13 | 111 | 17 | 86 | 8 |

**Figure 10.1 NHSN CLABSI report from Acute Care Hospitals in 2022.**

**Source: National Healthcare Safety Network (NHSN). (2024b, June 26). HAI Progress Report, 2022 Data, 2022 National and State HAI Progress Report SIR Data – Acute Care Hospital, [Excel file]. Retrieved from https://www.cdc.gov/nhsn/datastat/progress-report.html**

ADT information, orders, lab results, clinical documentations, surgical reports, coding (ICD-10 pre- and post-diagnosis, CPT-4 Procedure codes) for the finance department, etc. Based on the interface specification, each required data field from the sourcing system was reviewed and processed to a real-time integration feed through an enterprise interface engine. For instance, in order to pull an SSI rate, the following required or optional data should be prepped from multiple applications:

- Patient demographics – First and Last name, Date of Birth, Gender, MRN, Visit ID (required)
- ADT information – Admission and Discharge Dates (required), Unit Transfer Date (optional)

- Surgical information – Date of Surgery, Service, Patient type (Inpatient, Outpatient, or Same day admit), Surgery type (emergency, urgent, scheduled), Procedure Name(s), Laterality, Wound classification, Anesthesia type, ASA score
- Lab and/or pathology results – From specific blood, cytology, urine culture, specimen, etc.
- ED visit/ readmission – Date (optional)

This application launched a dynamic, seamless, real-time, and automated monitoring system. However, the challenge of the integration is that once the systems are integrated, any changes to the systems impact the other integrated applications up or downstream. In addition, any software upgrade, adding new lab results within LIS, or vendor changes require intensive re-evaluation of the interface changes, regression testing, and post go-live validations. EMR software upgrade requires integration testing for infection control software (VigiLanz, 2024). Lab system software vendor change also requires thorough integration testing so as to not miss any critical report functionalities.

## *Case Study: Medical Device Integration with EHR*

There are multiple examples of integrating EHR with medical devices, wireless technologies, and data warehouses to create a seamless healthcare environment while reducing human errors and redundant processes. Various types of medical devices can transfer data to the EHR via wired or wireless hospital network, or even through Cloud servers. Figure 10.2 depicts an example of the EHR integration process. A colonoscopy procedure was completed, and the provider completed operative notes along with indexed images. The medical content is available in the inpatient clinical documentation as a PDF file, and nurses can access the notes from WOWs on the hospital network.

Through point-of-care testing (POCT) devices, data can be transferred to the Cloud server, which can be accessed by the hospital clinical team as well as the patient (Kasoju et al., 2023). As per a report by Trimedx, 74% of healthcare organizations have more than half of their medical devices connected to the hospital network (Trevino, 2023). Patients with chronic diseases such as Diabetes Mellitus (DM) or Chronic Heart Failure (CHF) can obtain provider feedback effectively

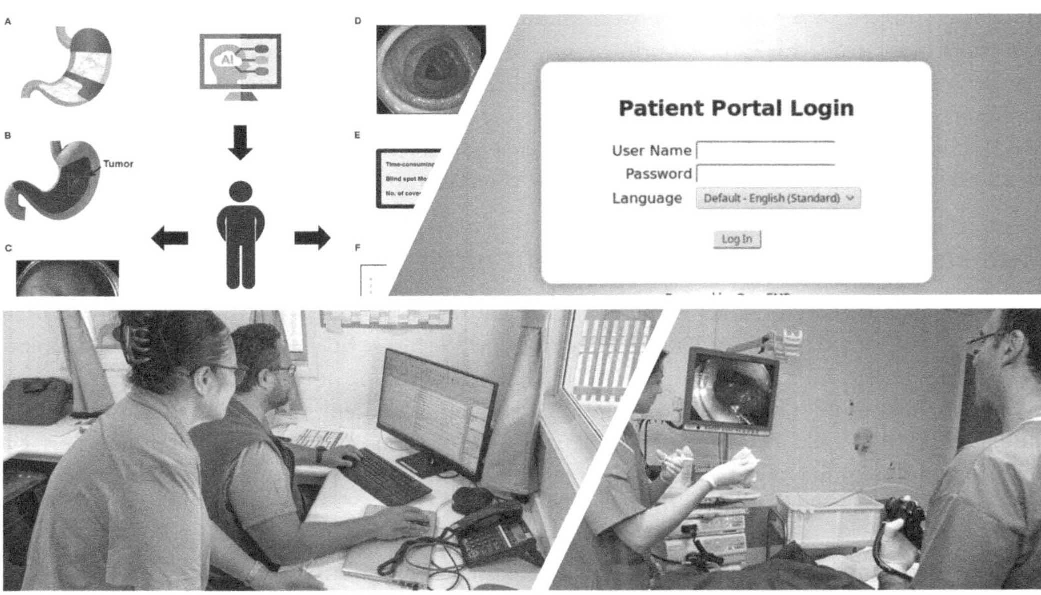


**Figure 10.2 Data access through POCT devices and patient portal via cloud computing.**

via device integration. For instance, an interactive web application for diabetes management is used by patients to communicate with healthcare providers by specifying the various types of insulin pumps and continuous glucose monitors used (Tidepool, n.d.). The application can be launched on either the iOS or Android mobile platforms for easier data access.

Another example is an infusion smart pump integration with the Intake and Output (I/O) flowsheet integration. When nurses use infusion pumps, medication orders in the EHR can be pulled and selected on the smart pump device screen, as long as the information (medication name, dose, volume, concentration, drip speed, etc.) matches the smart pump drug library in the database. Traditionally, the nursing staff manually transcribes total intake volumes in the I/O flowsheet in each shift. Integrating smart pump infusion data with the EHR I/O flowsheet will prevent potential transcription errors and create a seamless automated clinical documentation process. On the other hand, EMR records can trigger tasks on the device's end. If a patient is identified as high risk for falls based on the nursing documentation and flagged in the EHR, nursing staff can set the bed exit alarm on the identified patient's smart bed. If the patient attempts to be out of bed, an alarm will be generated via the nurse call system so the clinical team can be alerted in real time. This type of IoMT device allows the clinical team to increase patients' safety, patient care outcomes, as well as efficiency.

Hospital at Home is a new trend in which some patients can be treated and monitored in their homes as they get healthcare services at the hospital. The Center for Medicare & Medicaid Services (CMS) launched this program in November 2020, so that patients can receive acute-level care, oncology care, or postsurgical monitoring at home (American Hospital Association [AHA], 2020). Utilizing advanced technology and device integration, patients' physical conditions can be monitored remotely and electronically. Patients can be seen by the healthcare team remotely via telemedicine devices. This type of data integration increases patient satisfaction, efficiency, reduces ED visits by 48%, reduces costs by 42%, lowers 30-day hospital readmission rates, and decreases the length of stay (AHA, 2020). The assessed data can be recorded in EHR and shared with other healthcare providers or caregivers. Using the HL-7 FHIR integration technology, this streamlined process has been approved and allows for a feasible enhancement of patient care (Medroa Inacio et al., 2024).

Even though medical device integration with EHR has advantages, it may negatively impact patient privacy and safety (Abbing, 2020). The digital health medical devices that contain PHI must be connected to the hospital network in order to transmit patient data to the EHR. Because of its sensitive nature, this can be a prime target for hackers (Kasoju, et al., 2023). Clear rules and regulations of new digital health technology are essential but different countries have different guidelines, so it would be challenging to adopt on a global level (Abbing, 2020; Kasoju et al., 2023). For instance, if a nation neither accepts telemedicine as a healthcare practice nor reimbursement, telemedicine devices or Hospital at Home programs would not be deployed.

## *Case Study: Enterprise Master Patient Index (EMPI)*

EMPI is a data registry used across healthcare organizations to maintain consistent and accurate data on patients treated within its department (HIMSS, n.d.). In many circumstances, hospitals merge or migrate from a legacy application to a new system. One of the major tasks at this stage is to combine new patient records into a consolidated medical patient identification. For instance, if the existing MRNs used are five-digit numbers, and the previous system used six-digit numbers, the new merged system may need to begin a seven-digit numbering system or even add alphanumeric, so future MRNs do not overlap with the legacy patient MRNs.

Patients can request their old EHRs later, especially since Labor and Delivery (L&D) records can be requested for up to 21 years. Therefore, archiving prior applications is important. Further, patients can have future visits, so new EMPI should be assigned even to old patient records. If any unused patient identification fields exist, the old MRN may be moved to a different field and assigned a new EMPI to the MRN field. This way, multiple patient identification numbers can be retrieved. During the EMPI Implementation go-live, all the existing admitted or future cases should be remapped to the new MRNs. However, some vendors do not provide an auto-patient ID merge option. If so, patients' future appointment visits or inpatient records should be matched before and after the EMPI deployment. Moreover, the hospital IT team should set up a methodology to identify legacy MRNs.

This type of system change requires thorough assessment, planning, multiple dry runs, and issue tracking before execution. Once the system generates a unified enterprise-level MRN, the integration with other downstream systems would be seamless; however, it is a challenging and complex integration task to combine multiple systems into one system.

## Conclusion

Lack of infrastructure, interoperability, and potential mechanical failure are the biggest challenges of system dysfunction (Abbing, 2020). When patient health information is created, received, transmitted, or maintained by organizations, it is critical to set safeguards to adhere to any other laws or regulations in order to protect patient privacy, confidentiality, data integrity, and availability of the data (HIMSS, n.d.).

In today's complex and interconnected healthcare landscape, the integration of health information systems is no longer optional – it is essential for enhancing continuity of care, patient safety, and quality improvement. As demonstrated through case studies in infection prevention, medical device integration, and the implementation of EMPIs, seamless data exchange requires a robust infrastructure supported by interoperable systems. However, while integration allows for real-time clinical decision-making, streamlined workflows, and increased patient satisfaction, it also presents substantial challenges. These include system fragmentation, costly maintenance, data silos, manual documentation burdens, and vulnerabilities in cybersecurity. Moreover, the dynamic nature of healthcare demands constant adaptation – system upgrades, vendor transitions, and regulatory compliance must be navigated without compromising data integrity or patient care outcomes. Innovative technologies such as AI, smart pumps, IoMT devices, and HL7 FHIR interfaces offer tremendous potential to automate processes, reduce human error, and enable predictive, personalized care, especially in models like Hospital at Home. Yet, these advancements must be balanced with stringent data governance and global policy alignment to ensure privacy, security, and equity in digital health. The shift from best-of-breed systems to enterprise-wide integrated platforms reflects the need for more holistic solutions capable of bridging clinical, administrative, and operational functions. Ultimately, healthcare professionals must be actively engaged in system design, implementation, and evaluation to ensure that technologies serve patient-centered goals rather than add layers of complexity. As digital transformation accelerates, interdisciplinary collaboration, ethical vigilance, and continuous education will be key to unlocking the full promise of health IT while safeguarding the trust and safety of the populations we serve.

## References

Abbing, R. (2020). Innovative Technologies in Healthcare, Beware of the Pitfalls, *European Journal of Health Law*, *27*(1), 1–8.

American Hospital Association. (December, 2020). The Value Initiative Issue Brief Creating Value by Bringing Hospital Care Home, Retrieved from https://www.aha.org/system/files/media/file/2020/12/issue-brief-creating-value-by-bringing-hospital-care-home_0.pdf

Center for Disease Control and Prevention (CDC). (2023, November 7). 2022 National and State HAI Progress Report for Acute Care Hospitals - [Excel File], *CDC Stacks*, Retrieved from https://stacks.cdc.gov/view/cdc/166711

Freeman G. (2023). ComingSprit Ransomware Attack Holds Lessons for Cybersecurity. *Healthcare Risk Management*, *45*(1), 1–12.

HIMSS (n.d.). Interoperability in Healthcare. Retrieved September 5th 2024 from https://www.himss.org/resources/interoperability-healthcare

Kasoju, N., Remya, N.S., Sasi, R., Sujesh, S., Soman, B., Kesavadas, C., Muraleedharan, C.V., Verma, P.R.H., & Behari, S. (2023). Digital Health: Trends, Opportunities and Challenges in Medical Devices, Pharma and Bio-Technology. *CSI Transactions on ICT*, *11*(1), 11–30. https://doi.org/10.1007/s40012-023-00380-3

Li, E., Clarke, J., Ashrafian, H., Dazi, A., & Neves, A. L. (2022). The Impact of Electronic Health Record Interoperability on Safety and Quality of Care in High-Income Countries: Systematic Review. *Journal of Medical Internet Research*, *24*(9), e38144. https://doi.org/10.2196/38144

Medroa Inacio, P.M., Saltan, M., & Denecke, K. (2024). Integrating Laboratory Testing Results at Point-of-Care in Hospital@Home Care Settings: A FHIR-Based Approach, *Studies in Health Technology & Informatics*, *314*, 47–51.

National Healthcare Safety Network (NHSN). (2024a, July 1). CMS Requirements, CDC. Retrieved from https://www.cdc.gov/nhsn/cms/index.html

National Healthcare Safety Network (NHSN). (2024b, June 26). HAI Progress Report, 2022 Data, 2022 National and State HAI Progress Report SIR Data – Acute Care Hospital, [Excel file]. Retrieved from https://www.cdc.gov/nhsn/datastat/progress-report.html

Shrivastava, U., Song, J., Han, B.T., & Dietzman, D. (2021). Do Data Security Measures, Privacy Regulations, and Communication Standards Impact the Interoperability of Patient Health Information? A Cross-Country Investigation. *International Journal of Medical Informatics*, *148*. https://doi.org/10.1016/j.ijmedinf.2021.104401

Tidepool. (n.d.). Retrieved from https://www.tidepool.org/providers

Trevino, S. (2023, December 19). Advancing Medical Device Cybersecurity Beyond Compliance: Managing Risk with Governance, *HIMSS*. Retrieved from https://www.himss.org/resources/advancing-medical-device-cybersecurity-beyond-compliance-managing-risk-governance

VigiLanz. (2024, February 21). Inovalon's VigiLanz Solution Ranked No. 1 by KLAS Research in Pharmacy Surveillance and Infection Control and Monitoring, Retrieved from https://www.prnewswire.com/news-releases/inovalons-vigilanz-solution-ranked-no-1-by-klas-research-in-pharmacy-surveillance-and-infection-control-and-monitoring-302066731.html

# Chapter 11

# Artificial Intelligence in Healthcare

Kathleen McGrow

## Introduction to AI in Healthcare

Artificial Intelligence (AI) has emerged as a transformative force in healthcare, revolutionizing how we diagnose, treat, and manage diseases. AI encompasses a range of technologies that enable machines to perform tasks that typically require human intelligence. AI is a field of computer science that aims to create intelligent machines that can perform tasks that normally need human intelligence (Pan, 2016).

In healthcare, AI refers to the use of intelligent systems and algorithms to enhance healthcare delivery, decision-making, and patient outcomes. AI is relevant to healthcare and nursing informatics because it can change how healthcare delivery and management are done. With the rapid increase of digital data and technological innovations, AI can efficiently process and analyze large amounts of healthcare data, producing useful insights and supporting evidence-based care. The growing role of AI in healthcare delivery and decision-making comes from its ability to help healthcare providers in different ways. Integration of AI into healthcare shows promise to assist with diagnosis and treatment planning, by examining complex medical data, such as electronic health records (EHRs), medical images, and genomic information to find patterns and forecast outcomes (Alowais et al., 2023). AI-powered clinical decision support systems (CDSS) offer real-time suggestions and warnings, enabling healthcare providers to make well-founded decisions at the point of care (Wang et al., 2023).

## Nursing Informatics DIKW Framework

The Data, Information, Knowledge, Wisdom (DIKW) Framework is a conceptual model pivotal to nursing informatics. The DIKW framework is a theoretical model that illustrates the relationships between data, information, knowledge, and wisdom (Graves & Corcoran, 1989). This framework helps define how nursing informatics impacts nursing practice and care delivery. It starts with data,

DOI: 10.4324/9781003464457-11

the simplest element, which is uninterpreted and has no meaning without context (Garst et al., 2024). Data is transformed into information, which adds meaning (Garst et al., 2024). Information is then organized into knowledge, which is a set of connected pieces of information (Garst et al., 2024). Finally, wisdom is the ability to apply knowledge to human problems (Nelson, 2020).

The DIKW framework is a common tool in healthcare informatics to design and use technology solutions in healthcare. AI plays a significant role in this process. AI, part computer science and part cognitive science, encompasses the phenomena of computers performing tasks that require human intelligence (Cato et al., 2020). In the healthcare setting, AI is often paired with CDSS to move from knowledge to wisdom, which involves exercising judgment. The ability to use AI-assisted wisdom to solve problems and identify solutions is key for nurses to enable the delivery of nursing care that's more precise and efficient, benefiting both nurses and patients (Cato et al., 2020). Hence, nurse informaticists can use the DIKW framework to guide their work with AI and learn how to integrate AI into clinical workflows.

## Artificial Intelligence Technologies in Healthcare

Machine Learning (ML) is a subset of AI that enables machines to learn from existing data and improve upon that data to make decisions or predictions. ML in healthcare is used to draw insights from large medical data sets. Data insights facilitate clinicians' decision-making, improve patient outcomes, automate healthcare professionals' daily workflows, accelerate medical research, and increase operational efficiency. ML algorithms can discover patterns in datasets that allow medical professionals to identify new diseases and predict treatment outcomes (Alanazi, 2022).

*Supervised Learning* is a method where algorithms learn from labeled data. They make predictions based on input features and known target answers. In the healthcare sector, supervised learning has several applications. For instance, models can forecast disease progression, patient response to treatments, and identify risk factors (Rees et al., 2020). Additionally, supervised learning aids in the development of personalized treatment plans by tailoring recommendations based on individual patient characteristics.

*Unsupervised Learning* operates with input data and no corresponding output variables. It identifies patterns, clusters, and relationships without the need for predefined target labels. In healthcare, unsupervised learning is used for clustering patient profiles (Shickel et al., 2018). Algorithms group patients with similar characteristics, which aids in cohort analysis and the advancement of personalized medicine.

*Natural Language Processing (NLP)* can utilize both supervised and unsupervised learning approaches. NLP is a specialized branch of AI focused on reading, deciphering, understanding, and using human language. There are two primary approaches, including rule-based, which are programmed by developers, and ML-based, which learn using training data to solve tasks (Arivazhagan & van Vleck, 2023). NLP uses include chatbots, sentiment analysis, translation, and summarization of text. In healthcare, NLP enables organizations to extract vital data from documents quickly, organize uncategorized clinical information, give data insights, and streamline manual workflows. NLP can enhance the completeness and accuracy of EHRs by translating free text into standardized data.

*Generative AI (genAI)* is a kind of AI system that can create content such as text, images, or other media when given prompts (Ross et al., 2024a). Based on basic or foundational Language Models (LMs), genAI models learn patterns and structure from their large input training data and then generate new data that has similar characteristics. The advances in AI have been driven by enhanced computing power, abundant data, and better algorithms.

This figure illustrates the progression of artificial intelligence (AI) terminology and technologies, highlighting key milestones: Artificial Intelligence (1955), Machine Learning (1997), Deep Learning (2016), and Generative AI (2021). Each layer represents an advancement in how machines

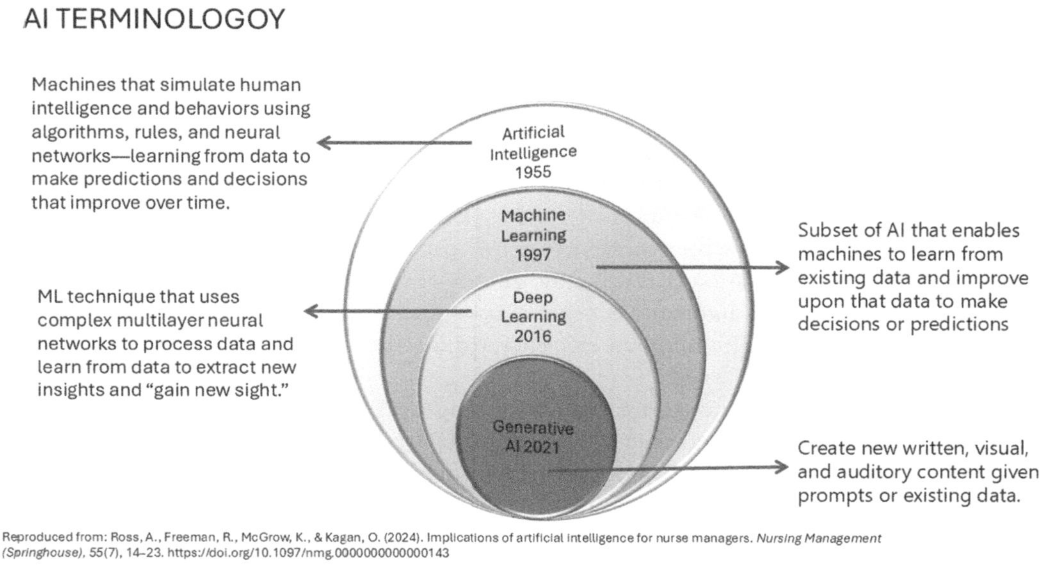


**Figure 11.1 The Evolution of Artificial Intelligence: From Foundational Concepts to Generative AI.**

simulate human intelligence, learn from data, extract insights, and create new content—providing context for nurse managers navigating AI's impact on healthcare leadership and decision-making.

Large Language Models (LLMs) are a type of genAI that may contain billions of parameters that are pretrained and learn patterns and relationships in language data and use this knowledge to generate human-like text. LLMs can be used for a wide range of applications in clinical settings, including NLP, text summarization, and language translation (Ross et al., 2024b).

*Large Multimodal Models (LMMs)* use LLMs as a central hub and extend their capabilities to handle multimodal tasks such as images, audio, and video (Huang et al., 2024). There is much research to be done to evaluate the capabilities of LMMs and their impact on clinical care. Some of the potential healthcare use cases include:

- Streamlining administration tasks such as billing, scheduling, and claims processing through automation.
- Improving patient engagement through chatbot use for follow-up care and patient questions.
- Enhancing clinical decision-making by thorough review of patient data, including EHR, laboratory, and imaging data, to facilitate decisions.
- Creating educational materials and content for clinicians.

LMMs offer various ways to assist the healthcare industry effectively and flexibly. This will allow healthcare organizations to improve efficiency and increase the standard of patient care.

## Robotics and Automation

The advent of robotics and automation has brought about a significant transformation in healthcare (Morgan et al., 2022). One of the key areas where this impact is felt is in surgical procedures. Robots are now assisting surgeons during minimally invasive procedures, offering benefits such as precision, reduced invasiveness, and faster recovery for patients (Morgan et al., 2022).

Another area where robotics has made a significant impact is in the field of telemedicine. Telepresence robots enable remote consultations between patients and healthcare providers, proving especially useful in rural or underserved areas (Bhaskar et al., 2020). These robots can overcome geographical limitations and provide specialized healthcare remotely.

In the realm of medication dispensing, robots have brought about a revolution. They accurately dispense medications, reducing human errors. This enhances patient safety and streamlines pharmacy workflows. Automated unit dose dispensing systems (UDDS) producing individually packaged and labeled drugs for patients have been shown to improve patient safety (Hänninen et al., 2023).

Robotic Process Automation (RPA) is another area where robotics and automation have made a significant impact. RPA automates repetitive tasks such as data entry and claims processing (Bhatnagar & Jain, 2019). This improves efficiency, reduces the administrative burden, and frees up staff time for more complex tasks.

In conclusion, robotics and automation are playing a pivotal role in transforming healthcare delivery by improving efficiency, accuracy, and patient safety. However, it is critical to acknowledge that while these technologies present considerable benefits, they necessitate meticulous planning and oversight to guarantee maximum advantages. The future of healthcare is indeed promising with the integration of these advanced technologies.

## AI Impact on Clinical Practice

AI algorithms can analyze and interpret vast amounts of patient data, including EHR, laboratory, and imaging, to identify patterns and biomarkers indicative of diseases. This enables clinicians to make more informed diagnostic decisions and provide targeted treatments tailored to each patient's unique condition. AI algorithms can assist clinicians in generating personalized treatment recommendations for patients. These recommendations are based on patterns and insights extracted from comprehensive patient data, enabling healthcare providers to make informed decisions. The integration of AI in healthcare holds excellent potential for improving disease diagnosis, treatment selection, drug discovery, and patient risk stratification (Kumar et al., 2023).

## Predictive Analytics

Predictive analytics in healthcare can help determine the risk of a patient developing a particular condition or complication, which can inform the shared decision-making process between clinicians and patients and improve patient satisfaction with their overall medical care (Alowais et al., 2023). AI-powered models can predict patient outcomes, assisting healthcare providers in crafting preemptive treatment plans. These AI-powered tools, when used at scale, ultimately help health practitioners make more informed decisions and enhance patient outcomes.

## Ethical Considerations

### *Transparency and Explainability*

Ethical guidelines for AI systems emphasize the importance of transparency and explainability (Ross et al., 2024a). Transparency refers to the openness about the functioning and decision-making process of AI systems, while explainability refers to the ability to provide understandable reasons for the decisions made by these systems. Developing transparency and explainability in AI systems is crucial for fostering trust. The aspects of the AI system that should be explained include the purpose, role of AI, inputs, behavior, data utilized, outputs, and limitations (Islam et al., 2022). AI-based guidelines should be clear, fair, unbiased, and guided by human knowledge and ethics.

### *Privacy and Security*

Privacy and security are paramount in the ethical and legal considerations of AI. AI systems often handle sensitive data, and it's crucial to ensure this data is protected and used responsibly. Ethical AI application necessitates adherence to principles of accountability, explainability, inclusivity, transparency, bias-free, and responsible use (Alowais et al., 2023). Moreover, privacy laws and regulations must be adhered to, ensuring that personal data is not misused.

### *Human–AI Collaboration*

Human–AI teaming (HAIT) is a socio-technical approach that views AI as a team member rather than a technology tool (Berretta et al., 2023). As AI becomes more integrated into healthcare decision-making processes, it's crucial that we understand its implications as much as possible. Human beings have a responsibility to comprehend the consequences of AI, and to design and apply AI in accordance with ethical values (Hayes et al., 2024).

## AI Implementation Challenges and Best Practices

### *Data Quality*

The success of AI implementations is deeply intertwined with the quality of data it processes. Data quality is a critical factor in AI because it directly impacts the performance, accuracy, and reliability of AI models (Stanfill & Marc, 2019). High-quality data enables models to make better predictions and produce more reliable outcomes, fostering trust and confidence among users. Poor data quality can lead to flawed results and cause poor performance and failure. Ensuring data quality also means addressing biases present in the data, which is essential to avoid perpetuating and amplifying these biases in AI-generated output (Stanfill & Marc, 2019). A diverse and representative dataset enhances an AI model's ability to generalize well across different situations and inputs, ensuring its performance and relevance across various contexts and user groups. Ensuring data quality is therefore not just a technical requirement but a strategic one as well. The goal of data quality management in healthcare organizations today is to ensure that the data meets the needs of the organization's business processes, decision-making, and planning (Stanfill & Marc, 2019).

### *Data Integration*

Data integration is the process of combining data from different sources and making it available in a unified format for analysis, reporting, and decision-making (Dhayne et al., 2019). This process is crucial for organizations that aim to consolidate data from various systems, applications, and databases to gain insights and support data-driven decision-making. AI and ML are essential for data integration as they significantly enhance the process by automating and streamlining various tasks. AI-powered data integration can result in better decision-making, improved operational efficiency, and a more agile response to changing business conditions.

### *Change Management*

Change management is a critical component when deploying AI in healthcare. The AI Maturity Roadmap provides a comprehensive framework for effective and sustainable AI deployment in healthcare (Durlach et al., 2024). This roadmap identifies six key focus areas: Culture, Governance, Business Implementation, Value, Maintenance and Operations, and Information Architecture. Each of these areas has granular themes and five levels of maturity, from "awareness" to "transformational" (Durlach et al., 2024).

Health systems are tackling AI adoption with varying degrees of readiness, necessitating diverse maturity strategies. Effective change management frameworks help leaders set clear aims and foster constructive conversations for widespread agreement and commitment to AI implementation. Moreover, the adoption of AI in healthcare faces challenges such as regulatory, reimbursement, return on investments, data sources and integration with EHR systems, need for education, fit with clinical workflows, and ethical considerations (Davenport & Glaser, 2022). Hence, effective change management is essential for the successful adoption of AI in healthcare.

The evaluation and continuous improvement of AI systems are crucial for their success (Reddy et al., 2021). This involves regularly assessing the performance of AI systems, identifying areas of improvement, and making necessary adjustments. Continuous improvement ensures that AI systems remain effective and relevant over time. It also helps in identifying and mitigating potential risks and issues early on, thereby enhancing the reliability and effectiveness of AI systems.

To address the challenges in implementing AI systems into healthcare settings, the Translational Evaluation of Healthcare AI (TEHAI) framework suggests a comprehensive evaluation approach with three main components being Capability, Utility, and Adoption (Reddy et al., 2021).

- Capability Assessment: Evaluate the technical ability of AI systems to perform their intended purpose, including data integrity, internal and external validity, and appropriate performance metrics (Reddy et al., 2021).
- Utility Evaluation: Assess the usability of AI systems, considering generalizability, safety, quality, transparency, privacy, and non-maleficence to ensure they are beneficial and ethical for clinical practice (Reddy et al., 2021).
- Adoption Consideration: Examine the "real-world" integration of AI systems in healthcare settings, focusing on their use, technical integration, service coverage, and domain alignment to facilitate widespread acceptance and effectiveness (Reddy et al., 2021).

These strategies aim to ensure AI systems are not only technically sound but also ethically aligned and practically useful in healthcare environments. Regular evaluation and continuous improvement are, therefore, key best practices for the successful implementation of AI.

## Future Directions and Opportunities for Nurses

Nurse informaticists can be instrumental in leveraging AI to enhance clinical workflows and patient outcomes. With their expertise in health information technology (HIT), data stewardship, and clinical processes, they are well-positioned to lead the way in adopting and assimilating AI innovations within healthcare settings. Nurse informaticists possess the necessary expertise and competencies to understand the specific requirements and hurdles associated with clinical practice. They are adept at working with interdisciplinary groups to facilitate the integration of AI technologies. Acting as a bridge between healthcare practitioners and technology creators, they can ensure AI applications align with nursing processes and essential clinical conditions. Their vital contributions can guide the development and tailoring of AI platforms to enhance user experience and maximize their benefits in healthcare. Furthermore, nurse informaticists play an essential role in data governance and management, safeguarding the quality, integrity, and security of healthcare data (American Nurses Association, 2022). These elements are crucial for the advancement of technology and are employed in AI applications. They work in conjunction with data scientists and information technology (IT) experts to create a strong data framework, setting benchmarks and procedures for systematically gathering, preserving, and distributing data to ensure AI algorithms are developed using dependable and inclusive datasets.

Nurse informaticists also contribute to the ethical and responsible use of AI in healthcare. They navigate the ethical considerations of privacy, consent, bias, and transparency, ensuring that AI systems prioritize patient safety, autonomy, and equitable care (The Ethical Use of Artificial Intelligence in Nursing Practice, 2022) with the help of tools like The 5 Rights of AI in Healthcare (Ross et al., 2024a). Nurse informaticists actively participate in discussions on ethical guidelines, governance frameworks, and regulatory compliance to address the potential risks and challenges associated with AI implementation. The introduction to AI in healthcare and its relevance to nursing informatics underscores its growing importance in healthcare delivery and decision-making. It highlights the specific role of nurse informaticists in leveraging AI technologies, including their expertise in driving AI adoption, ensuring data governance, and navigating ethical considerations. By harnessing AI capabilities, nurse informaticists contribute to improving clinical practice, patient care, and healthcare outcomes.

## Conclusion

In conclusion, the integration of AI into healthcare represents a transformative leap forward, offering unprecedented opportunities to enhance patient care and streamline medical processes. The application of the DIKW Framework in nursing informatics exemplifies the potential of AI to convert data into actionable wisdom, thereby empowering healthcare professionals to make informed decisions. Advancements in AI technologies, including ML, NLP, and genAI, have paved the way for more accurate diagnoses, efficient treatment plans, and improved disease management. Robotics and automation further contribute to this progress by enhancing surgical precision and facilitating remote consultations.

As we navigate the ethical landscape of AI in healthcare, it is imperative to maintain transparency and security to foster responsible AI use. The ethical and legal implications of AI adoption must be carefully considered to ensure patient privacy and data security. The future holds promising opportunities for nurse informaticists, who are at the forefront of this transformation, ensuring the ethical use of AI and optimizing clinical workflows for the betterment of patient care. The collective efforts in this field are not only reshaping the healthcare industry but also setting a precedent for the role of technology in enhancing human lives. As we stand on the cusp of this new era, AI will play a pivotal role in shaping the future of healthcare, promising better outcomes for patients and a more efficient healthcare system for all.

## References

Alanazi, A. (2022). Using machine learning for healthcare challenges and opportunities. *Informatics in Medicine Unlocked, 30*, 100924.

Alowais, S. A., Alghamdi, S. S., Alsuhebany, N., Alqahtani, T., Alshaya, A. I., Almohareb, S. N., Aldairem, A., Alrashed, M., bin Saleh, K., Badreldin, H. A., al Yami, M. S., Al Harbi, S., & Albekairy, A. M. (2023). Revolutionizing healthcare: The role of artificial intelligence in clinical practice. *BMC Medical Education, 23*(1), 689. https://doi.org/10.1186/s12909-023-04698-z

American Nurses Association. (2022). *Nursing informatics: Scope and standards of practice* (3rd ed.). American Nurses Association.

Arivazhagan, N., & van Vleck, T. T. (2023). Natural Language Processing Basics. *Clinical Journal of the American Society of Nephrology, 18*(3), 400–401. https://doi.org/10.2215/CJN.0000000000000081

Berretta, S., Tausch, A., Ontrup, G., Gilles, B., Peifer, C., & Kluge, A. (2023). Defining human-AI teaming the human-centered way: A scoping review and network analysis. *Frontiers in Artificial Intelligence, 6*. https://doi.org/10.3389/frai.2023.1250725

Bhaskar, S., Bradley, S., Sakhamuri, S., Moguilner, S., Chattu, V. K., Pandya, S., Schroeder, S., Ray, D., & Banach, M. (2020). Designing Futuristic Telemedicine Using Artificial Intelligence and Robotics in the COVID-19 Era. *Frontiers in Public Health, 8*. https://doi.org/10.3389/fpubh.2020.556789

Bhatnagar, R., & Jain, R. (2019). Robotic process automation in healthcare: A review. *International Robotics & Automation Journal, 5*(1), 12–14. https://doi.org/10.15406/iratj.2019.05.00164

Cato, K. D., McGrow, K., & Rossetti, S. C. (2020). Transforming clinical data into wisdom. *Nursing Management, 51*(11), 24–30.

Davenport, T. H., & Glaser, J. P. (2022). Factors governing the adoption of artificial intelligence in healthcare providers. *Discover Health Systems, 1*(1), 4. https://doi.org/10.1007/s44250-022-00004-8

Dhayne, H., Haque, R., Kilany, R., & Taher, Y. (2019). In Search of Big Medical Data Integration Solutions - A Comprehensive Survey. *IEEE Access, 7*, 91265–91290. https://doi.org/10.1109/ACCESS.2019.2927491

Durlach, P., Fournier, R., Gottlich, J., Markwell, T., McManus, J., Merrill, A., & Rhew, D. (2024). The AI Maturity Roadmap: A Framework for Effective and Sustainable AI in Health Care. *New England Journal of Medicine AI*. https://ai.nejm.org/doi/pdf/10.1056/AI-S2400177

Garst, C., Carroll, C., Carroll, W., Adams, S., & Cox, D. (2024, April 11). *Data from Novice to Expert: Aligning Benner with DIKW*. HIMSS. https://www.himss.org/resources/data-novice-expert-aligning-benner-dikw

Graves, J. R., & Corcoran, S. (1989). The study of nursing informatics. *Image: The Journal of Nursing Scholarship, 21*(4), 227–231.

Hänninen, K., Ahtiainen, H. K., Suvikas-Peltonen, E. M., & Tötterman, A. M. (2023). Automated unit dose dispensing systems producing individually packaged and labelled drugs for inpatients: A systematic review. *European Journal of Hospital Pharmacy, 30*(3), 127–135. https://doi.org/10.1136/ejhpharm-2021-003002

Hayes, P., Fitzpatrick, N., & Ferrández, J. M. (2024). From applied ethics and ethical principles to virtue and narrative in AI practices. *AI and Ethics*. https://doi.org/10.1007/s43681-024-00472-z

Huang, D., Yan, C., Li, Q., & Peng, X. (2024). From Large Language Models to Large Multimodal Models: A Literature Review. *Applied Sciences, 14*(12), 5068. https://doi.org/10.3390/app14125068

Islam, M. R., Ahmed, M. U., Barua, S., & Begum, S. (2022). A Systematic Review of Explainable Artificial Intelligence in Terms of Different Application Domains and Tasks. *Applied Sciences, 12*(3), 1353. https://doi.org/10.3390/app12031353

Kumar, Y., Koul, A., Singla, R., & Ijaz, M. F. (2023). Artificial intelligence in disease diagnosis: A systematic literature review, synthesizing framework and future research agenda. *Journal of Ambient Intelligence and Humanized Computing, 14*(7), 8459–8486. https://doi.org/10.1007/s12652-021-03612-z

Morgan, A. A., Abdi, J., Syed, M. A. Q., Kohen, G. el, Barlow, P., & Vizcaychipi, M. P. (2022). Robots in Healthcare: A Scoping Review. *Current Robotics Reports*, *3*(4), 271–280. https://doi.org/10.1007/s43154-022-00095-4

Nelson, R. (2020). Informatics: Evolution of the Nelson Data, Information, Knowledge and Wisdom Model: Part 2. *OJIN: The Online Journal of Issues in Nursing*, *25*(3). https://doi.org/10.3912/OJIN.Vol25No03InfoCol01

Pan, Y. (2016). Heading toward Artificial Intelligence 2.0. *Engineering*, *2*(4), 409–413.

Reddy, S., Rogers, W., Makinen, V.-P., Coiera, E., Brown, P., Wenzel, M., Weicken, E., Ansari, S., Mathur, P., Casey, A., & Kelly, B. (2021). Evaluation framework to guide implementation of AI systems into healthcare settings. *BMJ Health & Care Informatics*, *28*(1), e100444. https://doi.org/10.1136/bmjhci-2021-100444

Rees, C. E., Lee, S. L., Huang, E., Denniston, C., Edouard, V., Pope, K., Sutton, K., Waller, S., Ward, B., & Palermo, C. (2020). Supervision training in healthcare: A realist synthesis. *Advances in Health Sciences Education*, *25*(3), 523–561. https://doi.org/10.1007/s10459-019-09937-x

Ross, A., Freeman, R., McGrow, K., & Kagan, O. (2024a, July). Implications of artificial intelligence for nurse managers. *Nursing Management (Springhouse)*, *55*(7), 14–23. https://doi.org/10.1097/nmg.0000000000000143

Ross, A., McGrow, K., Zhi, D., & Rasmy, L. (2024b). Foundation Models, Generative AI, and Large Language Models. *CIN: Computers, Informatics, Nursing*, *42*(5), 377–387. https://doi.org/10.1097/CIN.0000000000001149

Shickel, B., Tighe, P. J., Bihorac, A., & Rashidi, P. (2018). Deep EHR: A Survey of Recent Advances in Deep Learning Techniques for Electronic Health Record (EHR) Analysis. *IEEE Journal of Biomedical and Health Informatics*, *22*(5), 1589–1604. https://doi.org/10.1109/JBHI.2017.2767063

Stanfill, M. H., & Marc, D. T. (2019). Health Information Management: Implications of Artificial Intelligence on Healthcare Data and Information Management. *Yearbook of Medical Informatics*, *28*(01), 056–064. https://doi.org/10.1055/s-0039-1677913

The Ethical Use of Artificial Intelligence in Nursing Practice. (2022). American Nurses Association. https://www.nursingworld.org/~48f653/globalassets/practiceandpolicy/nursing-excellence/ana-position-statements/the-ethical-use-of-artificial-intelligence-in-nursing-practice_bod-approved-12_20_22.pdf

Wang, L., Zhang, Z., Wang, D., Cao, W., Zhou, X., Zhang, P., Liu, J., Fan, X., & Tian, F. (2023). Human-centered design and evaluation of AI-empowered clinical decision support systems: A systematic review. *Frontiers in Computer Science*, *5*. https://doi.org/10.3389/fcomp.2023.1187299

# Chapter 12

# Emerging Technologies

Michael Joseph Dino

## Introduction to Humanoid Technologies in Nursing

### *Overview and Description*

The landscape of nursing practice is undergoing a profound transformation as technologies reshape how healthcare is delivered, learned, and experienced. Among the most promising developments in this evolution is the emergence of humanoid technologies (HTs)—anthropomorphic technologies that simulate human appearance, behavior, or interaction patterns to serve various roles within healthcare and practice environments (Dino et al., 2022). The integration of HTs into nursing practice represents a significant evolution in healthcare delivery, driven by practice-driven challenges and advancements in technology. As nurses navigate an increasingly complex healthcare ecosystem marked by the rising number of patients, healthcare data, staffing shortages, and evolving educational and training demands, HTs represent both an innovative solution and a paradigm shift for practice and learning, which warrants substantial attention.

HTs are physical or digital entities designed to simulate human-like appearance, behavior, or communication patterns (Dino et al., 2025). The use of HTs is particularly relevant in the caring professions, such as nursing, where interpersonal interactions and empathic care are crucial. Objects that resemble humans are more meaningful, helpful, and "trusted" to better elicit natural responses in simulated and actual nursing care scenarios where human interaction is important. HTs are specifically engineered to interact symbolically (basic) or meaningfully (advanced) with patients, healthcare providers, students, and other stakeholders within the healthcare ecosystem. For instance, human patient simulators (HPSs) in nursing schools offer a more realistic stimulus for students practicing therapeutic communication skills in a laboratory setting. Additionally, human-resembling robots are more widely accepted as companion agents by older adults in nursing homes than tablet computers attached to movable, roving poles.

HTs operate across a spectrum of uses and varying levels of complexity. On one hand, basic HTs may serve as inanimate models or references for patients during skills training. On the other hand, advanced HTs possess realistic visual representations that may range from photorealistic

 DOI: 10.4324/9781003464457-12

human appearances (physical) to stylized avatars (digital), may demonstrate natural language and artificial intelligence processing capabilities that enable contextual conversations, exhibit behavioral patterns that reflect understanding of healthcare protocols and nursing principles, and may adapt their responses based on user interactions and environmental contexts using large language models (Strohmann et al., 2023).

## History of Humanoid Technologies in Healthcare and Nursing

The desire to construct "mechanical representations" of humans traces back to medieval times. Leonardo da Vinci created what may be the earliest documented humanoid machine in 1495 with his "mechanical knight" design, which he likely built as a working prototype (Bucolo et al., 2020). This ingenious creation could perform basic human movements, including standing, sitting, lifting its helmet visor, and moving its arms autonomously through an intricate system of pulleys and cables (Clayton & Philo, 2010). Modern engineers have successfully recreated this design, demonstrating its feasibility. The following centuries witnessed the development of increasingly sophisticated mechanical humanoids, which served as the foundation for contemporary robotic technology. During the 18th and 19th centuries, inventors developed elaborate automata with complex internal mechanisms that could mimic human behaviors with remarkable precision (Bogue, 2020). A notable example from this era is Innocenzo Manzetti's automated flute player, completed in 1840 and still preserved today. This remarkable machine employed a combination of clockwork mechanisms, mechanical levers, connecting rods, and pneumatic tubes to control finger movements and lip positioning on the flute (Ronchi, 2020). Operating from a programmed cylinder similar to a music box, it could perform a repertoire of 12 complete musical pieces, demonstrating the sophisticated level of mechanical artistry achieved during this period (Bucolo et al., 2020).

Although they had been used in medical education for almost 30 years, nursing did not adopt them until much later (Nehring & Lashley, 2004; Palaganas et al., 2014). However, in the 1970s, student nurses were still training to practice nursing skills on inanimate objects (e.g., a pillow), a colleague, or a patient (Martins et al., 2012). HPSs and task trainers (e.g., simulator body parts) were first incorporated into nursing education in the mid-1990s.

Japan emerged as a pioneering force in modern-day HTs, primarily driven by its unique technology-driven culture, rapidly aging population, and declining birth rates. The country's drive for innovative solutions to support elderly care has led to substantial government and private sector investment in the development of robotics, an advanced version of HTs. In 2015, the Japanese research institute Riken developed Robear to provide support for nursing home caregivers and patients, marking one of the first purpose-built humanoid robots for nursing care (Korn et al., 2018). Simultaneously, "Softbank Robotics introduces Pepper, a humanoid robot designed to read emotions, interact with people and fulfill customer service roles", which would later find extensive applications in healthcare settings for patient interaction and emotional support (Pandey & Gelin, 2018).

The practical deployment of robots in nursing expanded significantly throughout the late 2010s and early 2020s, with applications ranging from direct patient care to administrative support. During the COVID-19 pandemic, humanoid robots gained new relevance in infection control, as they were used to take patients' temperatures and conduct video chats with patients to minimize the risk of infection between healthcare providers and patients (Khan et al., 2020). These robots demonstrated their versatility by maintaining communication and monitoring capabilities while physically distancing healthcare workers from patients who are potentially infectious (Wang & Wang, 2021). Research has begun to explore the use of robot HTs in specialized care settings, with studies examining their effectiveness in dementia care, rehabilitation support, and companion care programs for the elderly (Dino et al., 2022).

The advent of computers and the World Wide Web has introduced the concept of non-physical or digital HTs. The adoption of the Internet of Things (IoT) and artificial intelligence introduces the possibility of interacting with responsive virtual avatars or holographic representations of patients or nurses (Abbott & Shaw, 2016) in the digital space via the internet (Stuart et al., 2021) or the use of head-mounted devices (HMDs) (Dino, Dion, Abadir, Budhathoki, Huang, Ong, et al., 2024a).

## Theoretical Frameworks and Models Supporting Humanoid Technologies

### *Anthropomorphism*

The effectiveness of HTs in nursing would fundamentally depend on their realism, technological capabilities, and their ability to complement rather than replace human caring relationships. The most significant and distinguishable feature of HTs is their anthropomorphic (or human-like) characteristics. Scholars have introduced the Anthropomorphic Robot (ABOT) score, a simple rating system that measures how human-like a physical HT (such as a robot) appears to its users (Phillips et al., 2018). Developed by researchers at Brown University, it works by having users answer 18 questions about a robot's physical appearance. Then, an algorithm calculates a score from 0 to 100, where 100 indicates that the HT appears completely human-like (Phillips et al., 2018). Measuring anthropomorphism is particularly useful in nursing, as the level of human appearance of HTs in healthcare is shown to impact human–technology interaction and the quality of care (Bartneck et al., 2010). In the 1970s, roboticist Masahiro Mori introduced the concept of the Uncanny Valley (Figure 12.1) – a fascinating psychological phenomenon that describes the unsettling feeling people experience when encountering robots or artificial beings that appear almost, but not quite, human (Mori et al., 2012). Mori hypothesized that a person's response to a humanlike robot would abruptly shift from empathy to revulsion as it approached, but failed to attain a lifelike appearance (Betriana et al., 2021). The uncanny valley postulated that as HTs appear more humanlike, they become more appealing, but only up to a certain point, where humans start to feel uncomfortable or scared (Mori et al., 2012).

### *Reality–Virtuality Continuum*

The reality–virtuality continuum (Figure 12.2), originally conceptualized by Paul Milgram (Milgram et al., 1995), provides a framework for understanding how HTs can exist across different levels of virtual embodiment and interaction with reality. It is a spectrum that illustrates the possibility of digital forms of HTs existing in various types of digital and physical spaces. The reality–virtuality continuum is a continuous scale ranging from completely virtual to completely real, with HTs appearing anywhere along this spectrum (Skarbez et al., 2021). At one end, HTs are situated in completely virtual worlds where everything is computer-generated. At the other end, HTs might appear as holograms or digital overlays in the real world through the use of augmented reality.

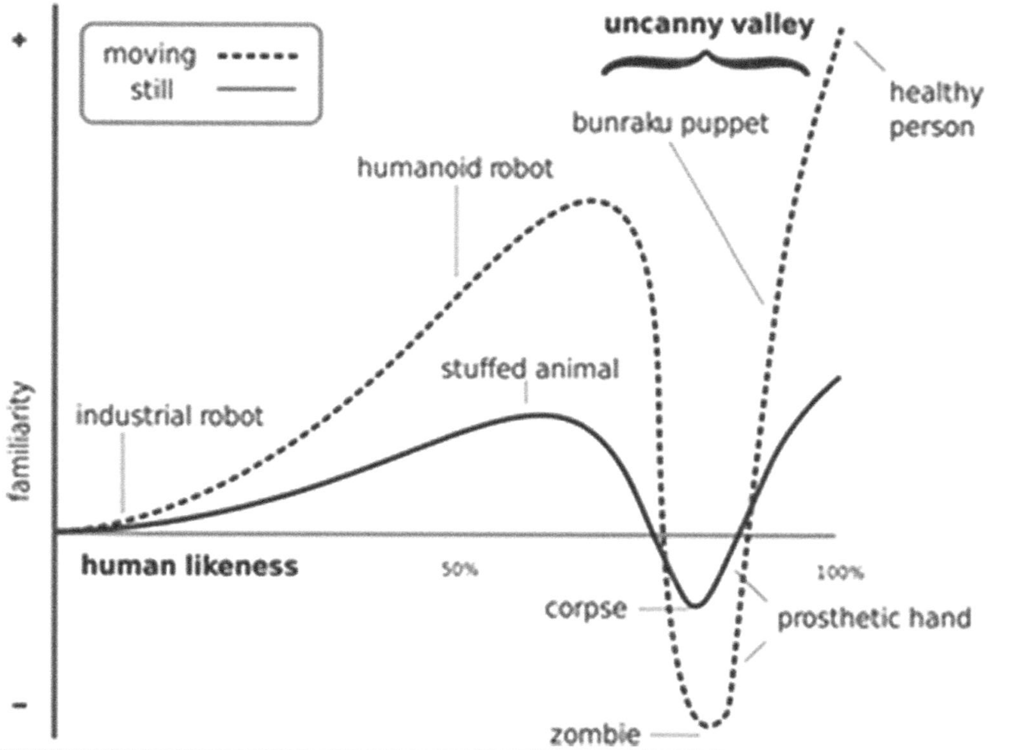


Figure 12.1 Uncanny valley. (Mori et al., 2012).

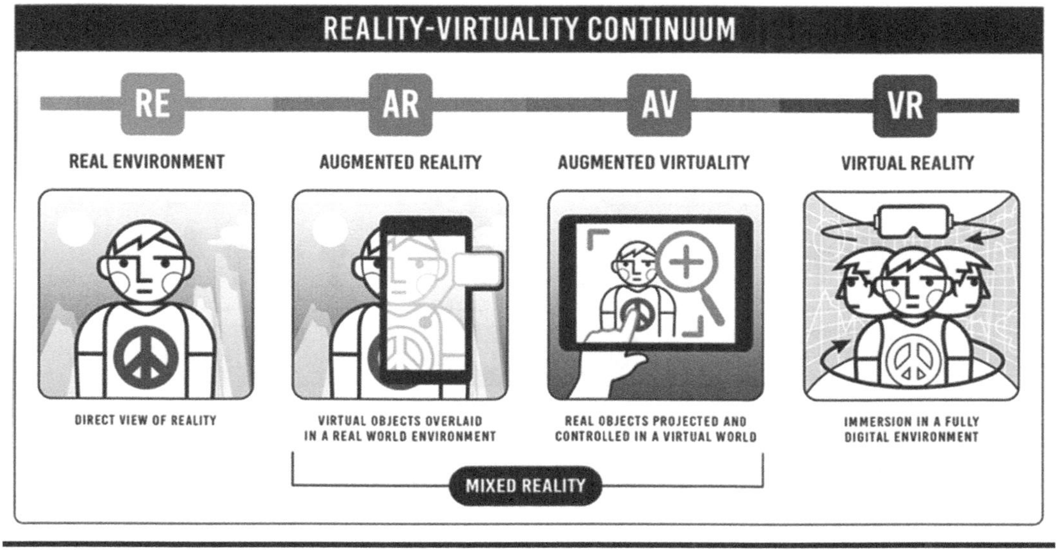


Figure 12.2 Reality–virtuality continuum. (Milgram et al., 1995).

The area between the two extremes, where both the real and the virtual are mixed, is called mixed reality. In this middle ground, HTs can interact with both real and virtual objects simultaneously.

## Human–Technology Interaction

Human–computer interaction (HCI) plays a fundamental role in determining whether technologies such as HTs will be usable and successful for their intended uses and users (Gulliksen, 2017; Siek, 2018; Søgaard Neilsen & Wilson, 2019). Research has demonstrated that HCI significantly influences users' intentions to adopt technology and their actual usage patterns, which must occur before any technology-based intervention can effectively impact (Brandsma et al., 2020; Singleton et al., 2019). The modified HCI model by Bálint (1995), shown in Figure 12.1 (tagged as the Human–Technology Interaction, Figure 12.3), provides a comprehensive framework for examining both measurable and experiential factors that influence the implementation of HT programs. Furthermore, the framework positions HT components—including content design, technological platform, and implementation environment—as precursors to health-related outcomes spanning physical, cognitive, and behavioral domains (Macabasag & Dino, 2018). Finally, the model acknowledges that human characteristics, including demographics, technology familiarity, and wellness status, serve as secondary variables that may influence the expected relationships between HT interventions in nursing and their outcomes.

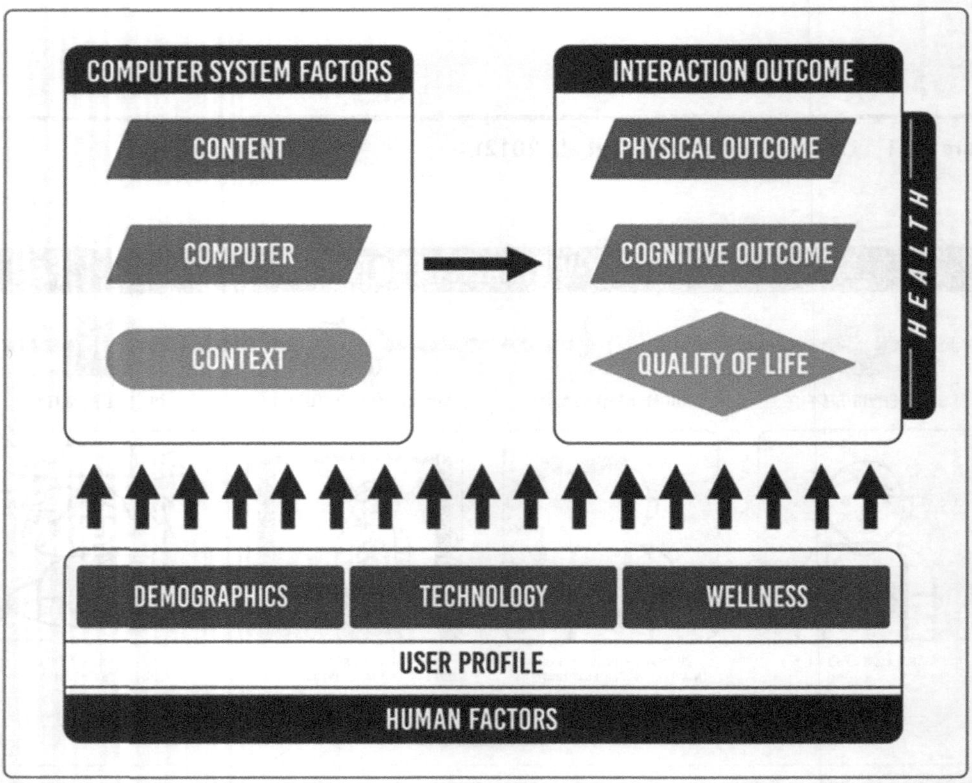


**Figure 12.3 Human–technology interaction. [adapted by (Dino, Dion, Abadir, Budhathoki, Huang, Padula, et al., 2024b) from (Bálint, 1995).]**

## Nursing Practice Applications

HTs in nursing can be categorized as either physical or digital. Physical HTs consist of tangible devices and equipment, whereas digital HTs exist as software-based or virtual applications.

### *Physical Humanoid Technologies – Common Examples are Robots and Human Patient Simulators.*

#### Humanoid Service Robots (HSRs)

Robotic systems refer to the "actuated mechanisms programmable in two or more axes with a degree of autonomy, moving within its environment to perform intended tasks; a robot includes a control system and an interface of the control system" (International Organization for Standardization, 2012 cited in Tanioka et al., 2017). HSRs are robots designed with human-like morphology and motion capabilities, inherently offering greater compatibility in human environments. However, the attributes of a humanoid robot are said to have fewer flaws compared to those of an actual human (Denny et al., 2016). Previous research indicates that the level of human likeness or anthropomorphism, the type of interaction with the humanoid robots, and the level of personal characteristics, such as power and status, influence how individuals form and report their attitudes toward robots (Ozturkcan & Merdin-Uygur, 2022).

HSRs have been increasingly utilized in various disciplines, particularly in the healthcare industry. The use of tele-operated HSRs, a specific type of robot controlled remotely by a human being, can perform tasks typically done in uncontrolled environments. This presents an advancement in assisting healthcare providers and patients during high-risk situations, including those involving highly infectious diseases. This type of HSR allowed healthcare providers to perform some of their duties at a safe distance from the infected patients (Kraft & Smart, 2016). HSRs are also used to implement techno-psychological distraction for children to reduce their pain as a result of stress and anxiety during a medical procedure (Azeta et al., 2018). Previous research has found that children are more likely to smile when encountering medical procedures with a robot (Beran et al., 2013, 2015; Yasemin et al., 2016). HSRs are also being designed to ease the burden on healthcare workers, who perform tasks that require both physical and fine motor skills, such as patient transfer and bed baths (Azeta et al., 2018).

Famous examples of HRs include Diligent Robotics' Moxi (Diligent Robotics Inc., 2024) and SoftBank's Pepper (SoftBank Robotics, 2014). **Moxi** features a minimalist architecture comprising a head, torso, and storage base, making it easy to navigate hospital corridors, aiding healthcare workers in delivering supplies and performing routine tasks (Diana, 2024). **Pepper**, similar to Moxi, assists with hospital activities, including guiding patients, providing directions, answering basic questions, and offering emotional support (Mantas et al., 2025). Pepper has also been utilized in elderly care and rehabilitation, often serving as a mediator between the elderly and their healthcare providers (T. Tanioka, 2019). Lesser-known examples include **RIBA**, a high-load capacity robot designed to safely and efficiently lift and transfer patients using its "humantype" arms (Mukai et al., 2010, 2011). RIBA is equipped with tactile sensors that detect the patient's contact position, allowing for motion adjustments to be made accordingly. Another example is **Cody**, a robot assistant developed to assist caregivers with patient hygiene using its compliant arm and gentle force to perform "wiping motions" (Chih-Hung King et al., 2010). **ARI**, another humanoid SR, is a high-performance robot that utilizes reinforcement learning to learn from each patient interaction, adapting its behavior to each user. ARI was widely used during the COVID-19 pandemic, particularly for interacting with and supporting patients remotely (Holland et al., 2021). These applications of humanoid SRs have highlighted the dire need for technological adoption in the healthcare industry and the apparent lack of focus on technological innovations, particularly during times of need (Mukherjee et al., 2022), such as the COVID-19 pandemic (Defi et al., 2022; Shen et al., 2021). These robots have made swift progress in extending vast opportunities and providing a helping hand to the strained global healthcare system, particularly in light of the pressing challenges posed by limited resources and demands for improved quality (Ozturkcan & Merdin-Uygur, 2022).

Interestingly, scholars have summarized the healthcare robots used by nurses in a published study (Dino et al., 2022) and have advanced the design spectrum of healthcare robots (Figure 12.4), which contain both HSRs and non-HSRs (Appendix A). Based on this paper, "current robotic systems are less anthropomorphic, operated through real-time direct and supervisory inputs, and mainly equipped with visual and auditory sensors and actuators with limited capability in performing health assessments" (Dino et al., 2022).

## Human Patient Simulators

HPS are sophisticated, computerized mannequins designed to replicate realistic physiological responses and clinical scenarios for healthcare education and training. These high-fidelity simulators feature programmable vital signs, responsive airways, palpable pulses, and the ability to exhibit various pathological conditions. Unlike traditional static training models, HPS can breathe, have heart rhythms, respond to medications, and even speak through voice simulation technology. Instructors control them through computer interfaces that allow real-time manipulation of patient conditions, creating dynamic learning environments that closely mirror actual clinical situations.

In nursing education, HPS serve multiple critical functions, including skills training, clinical decision-making practice, emergency response preparation, and interprofessional team collaboration exercises (Stenseth et al., 2025). Common examples include SimMan by Laerdal, which can

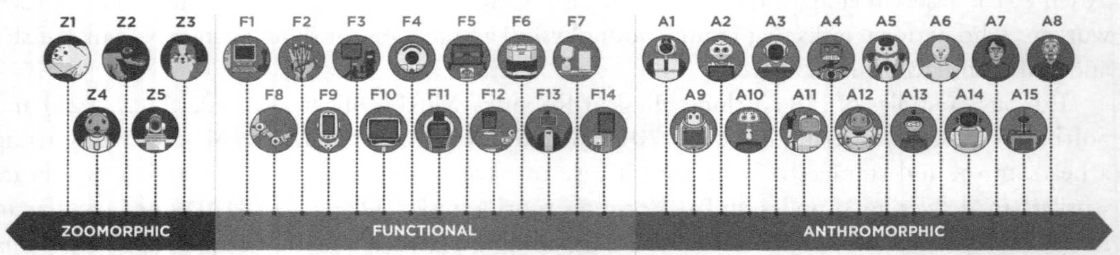


**Figure 12.4 Design spectrum of healthcare robots.**

*Note. Zoomorphic: Z1 = Paro, Z2 = Pleo, Z3 = Joy for All, and Z4 = AIBO; Functional: F1 = JavaTherapy System, F2 = Rutgers Master II (RMII), F3 = InMotion2 (MIT-Manus), F4 = Home robot with ambient facial features, F5 = NeuroVR; F6 = TUG Automated Robotic Delivery System, F7 = ElliQ, F8 = Experimental robot with tactile sensors, F9 = Giraff/ROBIN, F10 = EyeGo System, F11 = VGo, F12 = ReMeDi, F13 = Tele-robotic Intelligent Nursing Assistant (TRINA), and F14 = Telepresence Robot; Anthromorphic: A1 = Robotic Nursing Assistant, A2 = Pepper, A3 = Alice/"Eva", A4 = IRL-1, A5 = Nao, A6 = Telenoid R1, A7 = Hiroshi Ishiguro Geminoid, A8 = Philip K. Dick, A9 = iRobi, A10 = HOBBIT, A11 = Moxie, A12 = Ifbot, A13 = Kompai, A14 = Oni Robot, and A15 = ALECSA.*

simulate cardiac arrest scenarios and medication responses, and CAE Healthcare's Lucina for maternal–fetal care training. These simulators are used in scenarios ranging from routine vital sign assessment and medication administration to complex emergency situations like respiratory failure, cardiac events, and postoperative complications. Nursing students can practice procedures such as intubation, IV insertion, wound care, and patient assessment in a controlled environment where mistakes become learning opportunities rather than risks to patient safety (Koukourikos et al., 2021).

The integration of HPS has significantly transformed nursing education by bridging the gap between theoretical knowledge and clinical practice. Research demonstrates that simulation-based learning improves student confidence, clinical reasoning skills, and technical competency while reducing anxiety about real patient encounters (Tseng et al., 2021). HPS enables standardized learning experiences, ensuring that all students encounter similar clinical scenarios, regardless of the clinical site's availability or patient census. The technology has also enhanced patient safety by allowing nurses to refine their skills and practice rare or high-risk procedures before working with actual patients. Furthermore, simulation promotes interprofessional collaboration as nursing students can train alongside medical students, respiratory therapists, and other healthcare professionals, fostering the teamwork essential in modern healthcare delivery.

## *Digital Humanoid Technologies – Common Applications are Holograms and Virtual Agents.*

### *Holograms*

Recent technological advancements have introduced HTs even in digital and virtual spaces. Among the promising innovations is the hologram, a three-dimensional image produced through a coherent light source (i.e., light beams) that creates an illusion of physical presence (Mohammad et al., 2023). Haleem et al. (2022) described two primary methods of creating holograms: computer-generated holograms, which are used in augmented reality glasses, and optical display holograms, which do not require wearable devices. These holograms may appear as *clichéd* (stylized and less detailed) or *realistic* (high-fidelity visualizations), depending on their intended use. Three notable functions of this in the nursing field are for (1) visualization, (2) assessment, and (3) communication. The advanced, realistic, and volumetric interfaces of holograms allow learners and clinicians to study complex anatomical structures and engage with various patient scenarios. Evidence also suggests that holograms potentially improve knowledge scores and spatial awareness when compared to traditional learning modalities (Moro et al., 2016, 2019). Examples of these are **HoloAnatomy**, developed by Case Western Reserve University, which utilizes a hologram to learn different anatomical structures of the body (Gibson, 2022). Similarly, **the Project Polaris** at the National University of Singapore's Yong Loo Lin School of Medicine helps medical and nursing students learn medical procedures and visualize anatomical structures (XR Today, 2022).

Beyond visualization, a hologram plays a crucial role in improving communication for learners and instructors. It enables interactive simulations that replicate real-life patient interactions between students and a virtual patient, or between a learner and a virtual instructor, providing a safe and controlled environment for learning and training. One example of this is the University of Central Florida's **Dr. Hologram** patient simulation, which utilizes the PORTL device. This device presents people in life-size, volumetric 4K, both pre-recorded and live. It has a feature called *holoportation*, which is primarily applicable in rural areas (Lee, 2021). **Embodied Labs**, founded in 2016 by Carrie Shaw, trains future nurses to improve their communication skills when working with geriatric and hospice patients (Embodied Labs, n.d.). Another example is **Holoconnects**, through its development of *HoloBox*, alleviates shortages in healthcare providers by improving the accessibility of doctor–patient engagement, particularly in remote locations where urgent care is not readily available (Kite-Powell, n.d.). In addition to visualization and communication, Hologram supports objective and standardized assessment by offering consistent simulations that measure clinical reasoning and procedural accuracy. **HoloPatient** was developed by the National Health Service (NHS) in England and Health Education England (HEE) to deliver care to COVID-19 patients using HoloLens (Son et al., 2023). The patient demonstrates the four stages of the illness, enabling learners to recognize the signs and symptoms of COVID-19. Another initiative by the same company, **HoloScenarios**, was developed in partnership with Cambridge University Hospitals and others to address respiratory and emergency conditions (University of Cambridge, 2022).

Empirical studies have indicated that a holographic learning environment yielded notable advantages in nursing practice and education. Chen et al. (2021) noted that adding three-dimensional hologram modules to courses in health assessment resulted in statistically significant increases in knowledge and skill gain. Ditzel and Collins (2021) also reported an improvement in clinical reasoning ability among students who were trained using holographic standardized patients, highlighting the advantages of stable and immersive practice situations. Furthermore, research has demonstrated that incorporating holographic technology into nursing education enhances critical thinking skills, confidence, and knowledge (Son et al., 2023). These results suggest that holograms hold significant promise for improving nursing education, developing clinical expertise, and bridging the theory–practice gap in modern healthcare education.

### *Virtual Agents Projected via Reality–Virtuality Technologies*

Virtual Agents (VAs) are digital HTs that have evolved from simple task-oriented chatbots into more sophisticated systems capable of sustaining natural language interactions with users while showcasing a digital anthropometric interface. While virtual assistants like Siri and Alexa primarily offer utility-based support, VAs present a more natural front for providers and patients. VAs are designed to proactively interact, display empathy, and build trust, emulating social dynamics found in human relationships. Most VAs are made available to users as a stand-alone mobile application via smart devices (e.g., smartphones), integrated into websites, or projected to users via HMDs (Shorey & Ng, 2021).

VAs vary based on their application in educational and clinical settings. **Simulation-based VAs** are primarily designed for training purposes. This approach promotes experiential learning, enabling students to explore various scenarios and enhance their clinical skills through automated feedback (Georg & Zary, 2014). **Narrative-based VAs**, on the other hand, focus on story-driven clinical scenarios for improved engagement and information retention (Guise et al., 2012). Additionally, **standardized virtual patients (VAs)** are available to cater to traditional role-play scenarios with digital elements, facilitating remote participation in nursing education assessments (Torbatinezhad et al., 2018).

VAs function primarily as an **educational tool** to provide scenario-based simulations to improve the decision-making processes of healthcare professionals and students. One of the functionalities of VAs is providing an interactive learning environment. This environment offers well-defined protocols and algorithms that mimic real patient behavior and responses, providing immediate feedback and a dynamic educational experience (Han et al., 2022) Moreover, scenarios can cover patient history, diagnostic assessments, treatment planning, and follow-up care to promote clinical reasoning (Ionite et al., 2022) Similarly, this interactive fosters a feedback mechanism that enables students to reflect on their clinical judgment and improve their decision-making skills in real-life

**Figure 12.5 Virtual humanoid coaches.**

situations (Miles et al., 2020). Another functionality of VAs is that they cater to **customization and adaptation.** VPs foster personalized learning, tailored to meet specific learning objectives, and also depend on the user levels. Aspects that cater to customization are patient demographics, clinical history, and treatment outcomes (Kim et al., 2020). Lastly, VPs can be integrated with **assessment metrics** for broader competencies such as clinical integration and situational awareness in the clinical setting (Siah et al., 2022).

Interestingly, a group of scholars has utilized VAs as virtual coaches in community health programs in the Philippines (Dino, Dion, Abadir, Budhathoki, Huang, Padula, et al., 2024b). Virtual coaches (Figure 12.5) are "virtual humanoid coach-driven" systems that can effectively deliver health intervention programs, specifically designed to address healthcare challenges in community settings, such as compliance with health-enhancing physical activities (Dino et al., 2025). In previous studies, these virtual coaches utilize mixed reality technology to provide personalized health guidance (Dino, Dion, Abadir, Budhathoki, Huang, Padula, et al., 2024b).

Virtual Agent Nurses, also known as Virtual Nurses (VNs), are humanoid nurse models facilitated through technology, where registered nurses remotely conduct comprehensive care responsibilities, primarily patient assessments, and management tasks. Several variations for VNs exist. **Synchronous VNs** address immediate healthcare needs in real time either through video conferencing or telehealth platforms (Kleib et al., 2024; Rouleau et al., 2024). On the other hand, **Asynchronous VNs** do not involve real-time engagement and primarily focus on reviewing patient data and providing follow-up care (Boston-Fleischhauer, 2025). Most VNs are used to deliver patient care and support. Most of them are used for consultation via telecommunication services to facilitate direct patient care without physical visits. These telehealth services were particularly beneficial during the COVID-19 pandemic, assisting in the continuity of care through virtual channels (Sumargono et al., 2022). Furthermore, VNs can monitor the patient's status, adherence to treatment, and continuity of symptom management. VNs can check and evaluate their health progress regularly without the constraints of physical spaces (Shah et al., 2021).

## Impact, Challenges, and Future Directions

HTs are transforming nursing practice by addressing critical healthcare challenges, including staffing shortages, aging populations, and increasing care demands. These systems provide 24/7 patient monitoring, medication reminders, and basic care assistance, effectively reducing the burden on human caregivers while maintaining quality care delivery. In rehabilitation and elder care settings, humanoid robots serve dual roles as therapeutic assistants and social companions, guiding patients through exercise routines and providing emotional support to combat isolation. The technology has demonstrated effectiveness comparable to traditional care methods, while offering advantages such as consistency, personalized pacing, and comprehensive data collection that enhance clinical decision-making. Virtual humanoid coaches and robotic assistants are particularly impactful in community-based programs, where they expand access to healthcare services and support aging-in-place initiatives.

Despite promising applications, significant barriers impede widespread adoption of HTs in nursing. Safety and reliability concerns represent the most critical challenge, as healthcare providers require fail-safe mechanisms and assurance that robots won't interfere with medical equipment or emergency procedures. Trust and acceptance issues persist among both healthcare professionals and patients, who express skepticism about robots' ability to provide appropriate care and handle complex situations. Ethical considerations surrounding human dignity, autonomy, consent, and the authenticity of artificial emotional interactions create moral dilemmas about the appropriate role of technology in healthcare. Technical limitations include difficulties recognizing complex emotional needs, understanding cultural nuances, and adapting to unexpected situations, while economic barriers involve high implementation costs, ongoing maintenance, and training requirements. Additionally, evolving regulatory frameworks create uncertainty regarding safety standards, liability, and quality assurance guidelines.

The future of HTs in nursing will focus on advanced AI integration featuring enhanced natural language processing, improved emotional intelligence, and ML capabilities that adapt to individual patient needs. Collaborative care models will emerge that optimize the unique strengths of both human nurses and robotic systems, creating more efficient care delivery without replacing human caregivers. Specialized applications will expand into dementia care, pediatric nursing, mental health support, and home healthcare, supported by improved safety systems with advanced sensors and better integration with hospital infrastructure. The healthcare companion robots' market, projected to grow steadily through 2030, will drive innovation and potentially reduce costs, making these technologies more accessible. Success will depend on developing comprehensive regulatory frameworks that address safety standards, liability guidelines, and ethical considerations while maintaining the compassionate, human-centered values essential to nursing practice. The ultimate goal remains to enhance rather than replace human nurses, empowering them with advanced tools that improve patient outcomes while preserving meaningful human connections in healthcare delivery.

## Summary

HTs in nursing represent a transformative force in healthcare delivery, offering solutions to critical challenges while introducing new complexities that must be carefully managed. The impact of these technologies extends beyond simple task automation to encompass fundamental changes in how nursing care is conceptualized, delivered, and experienced. Success in implementing HTs will depend on addressing current challenges through collaborative efforts among healthcare providers, technology developers, regulatory bodies, and patients themselves. The future of nursing will likely involve sophisticated human–robot collaboration models that leverage the unique strengths of both human caregivers and advanced technologies. As these technologies continue to evolve, the nursing profession must actively engage in shaping their development and implementation to ensure they enhance rather than diminish the human elements of care that are central to nursing practice.

The ultimate goal is not to replace human nurses but to empower them with advanced tools that improve patient outcomes, reduce workload burdens, and enable more meaningful human connections in healthcare delivery. The journey toward widespread adoption of HTs in nursing will require ongoing research, careful ethical consideration, and a commitment to maintaining the compassionate, human-centered values that define quality nursing care. With thoughtful implementation and continued innovation, these technologies have the potential to significantly improve healthcare outcomes while preserving the essential human elements of nursing practice.

## Appendix A Nursing Robots

| *Robot* | *Organization/ Developer* | *Description/ Hardware* | *Appeared in the Article(s)* | *Icon* |
|---|---|---|---|---|
| JavaTherapy System | (Reinkensmeyer et al., 2001) University of California | A unilateral rehabilitation device utilizing a force-feedback joystick connected to the patient's wrist via an orthopedic splint. It comprises a custom splint, mobile arm support, and a specialized base. | Carignan & Krebs (2006) |  |
| Rutgers Master II (RMII) | (Popescu et al., 2000) | A wearable exoskeleton for the hand delivering resistive forces to the fingers and thumb using pneumatic pistons. Features include infrared sensors and non-contact Hall-effect technology | Carignan & Krebs (2006) | 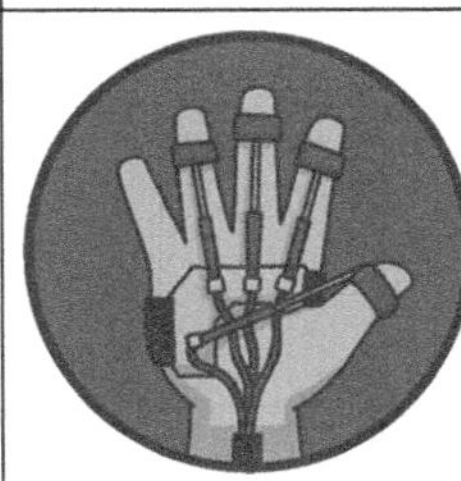 |
| VinMotion 2 (MIT-Manus) | Massachusetts Institute of Technology (MIT) Bionik Laboratories Corp. | A robotic system supporting bilateral arm rehabilitation by enabling horizontal reaching motions. It assists and tracks arm movements during therapy. | Carignan & Krebs (2006) | 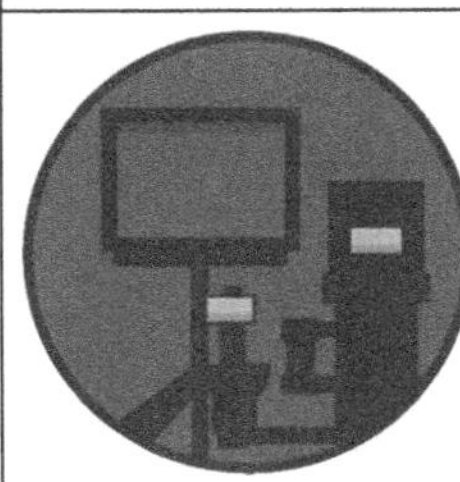 |

*(Continued)*

| *Robot* | *Organization/ Developer* | *Description/ Hardware* | *Appeared in the Article(s)* | *Icon* |
|---|---|---|---|---|
| "Home robot with ambient facial features" | (Takacs & Hanak, 2008) | An affordable robot with facial display, RFID, face recognition, and a built-in pill dispenser. It helps monitor food intake and conveys information in an elderly friendly format. | Takacs & Hanak (2008) | 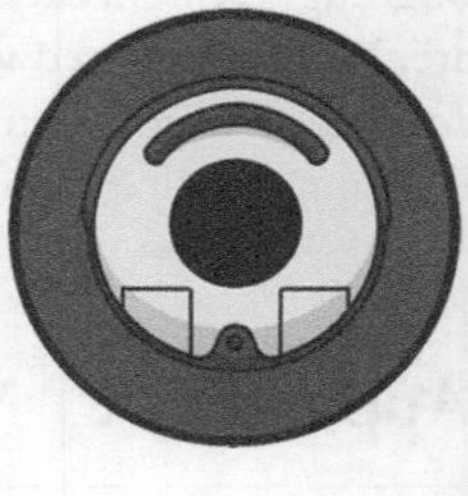 |
| NeuroVR | (Riva & Gaggioli, 2009) | An open-source platform offering 14 safe virtual environments to support rehabilitation. Tailored for clinical and therapeutic use. | Riva & Gaggioli (2009) |  |
| Robotic Nursing Assistant | | Designed with Mecanum wheels for multidirectional movement, this robot aids in lifting patients over 300 pounds, enhancing safety for users and caregivers. | Wood (2011) |  |
| TUG Automated Robotic Delivery System | Aethon | An autonomous delivery robot equipped with sensors and mapping capabilities to transport items like meals and medicine. It interfaces with building systems like doors and elevators via Wi-Fi. | Wood (2011) | 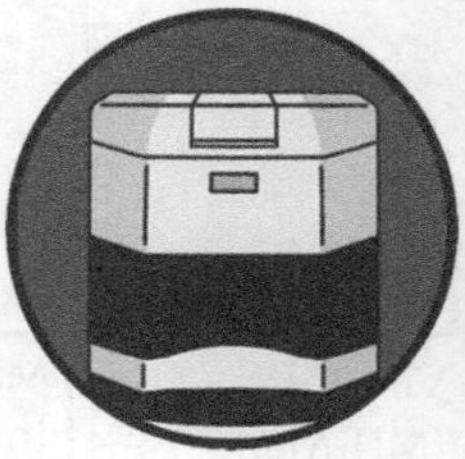 |

*(Continued)*

| *Robot* | *Organization/ Developer* | *Description/ Hardware* | *Appeared in the Article(s)* | *Icon* |
|---|---|---|---|---|
| Pepper | Softbank Robotics | Recognized as the first emotionally responsive robot designed for assistant roles, Pepper is a humanoid robot with a range of functions, including facilitating physical activities. It can detect and respond to basic human emotions. When operating continuously, Pepper functions for up to 12 hours and is capable of autonomously returning to its charging station when the battery runs low. | Ishiguro & Majima (2016), Broadbent et al. (2013), T. Tanioka et al., (2019), Sato et al. (2020), R. Tanioka et al. (2020), van der Putte et al. (2019), T. Tanioka et al. (2021) |  |
| Alice/"Eva" | Santa Monica Intelligent Technology Co., Ltd. | A 60 cm humanoid robot designed to assist the elderly through conversation and health monitoring. Reports medical data to caregivers. | Ishiguro & Majima (2016) |  |
| IRL-1 | (Lepage et al., 2016) | A research testbed robot with a mobile base, expressive face, dual arms, grippers, and a microphone array, allowing rich human–robot interaction. | Lepage et al. (2016) |  |

*(Continued)*

| *Robot* | *Organization/ Developer* | *Description/ Hardware* | *Appeared in the Article(s)* | *Icon* |
|---|---|---|---|---|
| iRobi | Yujin Robot | A multifunctional social robot with educational features. It includes an Intel processor, a camera, and is capable of teaching, singing, and dancing. | Broadbent et al. (2013) |  |
| Nao | Aldebaran | A versatile humanoid robot equipped with facial recognition and multiple sensors. Used in educational, research, and industrial applications. | Broadbent et al. (2013) | 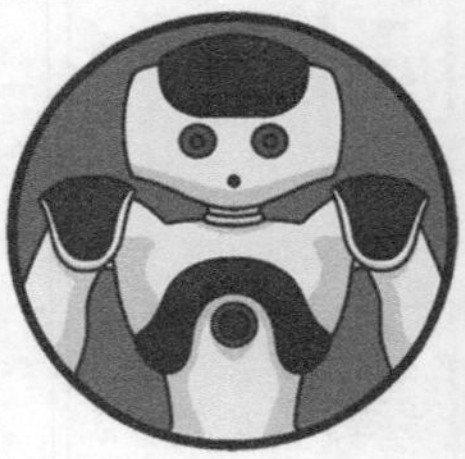 |
| Paro | Intelligent System Co. | A pet-like therapeutic robot that aids in reducing stress and anxiety, particularly for dementia patients. | Broadbent et al. (2013), Jensen et al. (2019) |  |
| Pleo | Innvo Labs | A dinosaur-shaped robot with tactile sensors, two infrared sensors, a camera, and motorized limbs. Designed for interactive companionship. | Broadbent et al. (2013) |  |
| Telenoid R1 | Osaka University and ATR Hiroshi Ishiguro Laboratory | A minimalist humanoid robot with 9 degrees of freedom. Capable of gestures like hugging and greeting in a compact 80 cm frame. | Broadbent et al. (2013) | 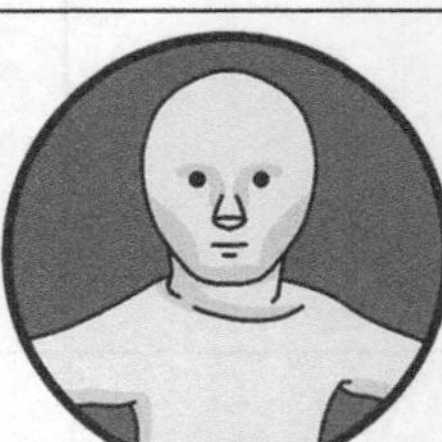 |

(*Continued*)

| *Robot* | *Organization/ Developer* | *Description/ Hardware* | *Appeared in the Article(s)* | *Icon* |
|---|---|---|---|---|
| Philip K. Dick | Hanson Robotics | A humanoid robot capable of expressive facial movements using 36 servomotors. Developed for cognitive and social interaction research. | Broadbent et al. (2013) |  |
| Hiroshi Ishiguro Geminoid | ATR Hiroshi Ishiguro Laboratory | A robotic twin of a real person, controlled via Android Science systems involving a robot, server, and teleoperation interface. | Broadbent et al. (2013) |  |
| Joy for All | Hasbro | A realistic robotic cat made to provide companionship to older adults. Known for its lifelike responses and playfulness. | Jensen et al. (2019) |  |
| HOBBIT | EU's 7th Framework Programme | A domestic robot equipped with various sensors and actuators for detecting falls and supporting the elderly within the home. | Jensen et al. (2019), Eftring & Frennert (2016) | 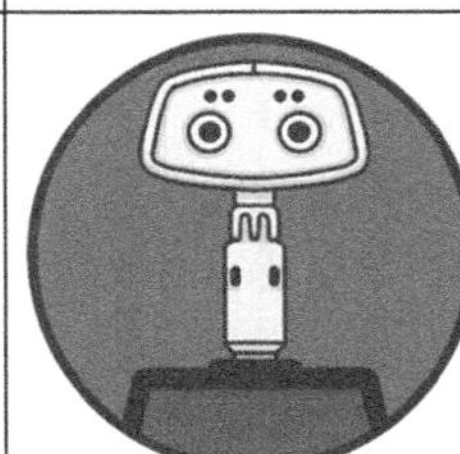 |
| ElliQ | Intuition robotics | A smart companion robot with voice interaction designed to reduce loneliness in older adults by facilitating social connections. | Jensen et al. (2019) |  |

(*Continued*)

| *Robot* | *Organization/ Developer* | *Description/ Hardware* | *Appeared in the Article(s)* | *Icon* |
|---|---|---|---|---|
| Moxie | Diligent Robotics | An interactive robot aimed at helping children with behavioral and developmental disorders, emphasizing trust through responsive interaction. | Pepito et al. (2020) | 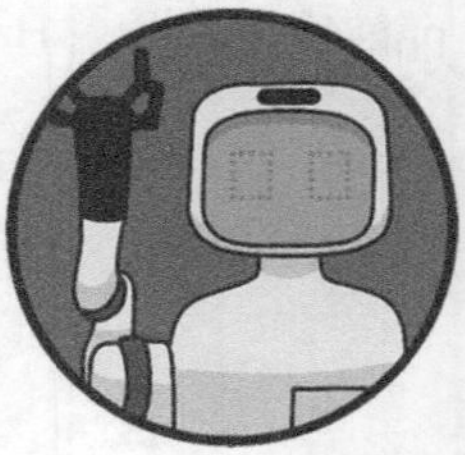 |
| AIBO | Sony | A robotic pet with adaptive personality and facial recognition. Learns behaviors and interacts emotionally over time. | Matsumoto et al. (2005) |  |
| ifbot | Business Design Laboratory (Japan) | A communication robot that detects emotions and expresses a variety of facial gestures, enhancing social interaction. | Matsumoto et al. (2005) | 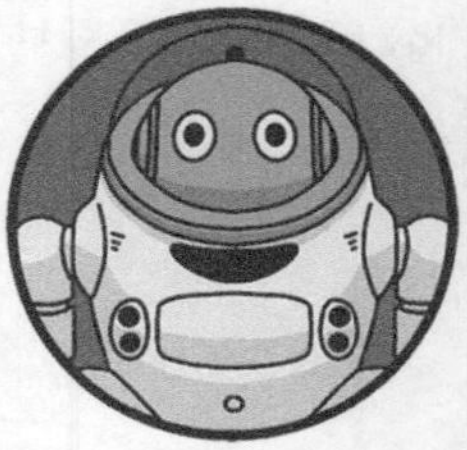 |
| Experimental robot with tactile sensors | (Mukai et al., 2006) | Features tactile sensing for detecting stress and controlling grip force, primarily used in robotic manipulation research. | Mukai et al. (2006) | 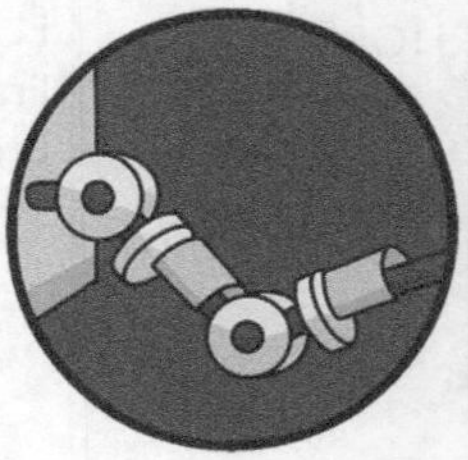 |
| Telepresence Robot for Interpersonal Communication (TRIC) | (Tsai et al., 2007) | Combines VR, robotics, and communication tech to connect elderly individuals with caregivers and family through a home-based system. | Tsai et al. (2007) |  |

(*Continued*)

| *Robot* | *Organization/ Developer* | *Description/ Hardware* | *Appeared in the Article(s)* | *Icon* |
|---|---|---|---|---|
| Kompai | Robosoft | A humanoid robot aiding individuals with disabilities, featuring speech recognition, autonomous navigation, and communication functions. | Granata et al. (2013), Zsiga et al. (2018) |  |
| Oni Robot | (not specified) | An emotional, game-playing robot designed to enhance interaction through expressive behavior. | Okano et al. (2013) | 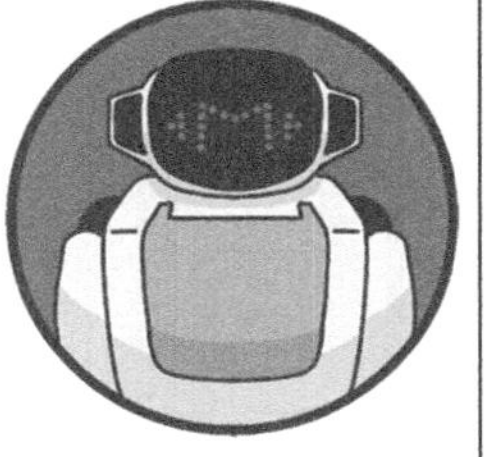 |
| Giraff/ROBIN | Camanio Care AB | A mobile telepresence system equipped with sensors for elderly care, enabling communication and activity monitoring at home. | Boman & Bartfai (2015), Moyle et al. (2020), Cortellessa et al. (2018) |  |
| ALECSA | LEGO Mindstorms NXT | An exercise-coaching robot built with LEGO Mindstorms, incorporating multiple sensors and an educational control unit (NXT Brick). | Pérez et al. (2015) |  |
| EyeGo System | (Wästlund et al., 2015) | A gaze-controlled wheelchair robot for individuals with severe cognitive impairments, enabling independent mobility. | Wästlund et al. (2015) |  |

*(Continued)*

| *Robot* | *Organization/ Developer* | *Description/ Hardware* | *Appeared in the Article(s)* | *Icon* |
|---|---|---|---|---|
| VGo | VGo Communications | A remotely operated robot that simulates human presence in distant locations, often used in medical environments. | Moyle et al. (2020) | 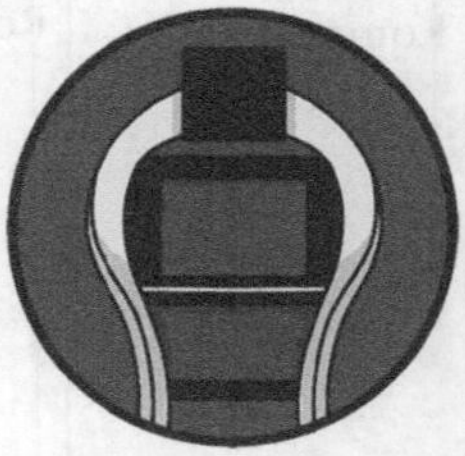 |
| ReMeDi | (Arent et al., 2016) | A telemedicine robot allowing physicians to perform palpation and ultrasound exams remotely via a mobile robotic platform. | Arent et al. (2016) |  |
| Tele-Robotic Intelligent Nursing Assistant (TRINA) | (Li et al., 2017) | A telepresence nursing assistant capable of clinical tasks, equipped with sensors and interface systems to aid healthcare providers. | Li et al. (2017) |  |
| Telepresence Robot | (Koceska et al., 2019) | Supports independent elderly living by reducing isolation and providing virtual human presence for daily interaction. | Koceska et al. (2019) |  |

# References

Abbott, M. B., & Shaw, P. (2016). Virtual Nursing Avatars: Nurse Roles and Evolving Concepts of Care. *Online Journal of Issues in Nursing, 21*(3), 7. https://doi.org/10.3912/OJIN.Vol21No03PPT39.05

Arent, K., Jakubiak, J., Drwiega, M., Cholewinski, M., Stollnberger, G., Giuliani, M., Tscheligi, M., Szczesniak-Stanczyk, D., Janowski, M., Brzozowski, W., & Wysokinski, A. (2016). Control of mobile robot for remote medical examination: Design concepts and users' feedback from experimental studies. *2016 9th International Conference on Human System Interactions (HSI)*, 76–82. https://doi.org/10.1109/HSI.2016.7529612

Azeta, J., Bolu, C., Abiodun, A. A., & Oyawale, F. (2018). A review on humanoid robotics in healthcare. *MATEC Web of Conferences, 153*(02004). https://doi.org/10.1051/matecconf/201815302004

Bálint, L. (1995). Adaptive human-computer interfaces for man-machine interaction in computer-integrated systems. *Computer Integrated Manufacturing Systems, 8*(2), 133–142. https://doi.org/10.1016/0951-5240(95)00007-G

Bartneck, C., Bleeker, T., Bun, J., Fens, P., & Riet, L. (2010). The influence of robot anthropomorphism on the feelings of embarrassment when interacting with robots. *Paladyn, Journal of Behavioral Robotics, 1*(2), 109–115. https://doi.org/10.2478/s13230-010-0011-3

Beran, T. N., Ramirez-Serrano, A., Vanderkooi, O. G., & Kuhn, S. (2013). Reducing children's pain and distress towards flu vaccinations: A novel and effective application of humanoid robotics. *Vaccine, 31*(25), 2772–2777. https://doi.org/10.1016/j.vaccine.2013.03.056

Beran, T. N., Ramirez-Serrano, A., Vanderkooi, O. G., & Kuhn, S. (2015). Humanoid robotics in health care: An exploration of children's and parents' emotional reactions. *Journal of Health Psychology, 20*(7), 984–989. https://doi.org/10.1177/1359105313504794

Betriana, F., Osaka, K., Matsumoto, K., Tanioka, T., & Locsin, R. C. (2021). Relating Mori's Uncanny Valley in generating conversations with artificial affective communication and natural language processing. *Nursing Philosophy, 22*(2). https://doi.org/10.1111/nup.12322

Bogue, R. (2020). Humanoid robots from the past to the present. *Industrial Robot: The International Journal of Robotics Research and Application, 47*(4), 465–472. https://doi.org/10.1108/IR-05-2020-0088

Boman, I.-L., & Bartfai, A. (2015). The first step in using a robot in brain injury rehabilitation: Patients' and health-care professionals' perspective. *Disability and Rehabilitation: Assistive Technology, 10*(5), 365–370. https://doi.org/10.3109/17483107.2014.913712

Boston-Fleischhauer, C. (2025). Virtual nursing: Organizational and professional crossroads for the immediate and beyond. *Nursing Administration Quarterly, 49*(2), 79–86. https://doi.org/10.1097/NAQ.0000000000000671

Brandsma, T., Stoffers, J., & Schrijver, I. (2020). Advanced technology use by care professionals. *International Journal of Environmental Research and Public Health, 17*(3), 742. https://doi.org/10.3390/ijerph17030742

Broadbent, E., Kumar, V., Li, X., Sollers, J., Stafford, R. Q., MacDonald, B. A., & Wegner, D. M. (2013). Robots with display screens: A robot with a more humanlike face display is perceived to have more mind and a better personality. *PLoS ONE, 8*(8), e72589. https://doi.org/10.1371/journal.pone.0072589

Bucolo, M., Buscarino, A., Famoso, C., Fortuna, L., & Gagliano, S. (2020). Automation of the Leonardo da Vinci machines. *Machines, 8*(3), 53. https://doi.org/10.3390/machines8030053

Carignan, C. R., & Krebs, H. I. (2006). Telerehabilitation robotics: Bright lights, big future? *The Journal of Rehabilitation Research and Development, 43*(5), 695. https://doi.org/10.1682/JRRD.2005.05.0085

Chen, C.-J., Chen, Y.-C., Lee, M.-Y., Wang, C.-H., & Sung, H.-C. (2021). Effects of three-dimensional holograms on the academic performance of nursing students in a health assessment and practice course: A pretest-intervention-posttest study. *Nurse Education Today, 106*, 105081. https://doi.org/10.1016/j.nedt.2021.105081

Chih-Hung King, Chen, T. L., Jain, A., & Kemp, C. C. (2010). Towards an assistive robot that autonomously performs bed baths for patient hygiene. *2010 IEEE/RSJ International Conference on Intelligent Robots and Systems*, 319–324. https://doi.org/10.1109/IROS.2010.5649101

Clayton, M., & Philo, R. (2010). *Leonardo da Vinci: The mechanics of man.* J. Paul Getty Museum.

Cortellessa, G., Fracasso, F., Sorrentino, A., Orlandini, A., Bernardi, G., Coraci, L., De Benedictis, R., & Cesta, A. (2018). ROBIN, a telepresence robot to support older users monitoring and social inclusion: Development and evaluation. *Telemedicine and E-Health, 24*(2), 145–154. https://doi.org/10.1089/tmj.2016.0258

Defi, I. R., Iskandar, S., Charismawati, S., Turnip, A., & Novita, D. (2022). Healthcare workers' point of view on medical robotics during COVID-19 Pandemic: A scoping review. *International Journal of General Medicine, 15*, 3767–3777. https://doi.org/10.2147/IJGM.S355734

Denny, J., Elyas, M., D'Costa, S. A., & D'Souza, R. D. (2016). Humanoid Robots: Past, present and the future. *European Journal of Advances in Engineering and Technology, 3*(5), 8–15.

Diana, C. (2024). Designing Robots that Work and Matter. In *Designing Interactions with Robotics* (p. 8). https://www.taylorfrancis.com/chapters/oa-edit/10.1201/97810033710.1-7/designing-robots-work-matter-carla-diana

Diligent Robotics Inc. (2024). *Moxi*. Diligent Robotics.

Dino, M. J. S., Davidson, P. M., Dion, K. W., Szanton, S. L., & Ong, I. L. (2022). Nursing and human-computer interaction in healthcare robots for older people: An integrative review. *International Journal of Nursing Studies Advances*, 100072. https://doi.org/10.1016/j.ijnsa.2022.100072

Dino, M. J. S., Dion, K. W., Abadir, P. M., Budhathoki, C., Huang, C.-M., Ong, I., Balbin, P. T., Himmelfarb, C. R. D., & Davidson, P. M. (2024a). Usability and acceptance as facilitators of behavioral intention to use a mixed reality exercise program in older adults: A structural equation model. *Computers in Human Behavior: Artificial Humans, 2*(1), 100071. https://doi.org/10.1016/j.chbah.2024.100071

Dino, M. J. S., Dion, K. W., Abadir, P. M., Budhathoki, C., Huang, C.-M., Padula, W. V., Himmelfarb, C. R. D., & Davidson, P. M. (2024b). The impact of a mixed reality technology-driven health enhancing physical activity program among community-dwelling older adults: A study protocol. *Frontiers in Public Health, 12*, 1383407. https://doi.org/10.3389/fpubh.2024.1383407

Dino, M. J. S., Dion, K. W., Abadir, P. M., Budhathoki, C., Huang, C.-M., Padula, W. V., Ong, I., Dennison Himmelfarb, C. R., Davidson, P. M., & Thiamwong, L. (2025). What drives older adults' acceptance of virtual humans? A conjoint and latent class analysis on virtual exercise coach attributes for a community-based exercise program. *Computers in Human Behavior, 164*, 108507. https://doi.org/10.1016/j.chb.2024.108507

Ditzel, L., & Collins, E. (2021). Holograms in nursing education: Results of an exploratory study. *Journal of Nursing Education and Practice, 11*(8), 43. https://doi.org/10.5430/jnep.v11n8p43

Eftring, H., & Frennert, S. (2016). Designing a social and assistive robot for seniors. *Zeitschrift Für Gerontologie Und Geriatrie, 49*(4), 274–281. https://doi.org/10.1007/s00391-016-1064-7

Embodied Labs. (n.d.). *Immersive Learning Solutions XR & VR Training*. Retrieved June 2, 2025, from https://www.embodiedlabs.com

Georg, C., & Zary, N. (2014). Web-based virtual patients in nursing education: development and validation of theory-anchored design and activity models. *Journal of Medical Internet Research, 16*(4), e105. https://doi.org/10.2196/jmir.2556

Gibson, E. (2022, January 30). HoloAnatomy: A virtual view of the human body. *TCU 360*. https://tcu360.com/2022/01/30/holoanatomy-a-virtual-view-of-the-human-body/

Granata, C., Pino, M., Legouverneur, G., Vidal, J.-S., Bidaud, P., & Rigaud, A.-S. (2013). Robot services for elderly with cognitive impairment: Testing usability of graphical user interfaces. *Technology and Health Care, 21*(3), 217–231. https://doi.org/10.3233/THC-130718

Guise, V., Chambers, M., & Välimäki, M. (2012). What can virtual patient simulation offer mental health nursing education? *Journal of Psychiatric and Mental Health Nursing, 19*(5), 410–418. https://doi.org/10.1111/j.1365-2850.2011.01797.x

Gulliksen, J. (2017). Institutionalizing human-computer interaction for global health. *Global Health Action, 10*(sup3), 1344003. https://doi.org/10.1080/16549716.2017.1344003

Haleem, A., Javaid, M., Qadri, M. A., & Suman, R. (2022). Understanding the role of digital technologies in education: A review. *Sustainable Operations and Computers, 3*, 275–285. https://doi.org/10.1016/j.susoc.2022.05.004

Han, L., Hazlewood, G. S., Barnabe, C., & Barber, C. E. H. (2022). Systematic review of outcomes and patient experience with virtual care in rheumatoid arthritis. *Arthritis Care & Research, 74*(9), 1484–1492. https://doi.org/10.1002/acr.24586

Holland, J., Kingston, L., McCarthy, C., Armstrong, E., O'Dwyer, P., Merz, F., & McConnell, M. (2021). Service robots in the healthcare sector. *Robotics, 10*(1), 47. https://doi.org/10.3390/robotics10010047

International Organization for Standardization. (2012). *8373: Robots and Robotic Devices* (Second Edition). International Organization for Standardization.

Ionite, C., Rotariu, M., Turnea, M., Ilea, M., & Condurach, I. (2022). A review about the effectiveness of virtual therapy in the recovery of patients with spinal cord injuries. *Journal of Men's Health, 18*(8), 1. https://doi.org/10.31083/j.jomh1808160

Ishiguro, K., & Majima, Y. (2016). Utilization of communication robot in patient education. *Studies in Health Technology and Informatics, 225*, 913–914.

Jensen, E. A. G., Smith, J., & Kovach, C. R. (2019). Social robots, robotic assistants, and home health monitoring devices: a gerontological research perspective. *Research in Gerontological Nursing, 12*(4), 163–166. https://doi.org/10.3928/19404921-20190612-02

Khan, Z. H., Siddique, A., & Lee, C. W. (2020). Robotics utilization for healthcare digitization in global COVID-19 management. *International Journal of Environmental Research and Public Health, 17*(11), 3819. https://doi.org/10.3390/ijerph17113819

Kim, Y., Kim, W. J., & Min, H. Y. (2020). Nursing students' experiences in virtual simulation practice. *The Journal of Korean Academic Society of Nursing Education, 26*(2), 198–207. https://doi.org/10.5977/jkasne.2020.26.2.198

Kite-Powell, J. (n.d.). *Holographic technology in this Holobox connects patients to doctors*. Forbes. Retrieved June 1, 2025, from https://www.forbes.com/sites/jenniferkitepowell/2024/05/28/a-holobox-at-crescent-regional-hospital-connects-patients-to-doctors/

Kleib, M., Arnaert, A., Nagle, L. M., Darko, E. M., Idrees, S., Da Costa, D., & Ali, S. (2024). Resources to support Canadian nurses to deliver virtual care: Environmental scan. *JMIR Medical Education, 10*, e53254. https://doi.org/10.2196/53254

Koceska, N., Koceski, S., Beomonte Zobel, P., Trajkovik, V., & Garcia, N. (2019). A telemedicine robot system for assisted and independent living. *Sensors, 19*(4), 834. https://doi.org/10.3390/s19040834

Korn, O., Bieber, G., & Fron, C. (2018). Perspectives on Social Robots: From the Historic Background to an Experts' View on Future Developments. *Proceedings of the 11th Pervasive Technologies Related to Assistive Environments Conference*, 186–193. https://doi.org/10.1145/3197768.3197774

Koukourikos, K., Tsaloglidou, A., Kourkouta, L., Papathanasiou, I. V., Iliadis, C., Fratzana, A., & Panagiotou, A. (2021). Simulation in clinical nursing education. *Acta Informatica Medica: AIM: Journal of the Society for Medical Informatics of Bosnia & Herzegovina: Casopis Drustva Za Medicinsku Informatiku BiH, 29*(1), 15–20. https://doi.org/10.5455/aim.2021.29.15-20

Kraft, K., & Smart, W. D. (2016). Seeing is comforting: Effects of teleoperator visibility in robot-mediated health care. *2016 11th ACM/IEEE International Conference on Human-Robot Interaction (HRI)*, 11–18. https://doi.org/10.1109/HRI.2016.7451728

Lee, J. (2021, July 29). New Lifelike Hologram Tech Expands UCF Students' Skills in Patient Care. *University of Central Florida News|UCF Today*. https://www.ucf.edu/news/new-lifelike-hologram-tech-expands-ucf-students-skills-in-patient-care/

Lepage, P., Letourneau, D., Hamel, M., Briere, S., Corriveau, H., Tousignant, M., & Michaud, F. (2016). Telehomecare telecommunication framework: From remote patient monitoring to video visits and robot telepresence. *2016 38th Annual International Conference of the IEEE Engineering in Medicine and Biology Society (EMBC)*, 3269–3272. https://doi.org/10.1109/EMBC.2016.7591426

Li, Z., Moran, P., Dong, Q., Shaw, R. J., & Hauser, K. (2017). Development of a tele-nursing mobile manipulator for remote care-giving in quarantine areas. *2017 IEEE International Conference on Robotics and Automation (ICRA)*, 3581–3586. https://doi.org/10.1109/ICRA.2017.7989411

Macabasag, R. L. A., & Dino, M. J. S. (2018). Understanding the essence of caring from the lived experiences of Filipino informatics nurses. *Nursing Science Quarterly, 31*(2), 166–174. https://doi.org/10.1177/0894318418755732

Mantas, J., Hasman, A., Zoulias, E., Karitis, K., Gallos, P., Diomidous, M., Zogas, S., Charalampidou, M., Kushniruk, A. W., Nair, H. S., & Borycki, E. M. (2025). The pepper robot in healthcare: A scoping review. In *Studies in Health Technology and Informatics*. IOS Press. https://ebooks.iospress.nl/doi/10.3233/SHTI250057

Martins, J. C. A., Mazzo, A., Baptista, R. C. N., Coutinho, V. R. D., Godoy, S. D., Mendes, I. A. C., & Trevizan, M. A. (2012). The simulated clinical experience in nursing education: A historical review. *Acta Paulista de Enfermagem, 25*(4), 619–625. https://doi.org/10.1590/S0103-21002012000400022

Matsumoto, K., Minato, J., Fuji Ren, & Kuroiwa, S. (2005). Estimating human emotions using wording and sentence patterns. *2005 IEEE International Conference on Information Acquisition*, 421–426. https://doi.org/10.1109/ICIA.2005.1635125

Miles, A., Hayden, S., Carnell, S., Halan, S., & Lok, B. (2020). What do speech pathology students gain from virtual patient interviewing? A WHO International Classification of Functioning Disability and Health (ICF) analysis. *BMJ Simulation and Technology Enhanced Learning*, bmjstel-2020-000616. https://doi.org/10.1136/bmjstel-2020-000616

Milgram, P., Takemura, H., Utsumi, A., & Kishino, F. (1995). *Augmented reality: A class of displays on the reality-virtuality continuum* (H. Das, Ed.; pp. 282–292). https://doi.org/10.1117/12.197321

Mohammad, H., Almarabeh, T., & Rajab, L. (2023). Rapid review of learning using hologram in higher education. *International Journal of Emerging Technologies in Learning (iJET), 18*(12), 242–247. https://doi.org/10.3991/ijet.v18i12.38913

Mori, M., MacDorman, K., & Kageki, N. (2012). The uncanny valley [From the Field]. *IEEE Robotics & Automation Magazine, 19*(2), 98–100. https://doi.org/10.1109/MRA.2012.2192811

Moro, C., Smith, J., & Stromberga, Z. (2019). Multimodal learning in health sciences and medicine: Merging technologies to enhance student learning and communication. In P. M. Rea (Ed.), *Biomedical Visualisation* (Vol. 1205, pp. 71–78). Springer International Publishing. https://doi.org/10.1007/978-3-030-31904-5_5

Moro, C., Stromberga, Z., Raikos, A., & Stirling, A. (2016). Combining virtual (Oculus Rift & Gear VR) and augmented reality with interactive applications to enhance tertiary medical and biomedical curricula. *SIGGRAPH ASIA 2016 Symposium on Education: Talks*, 1–2. https://doi.org/10.1145/2993363.2993364

Moyle, W., Jones, C., & Sung, B. (2020). Telepresence robots: Encouraging interactive communication between family carers and people with dementia. *Australasian Journal on Ageing, 39*(1). https://doi.org/10.1111/ajag.12713

Mukai, T., Hirano, S., Nakashima, H., Kato, Y., Sakaida, Y., Guo, S., & Hosoe, S. (2010). Development of a nursing-care assistant robot RIBA that can lift a human in its arms. *2010 IEEE/RSJ International Conference on Intelligent Robots and Systems*, 5996–6001. https://doi.org/10.1109/IROS.2010.5651735

Mukai, T., Hirano, S., Yoshida, M., Nakashima, H., Guo, S., & Hayakawa, Y. (2011). Tactile-based motion adjustment for the nursing-care assistant robot RIBA. *2011 IEEE International Conference on Robotics and Automation*, 5435–5441. https://doi.org/10.1109/ICRA.2011.5979559

Mukai, T., Onishi, M., Hirano, S., & Zhiwei, L. (2006). Development of Soft Areal Tactile Sensors for Human-Interactive Robots. *2006 5th IEEE Conference on Sensors*, 831–834. https://doi.org/10.1109/ICSENS.2007.355596

Mukherjee, S., Baral, M. M., Pal, S. K., Chittipaka, V., Roy, R., & Alam, K. (2022). Humanoid robot in healthcare: A Systematic Review and Future Research Directions. *2022 International Conference on Machine Learning, Big Data, Cloud and Parallel Computing (COM-IT-CON), 1*, 822–826. https://doi.org/10.1109/COM-IT-CON54601.2022.9850577

Nehring, W. M., & Lashley, F. R. (2004). Current use and opinions regarding human patient simulators in nursing education: An international survey. *Nursing Education Perspectives, 25*(5), 244–248.

Okano, T., Kitakoshi, D., & Suzuki, M. (2013). A preliminary study on preventive care system based on game playing with communication robots. *2013 Conference on Technologies and Applications of Artificial Intelligence*, 84–89. https://doi.org/10.1109/TAAI.2013.29

Ozturkcan, S., & Merdin-Uygur, E. (2022). Humanoid service robots: The future of healthcare? *Journal of Information Technology Teaching Cases, 12*(2), 163–169. https://doi.org/10.1177/20438869211003905

Palaganas, J. C., Epps, C., & Raemer, D. B. (2014). A history of simulation-enhanced interprofessional education. *Journal of Interprofessional Care, 28*(2), 110–115. https://doi.org/10.3109/13561820.2013.869198

Pandey, A. K., & Gelin, R. (2018). A mass-produced sociable humanoid robot: Pepper: The first machine of its kind. *IEEE Robotics & Automation Magazine*, *25*(3), 40–48. https://doi.org/10.1109/MRA.2018.2833157

Pepito, J. A., Ito, H., Betriana, F., Tanioka, T., & Locsin, R. C. (2020). Intelligent humanoid robots expressing artificial humanlike empathy in nursing situations. *Nursing Philosophy*, *21*(4). https://doi.org/10.1111/nup.12318

Pérez, P. J., Garcia-Zapirain, B., & Mendez-Zorrilla, A. (2015). Caregiver and social assistant robot for rehabilitation and coaching for the elderly. *Technology and Health Care*, *23*(3), 351–357. https://doi.org/10.3233/THC-150896

Phillips, E., Zhao, X., Ullman, D., & Malle, B. F. (2018). What is Human-like?: Decomposing Robots' Human-like Appearance Using the Anthropomorphic roBOT (ABOT) Database. *Proceedings of the 2018 ACM/IEEE International Conference on Human-Robot Interaction*, 105–113. https://doi.org/10.1145/3171221.3171268

Popescu, V. G., Burdea, G. C., Bouzit, M., & Hentz, V. R. (2000). A virtual-reality-based telerehabilitation system with force feedback. *IEEE Transactions on Information Technology in Biomedicine: A Publication of the IEEE Engineering in Medicine and Biology Society*, *4*(1), 45–51. https://doi.org/10.1109/4233.826858

Reinkensmeyer, D. J., Pang, T. J., Nessler, J. A., & Painter, C. C. (2001). *Java Therapy: Web-Based Robotic Rehabilitation.* https://wenku.baidu.com/view/48d4808ccc22bcd126ff0c44?pcf=2&bfetype=new&bfetype=new&_wkts_=1760046204995

Riva, G., & Gaggioli, A. (2009). Rehabilitation as empowerment: The role of advanced technologies. *Studies in Health Technology and Informatics*, *145*, 3–22.

Ronchi, M. R. (2020). *Vision for Social Robots: Human Perception and Pose Estimation* (Version Final) [California Institute of Technology; PDF]. https://doi.org/10.7907/N2V1-1G79

Rouleau, G., Wu, K., Parry, M., Richard, L., & Desveaux, L. (2024). Providing compassionate care in a virtual context: Qualitative exploration of Canadian primary care nurses' experiences. *DIGITAL HEALTH*, *10*, 20552076231224072. https://doi.org/10.1177/20552076231224072

Sato, M., Yasuhara, Y., Osaka, K., Ito, H., Dino, M. J. S., Ong, I. L., Zhao, Y., & Tanioka, T. (2020). Rehabilitation care with Pepper humanoid robot: A qualitative case study of older patients with schizophrenia and/or dementia in Japan. *Enfermería Clínica*, *30*, 32–36.

Shah, A., Guessi, M., Wali, S., Ware, P., McDonald, M., O'Sullivan, M., Posada, J. D., Ross, H., & Seto, E. (2021). The resilience of cardiac care through virtualized services during the COVID-19 pandemic: Case study of a heart function clinic. *JMIR Cardio*, *5*(1), e25277. https://doi.org/10.2196/25277

Shen, Y., Guo, D., Long, F., Mateos, L. A., Ding, H., Xiu, Z., Hellman, R. B., King, A., Chen, S., Zhang, C., & Tan, H. (2021). Robots under COVID-19 pandemic: A comprehensive survey. *IEEE Access*, *9*, 1590–1615. https://doi.org/10.1109/ACCESS.2020.3045792

Shorey, S., & Ng, E. D. (2021). The use of virtual reality simulation among nursing students and registered nurses: A systematic review. *Nurse Education Today*, *98*, 104662. https://doi.org/10.1016/j.nedt.2020.104662

Siah, R. C. J., Xu, P., Teh, C. L., & Kow, A. W. C. (2022). Evaluation of nursing students' efficacy, attitude, and confidence level in a perioperative setting using virtual-reality simulation. *Nursing Forum*, *57*(6), 1249–1257. https://doi.org/10.1111/nuf.12783

Siek, K. (2018). Expanding human computer interaction methods to understand user needs in the design process of personal health systems. *Yearbook of Medical Informatics*, *27*(01), 074–078. https://doi.org/10.1055/s-0038-1667073

Singleton, J. L., Remillard, E. T., Mitzner, T. L., & Rogers, W. A. (2019). Everyday technology use among older deaf adults. *Disability and Rehabilitation: Assistive Technology*, *14*(4), 325–332. https://doi.org/10.1080/17483107.2018.1447609

Skarbez, R., Smith, M., & Whitton, M. C. (2021). Revisiting milgram and kishino's reality-virtuality continuum. *Frontiers in Virtual Reality*, *2*, 647997. https://doi.org/10.3389/frvir.2021.647997

SoftBank Robotics. (2014, June 5). *What is Pepper*. SoftBank. https://www.softbank.jp/en/robot/

Søgaard Neilsen, A., & Wilson, R. L. (2019). Combining e-mental health intervention development with human computer interaction (HCI) design to enhance technology-facilitated recovery for people with depression and/or anxiety conditions: An integrative literature review. *International Journal of Mental Health Nursing, 28*(1), 22–39. https://doi.org/10.1111/inm.12527

Son, Y., Kang, H. S., & De Gagne, J. C. (2023). Nursing students' experience of using holopatient during the coronavirus disease 2019 pandemic: A qualitative descriptive study. *Clinical Simulation in Nursing, 80*, 9–16. https://doi.org/10.1016/j.ecns.2023.03.007

Stenseth, H. V., Steindal, S. A., Solberg, M. T., Ølnes, M. A., Sørensen, A. L., Strandell-Laine, C., Olaussen, C., Farsjø Aure, C., Pedersen, I., Zlamal, J., Gue Martini, J., Bresolin, P., Linnerud, S. C. W., & Nes, A. A. G. (2025). Simulation-based learning supported by technology to enhance critical thinking in nursing students: Scoping review. *Journal of Medical Internet Research, 27*, e58744. https://doi.org/10.2196/58744

Strohmann, T., Siemon, D., Khosrawi-Rad, B., & Robra-Bissantz, S. (2023). Toward a design theory for virtual companionship. *Human–Computer Interaction, 38*(3–4), 194–234. https://doi.org/10.1080/07370024.2022.2084620

Stuart, J., Aul, K., Bumbach, M. D., Stephen, A., & Lok, B. (2021). Building a handoff communication virtual experience for nursing students using virtual humans. *CIN Computers, Informatics, Nursing, 39*(12), 1017–1026. https://doi.org/10.1097/CIN.0000000000000760

Sumargono, E., Anastasia, M., Saleh, I., & Kholinne, E. (2022). The role of virtual clinics in postoperative total knee replacement surgery follow-up during COVID-19 pandemic. *Advances in Orthopedics, 2022*, 1–5. https://doi.org/10.1155/2022/9558511

Takacs, B., & Hanak, D. (2008). A prototype home robot with an ambient facial interface to improve drug compliance. *Journal of Telemedicine and Telecare, 14*(7), 393–395. https://doi.org/10.1258/jtt.2008.007016

Tanioka, R., Yasuhara, Y., Osaka, K., Kai, Y., Zhao, Y., Tanioka, T., Takase, K., Dino, M. J. S., & Locsin, R. C. (2020). Autonomic nervous activity of patient with schizophrenia during Pepper CPGE-led upper limb range of motion exercises. *Enfermeria Clinica, 30*, 48–53.

Tanioka, T. (2019). Nursing and rehabilitative care of the elderly using humanoid robots. *The Journal of Medical Investigation, 66*(1.2), 19–23. https://doi.org/10.2152/jmi.66.19

Tanioka, T., Yasuhara, Y., Dino, M. J. S., Kai, Y., Locsin, R. C., & Schoenhofer, S. O. (2019). Disruptive engagements with technologies, robotics, and caring: Advancing the transactive relationship theory of nursing. *Nursing Administration Quarterly, 43*(4), 313–321. https://doi.org/10.1097/NAQ.0000000000000365

Tanioka, T., Yasuhara, Y., Ōsaka, K., Itō, H., Locsin, R. C., Gomez, M., Schoenhofer, S. O., Bollos, L. V., & Fukurō Shuppan Publishing. (2017). *Nursing Robots: Robotic Technology and Human Caring for the Elderly*. Fukuro Shuppan Publishing, Okayama, Japan.

Tanioka, T., Yokotani, T., Tanioka, R., Betriana, F., Matsumoto, K., Locsin, R., Zhao, Y., Osaka, K., Miyagawa, M., & Schoenhofer, S. (2021). Development issues of healthcare robots: Compassionate communication for older adults with dementia. *International Journal of Environmental Research and Public Health, 18*(9), 4538. https://doi.org/10.3390/ijerph18094538

Torbatinezhad, H., Department of Educational Sciences, Farhangian University, Imam Khomeini Campus of Gorgan, Iran, Amani, H., & Department of Educational Sciences, Payam Noor University of Damghan, Iran. (2018). Computer-Assisted Instruction (CAI), Virtual Patients (VP), and Human Patient Simulation (HPS) in Medical Education Based on Gagne's Educational Design Pattern. *Jorjani Biomedicine Journal, 6*(2), 1–20. https://doi.org/10.29252/jorjanibiomedj.6.2.1

Tsai, T.-C., Hsu, Y.-L., Ma, A.-I., King, T., & Wu, C.-H. (2007). Developing a telepresence robot for interpersonal communication with the elderly in a home environment. *Telemedicine and E-Health, 13*(4), 407–424. https://doi.org/10.1089/tmj.2006.0068

Tseng, L.-P., Hou, T.-H., Huang, L.-P., & Ou, Y.-K. (2021). Effectiveness of applying clinical simulation scenarios and integrating information technology in medical-surgical nursing and critical nursing courses. *BMC Nursing, 20*(1), 229. https://doi.org/10.1186/s12912-021-00744-7

University of Cambridge. (2022, June 28). *'Hologram patients' developed to help train doctors and nurses.* https://www.cam.ac.uk/research/news/hologram-patients-developed-to-help-train-doctors-and-nurses

van der Putte, D., Boumans, R., Neerincx, M., Rikkert, M. O., & de Mul, M. (2019). A social robot for autonomous health data acquisition among hospitalized patients: An exploratory field study. *2019 14th ACM/IEEE International Conference on Human-Robot Interaction (HRI)*, 658–659. https://doi.org/10.1109/HRI.2019.8673280

Wang, X. V., & Wang, L. (2021). A literature survey of the robotic technologies during the COVID-19 pandemic. *Journal of Manufacturing Systems, 60*, 823–836. https://doi.org/10.1016/j.jmsy.2021.02.005

Wästlund, E., Sponseller, K., Pettersson, O., & Bared, A. (2015). Evaluating gaze-driven power wheelchair with navigation support for persons with disabilities. *Journal of Rehabilitation Research and Development, 52*(7), 815–826. https://doi.org/10.1682/JRRD.2014.10.0228

Wood, D. (2011). No longer rocket science: Robots have found their place in healthcare. *Telemedicine and E-Health, 17*(6), 409–414. https://doi.org/10.1089/tmj.2011.9981

XR Today. (2022). *NUS Medical School Adopts Microsoft HoloLens 2.* https://www.xrtoday.com/mixed-reality/nus-medical-school-adopts-microsoft-hololens-2/

Yasemin, M., Kasımoğlu, Y., Kocaaydın, S., Karslı, E., İnce, E. B. T., & İnce, G. (2016). Management of dental anxiety in children using robots. *2016 24th Signal Processing and Communication Application Conference (SIU)*, 237–240. https://doi.org/10.1109/SIU.2016.7495721

Zsiga, K., Tóth, A., Pilissy, T., Péter, O., Dénes, Z., & Fazekas, G. (2018). Evaluation of a companion robot based on field tests with single older adults in their homes. *Assistive Technology, 30*(5), 259–266. https://doi.org/10.1080/10400435.2017.1322158

# Chapter 13

# Telehealth Evolution towards Virtual Integrated Care

Mary Joy Garcia-Dia

## Introduction

At a recent healthcare conference, I conducted a poll where 70 participants participated. The results revealed the top three workplace challenges currently facing healthcare professionals. The foremost concern was burnout and workforce shortages (average rank: 1.74), reflecting the ongoing difficulties hospitals face in maintaining adequate nurse staffing to meet patient care demands (Steaban et al., 2024). Closely following were rising healthcare costs and resource constraints (1.67), which continue to strain budgets, staffing, and supply chains. Inefficiencies in care delivery (1.10), such as delays in admissions and fragmented workflows, also emerged as persistent issues impacting patient flow and satisfaction. Although ranked lower (0.86), disparities in health equity and access remain a critical long-term concern, particularly as they intersect with social determinants of health.

These findings underscore the systemic pressures that healthcare environments continue to face, affecting both the mental well-being of clinical teams and leadership's goals, in general, in driving effective changes in a post-pandemic world.

When asked to identify emerging technologies that could help address these challenges, participants highlighted a range of innovations. These included electronic medical records (EMRs), clinical automation tools, and integrated technologies such as GPS apps, voice assistants like Siri, and smart home devices. Artificial intelligence (AI), the metaverse, and deep learning with speech recognition were also highly ranked. Telemedicine—encompassing hospital-at-home (HAH) programs, health trackers, smartwatches, and telesitting—stood out as a particularly promising and enduring solution (See Figure 13.1).

These responses align with the White House Office of Science and Technology Policy's broad definition of digital health technologies as tools that enhance health or healthcare delivery by connecting people with each other, with data, or with health information (Eswaran et al., 2022). Examples include telehealth, remote monitoring devices, mobile health apps, and electronic health records (EHRs).

 DOI: 10.4324/9781003464457-13

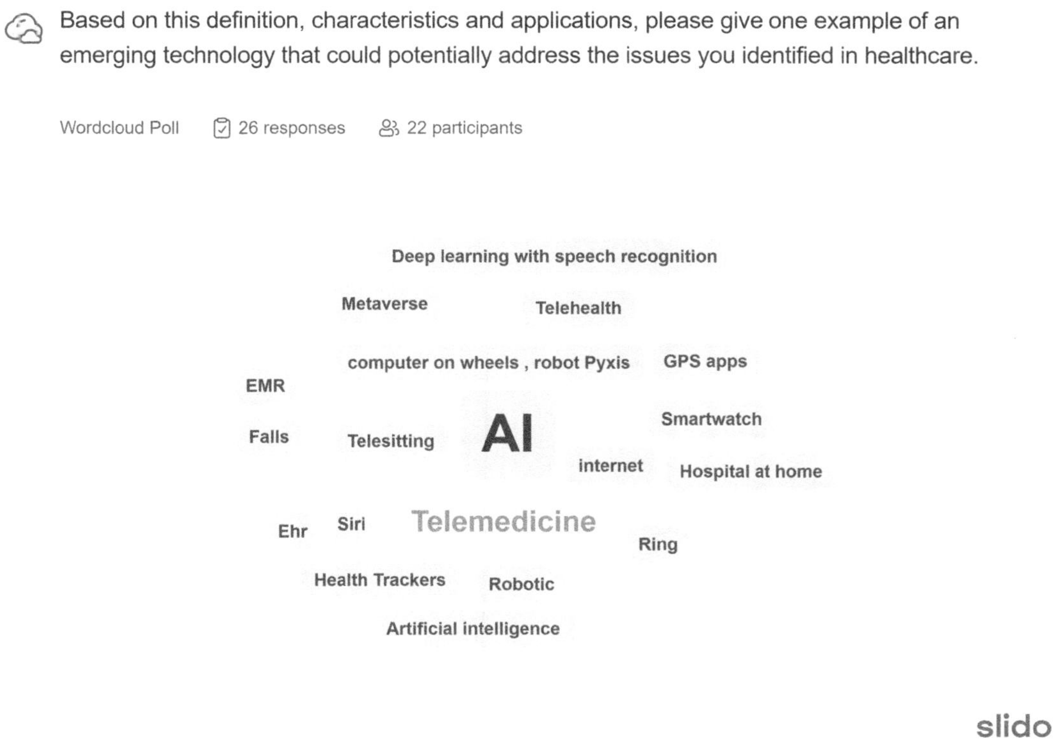


**Figure 13.1 Slido Poll Word Cloud Response: Example of an emerging technology that could potentially address the issues in healthcare (Garcia-Dia, 2025).**

As healthcare continues to evolve, innovation is increasingly driven by a diverse ecosystem of emerging technologies. Wu & Junior (2023) describe the modern healthcare system as a dynamic web of interconnected tools—from wearable devices and smartphones to AI-powered smart home systems. Unlike traditional technologies, emerging solutions are often complex and uncertain, making their evaluation and implementation extremely challenging.

Among the technologies identified, AI and telehealth/telemedicine emerged as the top two. This chapter focuses on the evolution of telehealth and the development of virtual care models since the COVID-19 pandemic. A separate chapter will explore the role of AI in healthcare.

## From Telehealth to Virtual Care

When we think of emerging technologies in healthcare, the concept of *innovation* often comes to mind. According to Merriam-Webster (2025), innovation refers to something new or a change made to an existing product, idea, or field. In a recent word cloud exercise, participants were asked to describe innovation in one word (See Figure 13.2). The most common responses were "advancement" and "progress," followed by terms like "efficiency," "improvement," "collaboration," and "future." These responses reflect the dynamic and transformative nature of digital technologies, many of which are rooted in telehealth practice, where clinicians consult with each other or communicate with the patients or family members through audio/video tools.

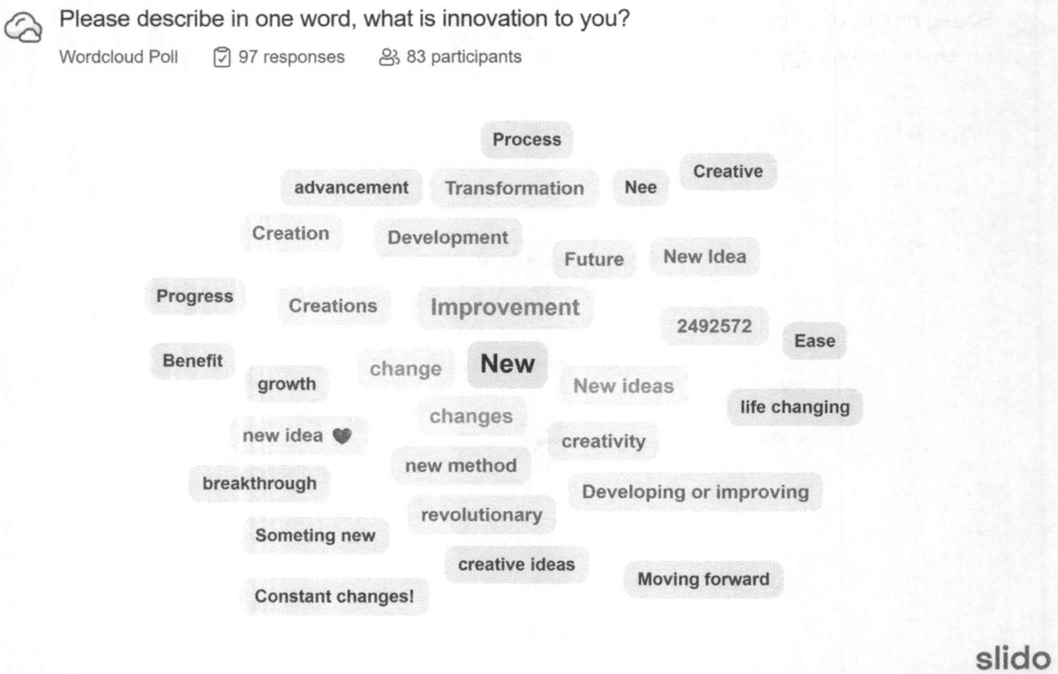


**Figure 13.2 Slido Poll Word Cloud Response: What is innovation to you? (Garcia-Dia, 2025).**

Telehealth has become a cornerstone of healthcare innovation, especially in the wake of the COVID-19 pandemic. It encompasses a wide range of services and tools that enable remote care, including videoconferencing, remote patient monitoring (RPM), and mobile health applications. These technologies have not only expanded access to care but also redefined how healthcare is delivered, shifting from traditional in-person visits to virtual interactions. The evolution from telehealth to *virtual care* represents a broader transformation. While telehealth often refers to specific technologies or services, virtual care encompasses a more integrated, patient-centered approach. It includes real-time video visits, asynchronous messaging, remote monitoring, and digital tools that support continuous engagement between patients and providers.

This shift has also redefined the role of nurses and other healthcare professionals. Nurses are now leveraging telehealth tools to deliver care, educate patients, and coordinate services in ways that were not possible before. As more consumers adopt mobile devices and digital health tools, the demand for virtual care continues to grow, extending care beyond hospital walls and into patients' homes and daily lives. In the following sections, we will explore how virtual care is being implemented across different settings, the technologies enabling this transformation, and the best practices that support its success.

## Telehealth

The United States Office of the National Coordinator for Health Information Technology (ONC) defines *telehealth* as the use of videoconferencing, RPM, store-and-forward technologies (such as sending wound images for evaluation), and mobile health (mHealth) applications (Groom et al., 2021). These tools enable healthcare providers to deliver care remotely, expanding access and improving efficiency.

*Telemedicine*, a term often used interchangeably with telehealth, refers specifically to clinical services delivered remotely. It originates from the Greek word *tele* (meaning "distance") and the Latin *medicus* (meaning "physician"), essentially translating to "healing at a distance" (Rampton et al., 2022). While some organizations distinguish between the two, defining telehealth as the broader category that includes non-clinical services such as education and administration, legislation often uses the terms interchangeably (Eswaran et al., 2022).

The World Health Organization (WHO) uses the term *digital health* as an umbrella concept that includes telehealth, telemedicine, mobile health, EHRs, and health data systems (Eswaran et al., 2022). While patients may not differentiate between these terms, it is essential for healthcare professionals, researchers, and policymakers to understand their distinctions. These definitions influence care delivery models, regulatory frameworks, and reimbursement policies.

Telehealth gained significant momentum during the COVID-19 pandemic, becoming a vital component of primary care. It enabled virtual consultations, remote monitoring, and digital communication between patients and providers (Srivastava et al., 2023). According to Lebar et al. (2022), telehealth integrates electronic information and telecommunications technologies to enhance healthcare access, improve outcomes, reduce costs, and address longstanding barriers to care. Through telehealth, patients and their families can consult with providers, receive diagnoses, manage treatments, and access prescriptions, all from the comfort of their homes (ATA, 2020). This shift has empowered patients to become active participants in their care and has transformed traditional face-to-face interactions into dynamic, virtual engagements.

As telehealth continues to evolve, so does the role of nurses. Nurses are increasingly using telehealth tools to deliver care, educate patients, and support clinical teams. At the same time, the widespread adoption of mobile technology, including older populations, has accelerated consumer engagement in digital health. According to Wnag and Cohen (2022), 58.5% of adults used the Internet to look for health or medical information during July–December 2022, with a higher prevalence observed among women compared with men.

The expansion of care beyond hospital walls through remote monitoring and virtual visits has become a defining trend. Most healthcare organizations have now integrated virtual care into their service models, a shift that was rapidly accelerated by the pandemic.

## Virtual Care

The American Telemedicine Association (ATA) defines *virtual care* as healthcare services delivered remotely, allowing patients to receive care from the comfort and safety of their homes (ATA, 2020). Virtual care builds upon the foundation of telehealth by integrating a broader range of digital tools and services. These include videoconferencing, mobile apps, remote monitoring devices, and eHealth platforms.

Virtual care encompasses four primary modes of interaction: asynchronous communication, chat, phone, and video visits (ATA, 2020). Table 13.1 outlines four primary types of interaction utilized during telehealth services or virtual care, each with a description and the tools used to deliver them. This highlights the "people, process, technology" framework when implementing virtual care. There is a myriad of tools available that can support the interaction between patients, family, provider, and the clinical team.

**Table 13.1 Type of Interaction and Tools Used in Virtual Care**

| *Type of Interaction* | *Description* | *Tools* |
|---|---|---|
| **Virtual Visits** | Real-time, synchronous, and interactive meetings between a patient and a healthcare provider. | Video, telephone, and live chat |
| **Chat-Based Interactions** | Asynchronous communication where personal health data, vital signs, and diagnostic images are sent for later review. | Online platforms (e.g., email), mobile applications |
| **Remote Patient Monitoring (RPM)** | Continuous collection and transmission of health data from outside clinical settings, enabling chronic disease management and early intervention. | Wearable sensors, wireless devices, smartphones, and mobile apps |
| **Technology-Enabled Modalities** | Tools that support digital diagnostics, therapeutic interventions, and disease prevention. | Personal health devices, sensors, AI-enabled platforms, and machine learning |

Depending on the project's workflow, purpose, and targeted outcome, virtual care programs can combine synchronous and asynchronous modalities, enhanced by integration and decision support tools, while considering patient literacy, access, security, and privacy. The goal is to create a seamless, patient-centered experience that supports ongoing engagement and care coordination (Sabira et al., 2023).

Historically, nurses have played a pivotal role in telehealth. *Telenursing* began in the 1970s with nurses answering health-related questions by phone (Rutledge & Gustin, 2021). Today, telehealth nursing includes a wide range of responsibilities—from presenting patients to remote clinicians to designing and managing virtual care programs. According to the American Nurses Association (ATA, 2018), telehealth nursing is an essential component of ambulatory care, supporting individuals, families, and communities in non-acute settings (Rutledge and Gustin, 2021).

The COVID-19 pandemic significantly accelerated the adoption of virtual care. Healthcare systems implemented telehealth initiatives to address workforce shortages, reduce burnout, and improve both patient and provider satisfaction. As a result, the number of nurses delivering virtual care has grown substantially in response to the ongoing adoption and expansion of virtual integrated care programs enterprise-wide (Dicello et al., 2024; Nguyen et al., 2024). Interprofessional teamwork is crucial for addressing project readiness and change management challenges and opportunities (Dicello et al., 2024; Milton et al., 2022).

## Case Study

Using Walker and Avant's framework, the concept of teamwork and interprofessional collaboration will be utilized to showcase clinical and project scenarios in the following case studies (Bakht et al.,

2024). A model case illustrated these attributes in clinical settings, showing teamwork's impact on patient outcomes. Additional cases highlighted varying adherence to these attributes and their effects on teamwork effectiveness using related, contrary, and borderline cases.

## Virtual Nursing

*Virtual nursing* refers to the delivery of acute care services remotely, using digital technologies to support patients, families, and bedside care teams. Virtual nurses perform essential clinical tasks such as admission interviews, documentation, patient rounding, and discharge planning—all without being physically present at the bedside. This model enhances care delivery by reducing the workload on in-person staff and improving workflow efficiency. For virtual nursing to be successful, it must be grounded in the principles of effective teamwork. According to Bakht, Mir and Shah (2024), key attributes of high-functioning healthcare teams include communication, collaboration, trust, respect, shared decision-making, accountability, and flexibility. These qualities are especially critical in virtual environments, where coordination across physical and digital spaces is essential.

### *Model Case Study: Teamwork in Virtual Admission*

Using an interprofessional framework, a pilot program was launched to implement virtual nursing in a hospital setting. MJ, a 59-year-old emergency department nurse with over 15 years of experience, was selected to lead virtual admissions and discharges for medical-surgical units. MJ was initially unsure about using SmartScreen TV technology with patients, but received support from a nursing informatics specialist and a nurse educator. Her training emphasized the importance of communication—listening to patient concerns, interpreting verbal and non-verbal cues, and maintaining the same standard of care as in face-to-face interactions. Building trust with bedside nurses, patients, and families was a key focus. The emphasis with the virtual nursing workflow is that it is designed to reduce documentation burden, support administrative work at the bedside, and augment staffing.

MJ began each shift by rounding virtually, identifying patients ready for discharge, and collaborating with bedside nurses to update the admission lists. Inclusion and exclusion criteria were provided to help determine which patients were suitable for virtual care. Despite initial nervousness about using dual monitors and a headset, MJ quickly adapted. The IT department and nursing informatics team ensured high-quality audio and video connections, allowing her to conduct assessments and complete documentation efficiently. On the first day of implementation, the virtual nursing team, including IT, nursing operations, patient experience, and leadership, provided full support to ensure a smooth rollout. MJ successfully completed her virtual assessments and received positive feedback from both patients and staff. One patient noted in a satisfaction survey that they would gladly use a virtual nurse again. Bedside nurses expressed appreciation, with one remarking, "Having back-to-back admissions was tough—you saved my day!" The pilot demonstrated how virtual nursing, when supported by strong teamwork and infrastructure, can enhance care delivery as well as patient and staff satisfaction. Virtual care is not just a temporary solution—it represents a fundamental shift in how healthcare is delivered. By leveraging technology, healthcare providers can extend their reach, improve access, and deliver high-quality care in innovative and efficient ways.

## Remote Patient Monitoring

Remote Patient Monitoring (RPM) is a key component of virtual care, enabling healthcare providers to track patients' health data outside traditional clinical settings. This approach is especially valuable for managing chronic conditions such as hypertension and diabetes, where continuous monitoring can lead to early intervention, reduce readmission in the emergency department, and improve outcomes.

### Related Case Study: RPM Pilot for Hypertension and Diabetes

In a collaborative initiative, the academic medical center launched an RPM program in partnership with emergency department providers, nurse leaders, nursing informatics specialists, and the digital health team. The initiative targeted patients newly diagnosed with hypertension or diabetes, aiming to support them in managing their conditions at home. A steering committee worked with a telehealth software company in designing a patient-centered workflow. The program included:

- *Defining inclusion and exclusion criteria* with input from clinical subject matter experts.
- *Recruit participants* by coordinating with patient experience, providers, and nursing teams.
- *Setting up home monitoring equipment*, including blood pressure cuffs, glucose monitors, and iPads for connectivity in coordination with a third-party vendor.
- *Establishing remote monitoring protocols*, allowing virtual clinical nurses to remotely track patients' data and intervene when necessary.

Patients were enrolled in the program prior to discharge and monitored for 30 days. Of the 22 participants, 16 completed the 30-day monitoring period. The results were promising: 90% of participants said they would recommend the program, and the average care satisfaction rating was 4.6 out of 5. Patients appreciated the sense of security that came from knowing a care team was reviewing their health data daily. If a patient's vital signs or responses to assessment questions were outside the expected range, a virtual nurse would notify the provider team and initiate a follow-up via video or phone call.

To understand why some patients did not complete the program, the team conducted follow-up interviews. Common barriers included:

- *Busy schedules*, leading to missed check-ins for three or more consecutive days.
- *Requests for compensation*, despite the service being offered at no cost.
- *Travel or vacations*, which disrupted routine monitoring.
- *Perceived inconvenience*, with some patients finding the process cumbersome.

These findings highlight that while RPM can enhance care delivery, patient engagement is influenced by individual values, priorities, and attitudes toward health. Even with strong clinical support, adherence to remote monitoring depends on the patient's willingness and ability to integrate the program into their daily life.

## Telesitting

*Telesitting* is a remote patient observation system that uses two-way audio and video technology to monitor patients in real time. These systems are designed to enhance patient safety, particularly for individuals at risk of falls, disorientation, or self-harm. A visual indicator signals that monitoring is active, and while the system allows for live observation, it does not record audio or video, preserving patient privacy. Depending on the facility's infrastructure, telesitting systems may include advanced features such as AI-assisted sensors, ambient listening, and computer vision. These improvements enable a single telesitter to monitor multiple patients, with ratios ranging from 1:12 to up to 1:50 patients per observer. Telesitting platforms can work independently as a standalone system or integrate with nurse call systems and EHR application, depending on the design configuration and system infrastructure.

Telesitting is commonly used for patients with conditions such as delirium, dementia, or those with medical devices like central lines that could be accidentally dislodged. The goal is to reduce fall rates and alleviate the burden on bedside staff, allowing them to focus on direct care tasks.

### Contrary Case Study: Telesitting in Practice

When the telesitting program was introduced on Adam's unit, he collaborated with telesitter Gemma to assess the needs of a new patient, Mr. Diaz. A 69-year-old Hispanic male with early-onset dementia. Mr. Diaz had been transferred from a skilled nursing facility due to fever and was being evaluated for pneumonia. He met the criteria for telesitting and was enrolled in the virtual observation program.

Gemma and Adam reviewed Mr. Diaz's clinical profile, including his diet, activity level, IV lines, and preferred language (Spanish). Despite meeting the inclusion criteria, Mr. Diaz's cognitive impairment posed challenges. He frequently attempted to get out of bed and did not respond well to verbal redirection. During the trial, Gemma had to repeatedly alert Adam to intervene. At one point, she activated the emergency alarm to summon immediate assistance. It became clear that Mr. Diaz required a physical 1:1 sitter at the bedside for his safety.

This case illustrates that while telesitting can be effective for many patients, it is not universally suitable. Patients with severe disorientation or limited responsiveness may not benefit from remote monitoring alone. A hybrid approach—combining telesitting with frequent in-person rounding—may be appropriate in some cases, but others will require continuous bedside supervision. Review of literature has showcased the continuous use of telesitting in potentially enhancing patient safety by reducing falls with injuries and is considered acceptable and useful by nurses in general (Ergai et al., 2024).

## Hospital-at-Home

*Hospital-at-Home (HAH)* is an innovative care model that delivers hospital-level services to patients in their own homes. As an emerging transformative model in modern healthcare delivery, HAH offers acute-level services in the comfort of patients' homes. This approach is designed for individuals who meet specific clinical criteria and do not require intensive inpatient resources. HAH programs aim to reduce hospital admissions, improve patient satisfaction, and lower healthcare costs while maintaining high standards of care.

### Planning and Implementing a Hospital-at-Home Program

The planning and implementation of HAH requires a thorough environmental scan and gap analysis. Based on lessons learned, a detailed project plan outlines the scope, logistics, and operational strategies essential for its success (Falchenberg et al., 2024).

**Key Components of the HAH Program:**

1. *Target Population*: Adults aged 18 and older who are clinically stable and do not require advanced hospital-based interventions. Examples include patients needing IV therapy or wound care.
2. *Geographic Coverage*: Patients must reside within a five-mile radius of the hospital to ensure timely access to care and emergency services.
3. *Operational Hours*: Weekdays from 7:30 AM to 4:00 PM. Off-hours and weekends are supported by an emergency contact line or 911 services (a universal emergency call number in North America connecting individuals to reach police, fire, or emergency medical assistance).
4. *Staffing Model*: A multidisciplinary team including nurse practitioners or physician assistants, registered nurses, emergency medical technicians, attending physicians, and case managers or social workers.
5. *Transportation*: Ambulance services are used for patient transport and urgent needs.
6. *Medical Equipment and Supplies*: Includes vital sign monitors, oxygen tanks, wound care materials, diagnostic tools, emergency medications, and personal protective equipment.
7. *Technology and Documentation*: Providers use laptops or tablets with Wi-Fi access to connect to the EHR system. Documentation includes provider notes, nursing flowsheets, medication administration records (MAR), and patient education materials.

**Workflow and Coordination:**

- Patients are triaged in the emergency department or inpatient units to determine eligibility.
- Once enrolled, care is coordinated through dispatch services, case management, and patient access teams.
- The program includes protocols for emergency escalation and transfer to inpatient care if needed.

## Facilitators and Barriers

*Facilitators* to successful implementation include strong leadership support, seamless integration with existing EHR systems, and adequate technical infrastructure. Clinicians reported benefits such as improved care timeliness, better access to specialists, and enhanced family involvement.

*Barriers* included technical issues (e.g., poor audio quality, device charging), reimbursement challenges, and limited staffing for telemedicine roles. Patients and families also cited difficulties with Internet connectivity and a preference for in-person visits. Despite these obstacles, HAH programs have demonstrated potential in minimizing unnecessary hospital transfers, enhancing patient satisfaction, and ensuring continuity of care.

### *Borderline Case: Transitioning from Inpatient to a Home Environment*

This case study explores the practical implementation, challenges, and outcomes of such programs, focusing on the experience of DD and her mother, FD, as they navigated home-based healthcare while addressing barriers and utilizing facilitators.

FD, an 80-year-old woman diagnosed with pneumonia, also suffers from several co-morbidities, including diabetes, hypertension, and a cardiac stent post-coronary heart disease diagnosis. DD, the identified caregiver, opted for the HAH program to continue FD's intravenous (IV) antibiotic treatment at home. For DD, the program offered the benefit of treating her mother in a familiar environment, where her sister could assist due to proximity.

DD was comfortable with the HAH program when it was offered to them in continuing her mother's IV antibiotic treatment at home. She expressed that her mother would be more comfortable in a familiar environment, and her sister, who lives in the same apartment building, can easily walk over to her mother's place. A visiting nurse administers the IV antibiotic while a provider calls in using a hospital-issued laptop. In FD's case, her second-floor bedroom posed logistical challenges, necessitating the conversion of the living room into a "hospital room," which lacked conveniences like bedside tables, call bells, or sharps disposal units. Despite these obstacles, DD recognized the program's potential for minimizing hospital transfers and improving her mother's comfort and satisfaction.

The experience of DD and FD illustrates the importance of thoughtful implementation in achieving the goals of HAH programs. By leveraging advanced monitoring technologies, personalized interventions, and coordinated workflows, healthcare providers can meet the clinical and emotional needs of patients and their families effectively. DD noted her mother's improved comfort in a familiar environment, enhanced family engagement, and the convenience of at-home care.

For HAH programs to succeed, guidelines that ensure quality, safety, and consistency across care environments are essential. Implementation must align with robust change management strategies, project planning, IT infrastructure, staff training, and outcome evaluation. Interdisciplinary collaboration and continuous improvement remain central to integrating these models seamlessly into standard practices.

This case highlights the transformative potential of HAH programs when innovation is paired with practical strategies. When thoughtfully implemented, HAH can offer a scalable solution for delivering safe, quality care in the home environment.

## Conclusion

Telemedicine and virtual care are no longer emerging trends—they are now integral components of modern healthcare delivery. The rapid expansion of telehealth during the COVID-19 pandemic demonstrated its potential to improve access, enhance patient outcomes, and support overburdened healthcare systems. As digital health technologies continue to evolve, they offer scalable, patient-centered solutions that extend care beyond traditional clinical settings.

While the long-term vision is to integrate telemedicine seamlessly into standard care practices, current guidelines remain essential. These frameworks help ensure quality, safety, and consistency across diverse care environments. As healthcare organizations adopt virtual care models, it is critical to align implementation with robust change management strategies, project planning, IT infrastructure, staff training, and outcome evaluation.

Ultimately, the success of telehealth and virtual care depends on thoughtful integration, interdisciplinary collaboration, and a commitment to continuous improvement. By embracing innovation and leveraging technology, healthcare systems can meet the demands of today while preparing for the challenges of tomorrow.

## References

American Telemedicine Association (2018). *Telehealth nursing fact sheet.* ATA (American Telehealth Association) Telehealth Nursing Special Interest Group.

American Telemedicine Association (2020). Telehealth: Defining 21st century care. https://marketing.americantelemed.org/hubfs/Files/Resources/ATA_Telehealth_Taxonomy_9-11-20.pdf

Bakht, K., Mir, S., & Shah, S. A. (2024). Nursing teamwork: An in-depth concept analysis with Walker & Avant's framework. *Journal of Health and Rehabilitation Research*, 4(2), 1500–1505. https://doi.org/10.61919/jhrr.v4i2.1118

Dicello, D., Evans, R., Ferguson, S., Garcia-Dia, M. J., Manzano, W., Prado-Inzerillo, M., & Radosta, M. (2024). Virtual nursing to improve patient and team member experiences at NewYork-Presbyterian hospital. *New England Journal of Medicine*, 5(10). https://doi.org/10.1056/cat.23.0313

Ergai, A., Spiva, L., Thurman, S., Hatfield, M., McCollum, M., & Holmes, M. (2024). The Effectiveness of Remote Video Monitoring on Fall Prevention and Nurses' Acceptance. *Journal of Nursing Care Quality*, 39(1), 24–30. https://doi.org/10.1097/NCQ.0000000000000716

Eswaran, H., Dawson, L., Hernandez, M., Shoults, C., Hayes, C., Bogulski, C., & Allison, K. (2022). Telehealth: Current trends and definitions. *Rural Telehealth Evaluation Center*. Available at: https://idhi.uams.edu/rtec/wp-content/uploads/sites/4/2022/05/Telehealth-Definitions-Paper-06MAY2022-1.pdf. Accessed May 23, 2025.

Falchenberg, Å., Andersson, U., Boysen, G.N., Andersson, H., & Sterner, A. (2024 Sep 16). Hybrid emergency care at the home for patients - A multiple case study. *BMC Emergency Medicine*, 24(1), 169. https://doi.org/10.1186/s12873-024-01087-7. PMID: 39285362; PMCID: PMC11406757.

Garcia-Dia. (2025, June 27). Applications of AI in Nursing Education and Practice. [PowerPoint slides].

Groom, L. L., McCarthy, M. M., Witkowski-Stimpfel, A., & Bordy, A. A. (2021). Telemedicine and telehealth in nursing homes: An integrative review. *The Journal of the Post-Acute and Long-term Care Medical Association*, 22, 1784–1801. https://doi.org/10.1016/j.jamda.2021.02.037

Lebar, K., Chandra, S., & Hollander, J. E. (2022). Role of nursing in telehealth. *Nursing* 52(6), 42–126. Available at Role of nursing in telehealth Nursing: June 2022.

Merriam-Webster (2025). Innovation. Retrieved from https://www.merriam-webster.com/dictionary/innovation

Milton, J.M., Gillespie, B., Åberg, D., Erichsen Andersson, A. & Oxelmark L. (2022). Interprofessional teamwork before and after organizational change in a tertiary emergency department: An observational study. *Journal of Interprofessional Care*, 37(2), 300–311. https://doi.org/10.1080/13561820.2022.2065250

Nguyen, N. A., Holderread, B. M., & Pletcher, S. N. (2024). Virtual nursing initiatives in an urban hospital system: A discussion of successful interventions and future directions. *Telehealth and Medicine Today.* https://doi.org/10.30953/thmt.v9.530

Pew Research Center. (2024, November 13). *Internet, Broadband Fact Sheet*. https://www.pewresearch.org/internet/fact-sheet/internet-broadband/

Rampton, V., Bohmer, M., & Winkler, A. (2022). Medical Technologies Past and Present: How History Helps to Understand the Digital Era. *The Journal of Medical Humanities*, 43(2), 343–364. https://doi.org/10.1007/s10912-021-09699-x

Rutledge, C. M., & Gustin, T. (2021). Preparing nurses for roles in telehealth: Now is the time! *Online Journal of Issues in Nursing*, 26(1). https://doi.org/10.3912/OJIN.Vol26No01Man03

Sabira, F., Gupta, A., Gilbert, C., Huggins, C. E., Browning, C., Chapman, W., Haines, T., & Peeters, A. (2023). Virtual care initiatives for older adults in Australia: Scoping review. *Journal of Medical Internet Research*, 25, e38081. https://doi.org/10.2196/38081

Srivastava D., Van Kessel R., Delgrange M., Cherla A., Sood H., & Mossialos E (2023). A framework for digital health policy: Insights from virtual primary care systems across five nations. PLOS Digit *Health* 2(11), e0000382. https://journals.plos.org/digitalhealth/article?id=10.1371%2Fjournal.pdig.0000382

Steaban, R. I., Morrison, J., Simmons, S., Ivory, C., France, D., Leming-Lee, S., Hollingsworth, E. K., & Kleinpell, K. (2024). Strategies to evaluate new models of nursing care to meet hospital staffing and patient care needs. *Nurse Leader*. https://doi.org/10.1016/j.mnl.2024.05.007

Wnag, X. & Cohen, R. A. (2022). Health information technology use among adults: United States, July–December 2022. NCHS Data Brief No. 482. Retrieved from https://www.cdc.gov/nchs/data/databriefs/db482.pdf

Wu, S. & Junior, B.M. (2023). Emerging technologies and global health: A systematic review generating bibliometric evidence for innovation management. *BMJ Innovations*, 9, 165–176.

# Chapter 14

# The Evolving Role of Nurses in Informatics and Healthcare

Olga Kagan

## Introduction

This chapter focuses on exploring the value of nursing informatics (NI) and its crucial role in healthcare, particularly emphasizing education and preparing nurses for a digital future. It will delve into how NI enhances efficiency, quality of care, and decision-making processes, while also discussing educational strategies and leadership roles critical for leveraging technology in nursing practice.

## The Value of Nursing Informatics

Previous chapters offered the definition of NI and its importance in healthcare transformation as the field of NI continues to evolve. Before computers entered healthcare, NI pioneers (American Medical Informatics Association, n.d.) have recognized the inefficiencies of paper-based documentation, especially for data-driven knowledge generation and its dissemination on a larger scale as well as for capturing and codifying the work of nurses. Nurses' efforts in standardizing the language for nursing practice has shown to be most needed with the development of the electronic health records (EHR) and even more desirable as many emerging Artificial Intelligence (AI) algorithms are being trained on nursing data to ensure robust inputs and outputs. Newly generated knowledge can further inform practice, research, policy, and administrative decisions to ensure healthcare quality, safety, and access. Standardization of data also has the potential to transform how nursing care is reimbursed and valued, and to address the financial challenges that have contributed to the nursing shortage with direct impact on patient care, which is the main reason for the Commission for Nursing Reimbursement being established in April of 2023 (Commission for Nurse Reimbursement, n.d.).

DOI: 10.4324/9781003464457-14

Additionally, the National Council of State Boards of Nursing (NCSBN), a unique nurse identifier (UNI ID), assigned to every US nurse upon obtaining their first license, ensures concise communication among systems to protect a nurse's personal identifiable information (PII), aids interoperability across systems, permits free and easy lookup of nurse information, and allows aggregation of nurse-related data for research and decision-making purposes across health systems (Nursys®, n.d.; Sensmeier et al., 2019). These data-driven initiatives advance both the nursing profession and the patients we serve.

Similarly, defining the value in NI has been challenging. However, with automated data collection, analysis, modeling, and visualization at our fingertips, the outcome metrics can now tell the story of the value NI brings to its organizations and the nursing profession at large. Iuppa (2023a) offers three steps to define the value of NI: (1) Accurately Identify Value-Driven Metrics (what matters most), (2) develop a visual value story (impact story), and (3) effectively disseminate value contributions (socialize results). Furthermore, NI leaders' values can be recognized by building collaborative partnerships, participating in project governance, identifying care delivery opportunities, assuring value for stakeholders, and measuring results across the care continuum (McCleerey, 2019), as well as being in alignment with the organizational aims and success benchmarks. These value contributions need to be documented and disseminated by NI leaders within and outside of their organizations and be tailored to their audience (Iuppa, 2023b). NI is vital to the ongoing success of patient care outcomes as it intersects with existing and emerging technology and clinical engagement.

## Nursing Informatics Education and Competencies

Based on the poll during one of the sessions at the HIMSS 2024 conference, the audience identified informatics competency (52%) as one of the main barriers in successful transitions from informatics education to clinical practice, followed by other factors, including the adaptation to digital technologies, clinical judgment, as well as quality and safety education standards. This data reflect the impetus of professional nursing organizations to set new frameworks and models for competency-based education to prepare nurses for contemporary practice. It is evident in the publications of the third edition of the ANA Nursing Informatics Scope and Standards of Practice in 2021 (American Nurses Association, 2021) and the American Association of Colleges of Nursing (AACN) release of *The 2021 Essentials: Core Competencies for Professional Nursing Education* which provides the educational expectations for the preparation of nurses in baccalaureate, master's, and Doctor of Nursing Practice programs (American Association of Colleges of Nursing, 2021). As nursing education has been shifting to a competency-driven model, integration of AI and technology competencies in nursing education (Castonguay et al., 2023) has become one of the most pressing priorities for institutions of higher education (IHEs).

There is also an increasing demand for simulation learning and Academic Electronic Medical Records (AEMRs) to train nursing students and improve their clinical reasoning competencies (Elliott et al., 2018), enhance nursing students' confidence, digital literacy, and critical thinking skills in documenting and prioritizing care (Hong et al., 2022). All nurses need ongoing education on emerging technologies like remote monitoring, wearables, and automation to ensure patient safety, privacy, and data security. Training on the proper use, reporting, and documentation of observed malfunctions or inconsistencies of technologies at the point of care is paramount to maintain care quality and protect patient information.

Reflecting the most recent definition of the NI specialty, nurses are expected to transform data into needed information and leverage technologies to improve health and healthcare equity, safety, quality, and outcomes (American Nurses Association, 2021). Graduate NI students have more than one pathway to becoming proficient, either as Informatics Nurses (NIs) or Informatics Nurse Specialists (NIS). NI is a registered nurse with an interest or experience in an informatics field, most often NI, and INS is a registered nurse with formal graduate education in informatics who is expected to have experience in informatics projects or processes and has achieved and maintains applicable certifications (American Nurses Association, 2021). Some of the key concepts these professionals need to be knowledgeable about are data, information, knowledge, wisdom (DIKW), clinical decision support (CDS) and expert systems, big data, data lakes, analytics, artificial/augmented intelligence, machine learning (ML), natural language processing (NLP), and deep learning, forecasting, and predictive analytics as well as user experience (UX).

Informatics professionals, such as NI/NIS, offer a unique combination of nursing and informatics practice expertise, expert understanding of healthcare delivery and operational flow, scientific research and discovery, policy influence, organizational strategy and leadership, education, and more. IHE need to prepare NI/NIS to be marketable for a wide range of positions across in-patient, outpatient, and industry settings within public and private sectors, including roles in management, administration, and leadership, clinical informatics, data management and analytics, patient safety and quality, research and evaluation, compliance and integrity management coordination, consultation, facilitation, education, population health, and integration.

Nurses can be instrumental in driving the future of nursing by 1) engaging in implementing educational competency-based content; integrating NI competencies across academia, professional development, and practice; contributing to the evolving NI competencies for undergraduate and graduate-level education and practice going forward; and providing input to policy development with healthcare consumers and nurses in mind.

## Leadership and Roles in Nursing Informatics

Nurse leaders play an integral role within the healthcare ecosystem. While not all nurse leaders hold titles such as Chief Nursing Informatics Officer (CNIO) or Director of Informatics, or report directly to CNIO or CNO, nurses lead teams, projects, and direct patient care in an increasingly digitized environment. Based on research and current trends of digital expansion within healthcare, organizations have become more reliant on nurses to support strategy, implementation, and optimization of health information technologies, that is, within the scope of the senior leadership roles such as CNIO (Strudwick et al., 2022). However, these roles are not always standardized, widely adopted, or funded by organizations.

Additionally, as new roles emerge, leaders are charged with responsibilities to develop required competencies, practice standards, and educational opportunities for these nurses. One example is the Alliance for Nursing Informatics (ANI) Emerging Leaders Program, founded in 2010, sponsored by the American Medical Informatics Association (n.d.) and the Healthcare Information and Management Systems Society (HIMSS) to develop professionals capable of assuming national leadership positions in informatics-related organizations (Sensmeier, 2019). Nurses also bring tremendous value to non-nursing organizations, where they offer unique perspectives by serving on boards of nonprofit or for-profit organizations to achieve the goals of improved health and efficient and effective healthcare systems at the local, state, and national levels (Nurses On Boards Coalition, n.d.).

## Impact of Big Data on NI specialty

With every patient encounter, nurses collect large amounts of structured data, organized in predefined formats like rows and columns in a database that is easy to analyze, and unstructured data, without a set format, like narrative notes that require advanced techniques like ML to analyze. This data is used to train various ML algorithms to help automate tasks and reduce documentation burden and perform other menial tasks. Consequently, big data has the potential to have a significant positive impact on nursing practice, but only if nurses are active partners in this relationship. Nurses are in the position to ensure that entered data is complete, accurate, timely, and free from bias. Nurses are gaining an understanding that the data they collect daily become the basis of training intelligent algorithms, such as an AI-powered sepsis clinical decision support system (CDSS) tool, which must be robust and reliable to help address the problems nurses face in clinical practice (Kagan et al., 2024; Ross et al., 2024).

To further demonstrate the significance of the amount of data that nurses have the power to influence, let's look at terabytes. A terabyte (TB) is 1012 or 1,000,000,000,000 (1 trillion) bytes; to simplify, 1 terabyte equals two million books, and 1 terabyte = 1,000 gigabytes. Terabytes are often used to measure the hard drive storage capacity. Some servers and workstations can have multiple hard drives with a total storage capacity of over several TB. TB is also used to measure bandwidth aka data transfer rate over a specific amount of time, or internet connection. With more affordable and faster software capabilities to aggregate and analyze large data, nurses with education in informatics and related fields have opportunities to mine data to find solutions for problems that impact nurses' work and the patients they serve. This type of prescriptive data eliminates bias and helps answer very focused research questions (Simpson, 2019). Thus, NIs working in data science and NI researchers are able to disseminate newfound information to facilitate and improve evidence-based practice at the bedside faster and more efficiently.

Senior nurse leaders, serving as CNIOs, CNOs, Directors of Nursing Informatics, and other administrative positions, are uniquely positioned to advocate for NI roles and education that is specific to data science and other STEM-related (science, technology, engineering, and math) majors, and supply the tools needed to conduct and implement large data projects.

For example, there is a significant movement among nurse leaders to advocate for nursing to be recognized as a STEM degree (Dreisbach et al., 2022), which would unlock significant funding opportunities and support our profession, including in education, practice, and research. For example, with funding, we can achieve health informatics literacy for undergraduate nurses and upskill nurses currently practicing at the bedside because informatics and computer skills are essential underlying components that support evidence-based practice (Abdekhoda, 2021). Additionally, grant money can provide scholarships to more nurses to pursue informatics-related studies and advanced degrees and to fast-track big data exploration in research.

## Future Directions and Conclusion

NIs has rapidly evolved over the past few years due to technological advancements, healthcare policy changes, and a focus on data-driven patient care. The COVID-19 pandemic accelerated the adoption of EHRs, telehealth, wearable devices, and AI-powered tools, enhancing patient care and efficiency. There has been an increase in healthcare informatics programs in America, with an estimated global healthcare informatics market expected to grow to $91.51 billion by 2031 (Coherent Market Insights, 2024). This progress is driven by the rising need for informatics professionals in such areas as data quality and analytics, consumer health information and cybersecurity, and others

**Table 14.1 List of Professional Informatics Organizations**

| *Professional Organization* | *Abbreviation* | *Website* |
|---|---|---|
| American Health Information Management Association | AHIMA | https://www.ahima.org/ |
| American Medical Informatics Association | AMIA | https://amia.org/ |
| American Nursing Informatics Association | ANIA | https://www.ania.org/ |
| American Telemedicine Association | ATA | https://www.americantelemed.org/ |
| Alliance for Nursing Informatics | ANI | https://www.allianceni.org/ |
| Health Information and Management System Society | HIMSS | https://www.himss.org/ |
| International Medical Informatics Association | IMIA | https://imia-medinfo.org/wp/ |
| Project Management Institute | PMI | https://www.pmi.org/ |

to meet the increasing demands of healthcare organizations in integrating technology to improve patient care, efficiency, and data management (American Health Information Management Association, 2023). Nurses play a crucial role in using digital tools for documentation, care coordination, and patient management. NIs must be involved in the full lifecycle development and deployment of digital tools to ensure that critical technology decisions that directly and indirectly impact patient outcomes, safety, and care quality (Kagan et al., 2024).

Additionally, digital advancements have transformed nursing education through virtual simulations and remote learning. These changes bring both challenges and opportunities, requiring the NI community to adapt and maintain its competitive edge. There are a number of professional organizations (Table 14.1) that support nurses with an interest in informatics and NI professionals on the national and state levels by offering interprofessional collaboration, educational resources forums, professional development, and leadership opportunities (Kagan et al., 2023). Nurses with a solid informatics foundation gained via advanced education, and clinical experience uphold the highest standards and professionalism and serve as role models and stewards of the NI specialty.

## References

Abdekhoda, M. (2021). Investigating the impact of health informatics literacy on the evidence-based practice of nursing. *Online Journal of Nursing Informatics*, *25*(2). https://gkc.himss.org/resources/investigating-impact-health-informatics-literacy-evidence-based-practice-nursing

American Association of Colleges of Nursing. (2021). *The 2021 essentials: Core competencies for professional nursing education*. https://www.aacnnursing.org/Portals/0/PDFs/Publications/Essentials-2021.pdf

American Health Information Management Association. (2023). *Health information workforce shortages persist as AI shows promise: AHIMA survey reveals*. https://www.ahima.org/news-publications/press-room-press-releases/2023-press-releases/health-information-workforce-shortages-persist-as-ai-shows-promise-ahima-survey-reveals/

American Medical Informatics Association. (n.d.). *Nursing Informatics History Project*. Retrieved from https://amia.org/nursing-informatics-history-project

American Nurses Association. (2021). *Nursing informatics: Scope and standards of practice* (3rd ed.).

Castonguay, A., Farthing, P., Davies, S., Vogelsang, L., Kleib, M., Risling, T., & Green, N. (2023). Revolutionizing nursing education through AI integration: A reflection on the disruptive impact of ChatGPT. *Nurse Education Today, 129*, 105916. https://doi.org/10.1016/j.nedt.2023.105916

Coherent Market Insights. (2024). *Healthcare informatics market size and trends*. Retrieved from https://www.coherentmarketinsights.com/industry-reports/healthcare-informatics-market/market-size-and-trends

Commission for Nurse Reimbursement. (n.d.). *Commission for Nurse Reimbursement*. Retrieved from https://commissionfornursereimbursement.com/

Dreisbach, C., Wright, M. L., Walker, R. K., Byon, H. D., & Keim-Malpass, J. (2022). Nursing science as a federally-recognized STEM degree: A call to action for the United States with global implications. *International Journal of Nursing Studies Advances, 4*, 100084. https://doi.org/10.1016/j.ijnsa.2022.100084

Elliott, K., Marks-Maran, D., & Bach, R. (2018). Teaching student nurses how to use electronic patient records through simulation: A case study. *Nurse Education in Practice, 30*, 7–12. https://doi.org/10.1016/j.nepr.2018.02.003

Hong, S., Cho, I., Park, M., Lee, J. Y., Lee, J., & Choi, M. (2022). Simulation education incorporating academic electronic medical records for undergraduate nursing students: A pilot study. *Healthcare Informatics Research, 28*(4), 376–386. https://doi.org/10.4258/hir.2022.28.4.376

Iuppa, N. (2023a). Computing the value of nursing informatics. *Nursing Management, 54*(7), 10–13. https://doi.org/10.1097/nmg.0000000000000033

Iuppa, N. (2023b). Defining the value of nursing informatics in three easy steps. *Computers, Informatics, Nursing, 41*(4), 192–194. https://doi.org/10.1097/CIN.0000000000001018

Kagan, O., Connor, M., & Serwicki, V. (2023). The impact of leadership on the continued growth of the Nursing Informatics community in New York State and beyond. *Computers, Informatics, Nursing*. http://www.himss.org/resources/paving-way-himss-nys-chapter-spring-2022-virtual-nursing-symposium

Kagan, O., Owen, K., & Carroll, W. (2024). *The state of nursing informatics in 2024: Practice, research & education*. [Manuscript submitted for publication].

McCleerey, M. (2019). Vendor support of the expanded role of the CNIO. *Online Journal of Nursing Informatics, 23*(1). https://www.himss.org/resources/vendor-support-expandedrole-cnio

Nurses On Boards Coalition. (n.d.). *Nurses On Boards Coalition*. Retrieved from https://www.nursesonboardscoalition.org/

Nursys®. (n.d.). *Nursys®*. Retrieved from https://www.nursys.com/EN/ENDefault.aspx

Ross, A., Freeman, R., McGrow, K., & Kagan, O. (2024). Implications of artificial intelligence for nurse managers. *Nursing Management (Springhouse), 55*(7), 14–23. https://doi.org/10.1097/nmg.0000000000000143

Sensmeier, J. (2019). The value and impact of the Alliance for Nursing Informatics Emerging Leaders Program. *Computers, Informatics, Nursing, 37*(12), 612–614. https://doi.org/10.1097/CIN.0000000000000603

Sensmeier, J., Androwich, I., Baernholdt, M., Carroll, W., Fields, W., Fong, V., Murphy, J., Omery, A., & Rajwany, N. (2019). Demonstrating the value of nursing care through use of a unique nurse identifier. *Online Journal of Nursing Informatics, 23*(2).

Simpson, R. L. (2019). Big data fuels unstoppable change. *Nursing Administration Quarterly, 43*(4), 378–380. https://doi.org/10.1097/NAQ.0000000000000373

Strudwick, G., Lo, B., Kemp, J., Jessa, K., Tajirian, T., White, P., & Nagle, L. (2022). Opportunities and challenges to enhance the value and uptake of Chief Nursing Informatics Officer (CNIO) roles in Canada: A qualitative study. *AMIA Annual Symposium Proceedings, 2022*, 1012–1021.

# Chapter 15

# Evangelizing a Culture of Innovation

Hiyam Nadel and Olga Kagan

## Introduction

Innovation is not a new concept to healthcare informatics professionals, including nurses. Historically, informatics concepts such as data, systems, algorithms, information processing, and visualization have been utilized as early as the 1800s by one of the nursing pioneers, Florence Nightingale. During the Crimean War, she improved the standard of care of countless soldiers, while manually collecting, analyzing, and visually presenting data to support her work, with a long-lasting legacy in today's healthcare. Many have followed since then, prompting today's modern-day public health nursing, innovation theories, health IT advancements, professional nursing informatics organizations, and innovation books and programs. However, many challenges have existed over the years, and many remain unaddressed, hindering our ability to keep up with the rapidly changing landscape of healthcare technology. A 2024 poll at the Health Information Management Systems Society (HIMSS) conference session on innovation showed that major barriers included organizational support and culture (38%), followed by training and upskilling (27 %), staffing and retention (18%), economic stability or funding (13%), and regulatory barriers (2%). This chapter will cover the examples of how innovation leaders are tackling these challenges.

## How to Cultivate a Culture of Innovation?

In this chapter, several evolving definitions of innovation in healthcare, nursing, and technology, as well as innovation concepts, including human-centered design (HCD), Design Thinking (DT), and ROBUST acronyms are introduced.

*Healthcare innovation* is a term that refers to new or improved solutions that have the potential to accelerate positive health impact. Healthcare innovation can involve different aspects of healthcare, such as policies, systems, technologies, ideas, services, and products. Healthcare innovation

DOI: 10.4324/9781003464457-15

aims to solve existing or emerging health problems, improve the efficiency, effectiveness, quality, sustainability, safety, and/or affordability of healthcare, and achieve the health-related Sustainable Development Goals (Kimble L & Massoud, 2017; WHO, 2023).

*Nursing Innovation* is the application of creativity or problem-solving that results in a widely adopted sustainable strategy, product, or service that meets a need in a new and different way. Innovations are about improvement in quality, cost-effectiveness, cost avoidance, or efficiency (Kaya et al., 2016). Additionally, the need to develop new metrics and models around healthcare innovation, including emerging technologies and innovative solutions, will require ethical vetting. There needs to be a market for the solution. The solution must benefit frontline healthcare workers and meet the quintuple aim (Nundy et al., 2022). It involves an approach that includes creativity, controlled risk-taking, pivoting, and HCD (SONSIEL, 2023). One example is nurse-led solutions that emerged during MIT Hacking Medicine, NurseHack4Health, and Pitch-A-Thon events, some of which were directly in response to the COVID-19 pandemic, where tech solutions became essential in delivering care remotely (Koszalinski et al., 2021; Kagan et al., 2021).

*Healthcare Technology Innovation* is a dynamic and multifaceted concept crucial in improving healthcare outcomes and systems worldwide. It involves introducing new ideas, methods, or devices that enhance healthcare quality, safety, and efficiency, ultimately improving patient outcomes and quality of life (Kimble, L. & Massoud, 2017; Rejon-Parrilla et al., 2022).

Healthcare attendees at the HIMSS24 conference session on innovation were asked: "*What word comes to mind when you think of nursing innovation?*" A word cloud generated in response to this question encompasses many of the concepts that are found in the definitions described above (Figure 15.1).

There is a need to create an innovative environment where diverse patient populations' needs are met within the high-tech environment and to successfully bridge the gap between leaders and staff, leading to improved retention and empowered employees. To empower healthcare leaders and

**Figure 15.1 "*What word comes to mind when you think of nursing innovation?*".**

***Source:*** **Poll results from the HIMSS24 session on *Leaders of change evangelizing culture of innovation*, attended by healthcare administrator/C-suite executives (51%), clinicians (20%), non-clinicians/industry (18%), academics (7%), and students (2%).**

nursing professionals and to boost their confidence, they require access to the necessary tools and insights to foster an environment that thrives on transformative ideas (Kagan et al., 2023). There are opportunities for organizations to thrive with innovative ideas as we delve into nursing leadership, innovation, and health IT. There are concepts and inclusive tools like DT, HCD, and the Society of Nurse Scientists, Innovators, Entrepreneurs & Leaders (SONSIEL) – that developed a ROBUST method to assist nurses and organizations in the innovation journey and to help overcome potential barriers by fostering a culture of innovation, advocating for necessary resources, and garnering organizational support.

Commercializing or receiving external funding for innovative solutions can generate revenue for institutions without causing additional burdens. These impactful solutions contribute to cost savings, quality of care, equitable treatment, and cost avoidance. For this, one needs to be familiar with the leadership strategies to evangelize the culture of innovation, where care is delivered domestically and globally to meet the needs of diverse populations utilizing health IT solutions. Healthcare leaders and nursing professionals must be equipped with the tools and insights needed to create an environment that thrives on innovation, where transformative ideas are nurtured and implemented. With an understanding of the diverse backgrounds and needs of the populations, nurses can develop inclusive and effective solutions. Encouraging creativity, risk-taking, and collaboration among nursing, interdisciplinary, and interprofessional teams can spark groundbreaking ideas and drive continuous improvement. Leaders who possess a comprehensive understanding of how to champion and implement a culture of nursing innovation within their organizations, as well as armed with tools and practical strategies, will be poised to create an environment where nurses can genuinely thrive as innovative leaders, driving positive change in the healthcare landscape for the benefit of all populations.

## *Design Thinking Framework*

To set the stage for a culture shift, one must be familiar with the DT framework, HCD, and the SONSIEL-developed ROBUST method, which will take center stage.

DT offers a human-centered approach to problem-solving and innovation. It encourages nurses to empathize with patients and colleagues, identify unmet needs, and create solutions that resonate deeply with the people they serve. There are various stages of the innovation journey, addressing challenges and opportunities that nurses may encounter. DT is a five-step method that includes empathizing, defining, ideating, prototyping, and testing as a quick way to establish what works best before developing a full product or service. DT helps balance consumer needs and usability, while encouraging diverse thoughts and ideas. Considering the quintuplet aims, DT has also evolved to more of a humanity-centered approach as we move to care for communities and society as a whole.

If opportunities are available within the existing place of employment, nurses must be encouraged to actively participate in their community of peers, sharing their experiences, insights, and questions. This interaction allows for a dynamic exchange of ideas and practical strategies, fostering a collaborative learning environment and an outlet to innovate within the organization's boundaries (Nadel et al., 2023). Described an efficient way to engage many clinical and administrative staff in the innovation process. Open innovation allowed frontline healthcare workers to share ideas and feel heard. Trained staff in HCD thinking and strengthened partnerships within and beyond the hospital system.

If opportunities do not exist within the system or there is apparent resistance to change, explore outside resources and organizations or spearhead innovation initiatives by garnering support from key stakeholders and creating a shared vision for the future of nursing practice.

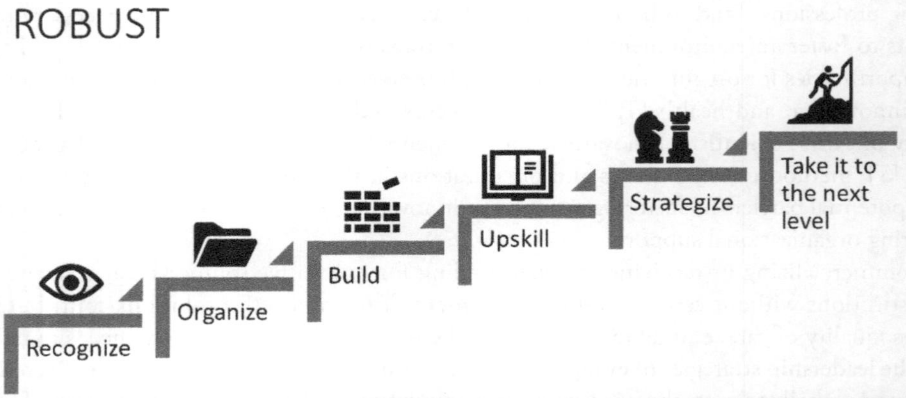


**Figure 15.2 ROBUST. Society of Nurse Scientists, Innovators, Entrepreneurs, & Leaders (SONSIEL), (2023).**

## *Human-Centered Design*

HCD is a product development methodology that must be applied in healthcare innovation to help create innovative solutions through empathy, with a focus on the human perspective that allows for continuous iteration based on feedback to meet the changing needs of the end user. It allows one to understand how the product is viewed, its usefulness, effectiveness, and level of engagement. Designers often utilize an empathy map to understand user behavior, limit miscommunication and misunderstanding, and improve the user experience. An empathy map helps identify customers' thoughts, feelings, and behaviors. Empathy maps help us understand pains and gains and refine our audience persona to better hone in on the kind of product, service, or experience they might find valuable (Brown, 2009; Gray, n.d.). One example is mapping a patient journey as patients navigate a digital patient portal from previsit, such as finding a provider, making an appointment, and completing web-based forms, to an actual visit, from parking the vehicle or taking public transportation using an app to using a kiosk to check-in, receiving real-time updates of wait time on their smartphone, interacting with providers when prompted; and finally, post-visit as they access electronic discharge instructions, satisfaction survey, and payments of copays or deductibles. To map a patient journey in this case, several stakeholders might need to be involved, including but not limited to patients and caregivers, providers, nurses, administrative assistants, paraprofessionals, and parking attendants.

## *ROBUST*

Several barriers and challenges to innovation exist in healthcare, including staff retention, morale, and economic stability, just to name a few. Employees must feel heard, valued, and empowered to create change and ensure staff retention. To mitigate these barriers, we suggest following the ROBUST methodology as identified by SONSIEL (Figure 15.2):

1. *Recognize the potential*: Leaders cannot always recognize nurses' potential to innovate, and nurses often do not view themselves as innovators. By simply asking for ideas and involving staff in developing solutions, and choosing the right solution from outside vendors, leaders can also close the gap between what they perceive as problems and what they hear are problems directly from the front lines. Then, ask the staff to come up with solutions for those problems rather than feel like, as a leader, you have to solve the problem for the staff.

2. *Organizational* buy-in from key stakeholders and leadership to be on board to provide funding to develop and implement the solutions. Leadership should be involved in vetting the feasibility of future ideas. Provide the resources to build the infrastructure needed for an innovation program.
3. *Build* a formal pathway to hear directly from the staff to identify the gaps and the solutions. Provide the resources and time to develop those solutions to ensure successful outcomes. Identify additional resources needed, but first, see what is available internally since many hospital systems have resources such as a model shop, metal shops, and IT staff that can assist in the initial prototype development. Identify the IT team to help navigate the requirements with digital solutions, such as interoperability and security.
4. *Upskill/skill workforce*: Skill building and upskilling are limited to nurses and their leaders using the DT methodology. Send staff to events such as the NurseHack4Health, ThinC conference, and the Pitch-A-Thon, where mentors are provided to learn DT methodologies, such as UX designers, entrepreneurs, and IT developers. Bring in innovation experts to run an innovation sprint or mini-hackathon for your organization, or create your own innovation committee to elicit and vet ideas.
5. *Strategy* and vision should align with the organization's mission, vision, and values, but ideas and solutions should also address the organization's pain points. A bottom-up approach to solving these problems engages the entire workforce, democratizes the process, and empowers and unites the staff toward a common goal.
6. *Take it to the next level and transform* by providing resources (time, funds) and implementing the innovation (Minimally Viable Product (MVP), pilot, Proof of Concept (POC), prototype) to allow feedback to iterate the next-level solution. Encourage and permit risk-taking and learning from failure. One of the critical learnings from DT is to challenge assumptions and attain agency on the future of healthcare. Ideas should be encouraged without the barriers of cost, regulations, or fear, not to squelch creativity. Once many creative ideas are generated, the leaders can vet them for feasibility.

Finally, challenges can be turned into opportunities. For example, commercialized solutions and grants can become new sources of revenue for the institution. These solutions will not only help overcome some of the barriers but they will also ensure quality and equitable care, reduction in waste, differentiation of the organization's reputation in the market, and innovation and scalability to make a greater impact.

## Looking Forward

We offer practical tips as one plans to embark on the journey of innovation. The first step is starting somewhere! Volunteer your time as many organizations actively pursue innovative initiatives where your expertise might be valuable and needed. Suppose prospects do not exist in your organization. In that case, there are several outside opportunities to consider, including but not limited to NurseHack4Health, MIT Hacking Medicine, Mayo Hack, Rutgers Hackathon, and innovation sprints or innovation workshops across academic and vendor organizations. One example of deploying open innovation within a healthcare system to actively elicit those ideas from the frontline was done at Massachusetts General Hospital (Nadel HM et al., 2023, BMJ Leader). Several professional organizations offer ample opportunities for creativity, networking, and learning (Table 15.1).

**Table 15.1 Professional Organizations with Innovation Initiatives**

| *Informatics* | *Innovation* | *Nursing* |
|---|---|---|
| 1. American Nursing Informatics Association (ANIA)<br>2. American Medical Informatics Association (AMIA)<br>3. Health Information Medical System Society (HIMSS)<br>4. American Health Information Management Association (AHIMA)<br>5. Alliance for Nursing Informatics (ANI) | 1. Society of Nurse Scientists, Innovators, Entrepreneurs & Leaders (SONSIEL)<br>2. Society of Inventors (SOI)<br>3. International Association of Innovation Professionals (IAOIP) | 1. American Nurses Association (ANA)<br>2. American Organization for Nursing Leadership (AONL)<br>3. International Council of Nurses (ICN) |

*Note:* This is not an exhaustive list of organizations.

The second step is to identify champions in your organization and, if you are in a leadership role, create opportunities for employees to innovate in a safe and welcoming environment, provide resources, and advocate for inclusive design and diverse interprofessional teams, especially if technology is used by multiple stakeholders.

Lastly, take controlled risks. This includes risk assessment, risk mitigation strategies such as having contingency plans, and the flexibility to adapt to changing circumstances. Failures or errors should be viewed as learning and growth opportunities and not as causes for punitive actions. We build a culture of innovation by embracing the growth mindset, celebrating small wins, and learning from failures.

## Conclusion

In conclusion, we leave you with a renewed sense of purpose and the confidence to lead positive change within your organizations, driving nursing innovation forward to enhance patient care and shape the future of healthcare in a highly technological ecosystem.

In this chapter, we addressed the innovation concepts and leadership strategies to evangelize the culture of nursing innovation to meet the needs of diverse populations with health IT solutions and services to better equip healthcare providers and nurses with the tools and insights needed to create an environment that thrives on innovation, where transformative ideas are nurtured and implemented.

## References

Brown, T. (2009). *Change by Design: How Design Thinking Transforms Organizations and Inspires Innovation.* Harper Collins.

Gray, D. (n.d.) Xplane. https://xplane.com/author/davegray/

Kagan, O., Nadel, H., Littlejohn, J., & Leary M. (2021). Evolution of nurse-led hackathons, incubators and accelerators from an innovation ecosystem perspective. *OJIN: The Online Journal of Issues in Nursing*, 26(3).

Kagan, O., Sciasci, N. G., Koszalinski, R. S., Kagan, D. H., Leary, M., & Nadel, H. (2023). Nurses' confidence in starting a new venture, startup or project in the context of nurse-led hackathons: Results of pre-hackathon survey. *Nursing Outlook*, 71(3), 101961. https://doi.org/10.1016/j.outlook.2023.101961

Kaya, N., Turan, N., & Aydin, G. (2016). Innovation in nursing: A concept analysis. *Journal of Community & Public Health Nursing* 2.

Kimble L, & Massoud M. R. (2017). What do we mean by Innovation in Healthcare? *EMJ*;1(1):89–91. https://doi.org/10.33590/emjinnov/10314103

Koszalinski, R. S., Kagan, O., Littlejohn, J., & Nadel, H. (2021). Collaborative COVID-19 Problem-solving: Nurses as content experts, mentors and judges. *OJIN*, 26(3). https://doi.org/10.3912/OJIN.Vol26No03PPT39

Nadel, H.M., Al-Sultan, N., Berger, A., McCree, P., Banister, G.,& Jung, O. (2023). Mission possible: Open innovation in nursing and patient care services at Massachusetts General Hospital. *BMJ Leader* 2023;0:1–5. https://doi.org/10.1136/leader-2023-000777

Nundy, S., Cooper, L.A., & Mate, K.S. The quintuple aims for health care improvement. *JAMA*. 2022;327(6):521.

Rejon-Parrilla, J. C., Espin, J. & Epstein, D. (2022). How innovation can be defined, evaluated and rewarded in health technology assessment. *Health Economics Review* 12, 1. https://doi.org/10.1186/s13561-021-00342-y

Society of Nurse Scientists, Innovators, Entrepreneurs, & Leaders (SONSIEL). (2023). *ROBUST*. https://www.sonsiel.org/publications

What is Healthcare Innovation? GCU. Published (September 6, 2017). Accessed December 17, 2023. https://www.gcu.edu/blog/medical-studies-sciences/what-healthcare-innovation

WHO. (2023). Health innovation for impact. Accessed December 17, 2023. https://www.who.int/teams/digital-health-and-innovation/health-innovation-for-impact

# Index

Page numbers in *italic* indicate figures. Page numbers in **bold** indicate tables.

## D

## F



## G



## H

## U



## V



## W



## Z